Ultimate Blazor WebAssembly for Web Development

Unlock the Full Potential of Blazor WebAssembly 8.0 and C# to Build High-Performance Web Applications with Ease

Chandradev Prasad Sah

www.orangeava.com

First published: May 2024

Published by: Orange Education Pvt Ltd, AVA™

Address: 9, Daryaganj, Delhi, 110002, India

275 New North Road Islington Suite 1314 London,
N1 7AA, United Kingdom

ISBN: 978-81-96862-06-0

www.orangeava.com

Dedicated To

My Beloved Father, Mother, Wife, and Daughter:

Without Their Moral Support, it was Very Difficult to Complete This Book

About the Author

Chandradev Prasad Sah holds B.E (Computer Science) from VTU. He is a web application developer with over 16 years of experience. He has a strong background in computer science and is a recognized expert in Blazor development, having completed over 50 web products using this framework.

Sah is a highly credentialed professional with certifications like MCC (Microsoft Community Contributor) and C# Corner MVP. He has also been awarded the Top Rated Plus Freelancer distinction.

A seasoned developer with experience at Dell, Intel, Walmart, and DXC, Sah now puts his knowledge to work as an independent consultant, providing services in Blazor, C#, WebApi Core, Azure, and AWS.

An active member of the Blazor community, Sah shares his knowledge and expertise by regularly publishing blog posts and content related to Blazor development on his personal blog.

About the Technical Reviewer

Trevoir Williams is a passionate software and system engineer dedicated to creating efficient and effective IT solutions that enhance service delivery in organizations. His educational achievements include a Master's degree in Computer Science (majoring in Software Development) and several Microsoft Azure Certifications.

With years of experience in software consulting, software engineering, database development, cloud systems, and server administration, Trevoir has the technical expertise to design and develop innovative systems. He is also a skilled musician.

Trevoir enjoys sharing his knowledge with students globally and is committed to teaching IT and development skills and guiding students in gaining the latest knowledge with practical application in the modern industry.

Acknowledgements

Writing a book is never a solitary endeavor. It requires the support, encouragement, and assistance of many individuals along the way.

I would like to express my deepest gratitude to my family: my father, Biswanath Sah, my mother, Sanmathi Devi, my wife, Runali Sah, and my daughter, Anvi Sah. Their love, encouragement, and unwavering belief in me fueled my determination at every turn. They are the guiding lights in my life, and this book is a testament to their enduring influence and the sacrifices they made.

Special thanks to my Technical Reviewer, **Trevoir Williams**, for his invaluable guidance, wisdom, and encouragement. Your insights and feedback have been instrumental in shaping this book and improving my craft as a writer.

I am also deeply grateful to the entire team at "AVA™ - An Orange Education Label", for their professionalism, expertise, and dedication to bringing this book to life. Their hard work and commitment to excellence have made this project a reality.

I also extend my gratitude to **Sonali and her team** and **Priyanka** for their assistance with research, proofreading, and providing valuable feedback throughout the writing process.

Lastly, I would like to thank the readers who will embark on this journey with me. Your interest and support mean the world to me, and I hope this book brings you knowledge, inspiration, and enjoyment.

Thank you all for being a part of this incredible journey.

Preface

The chapters are as follows:

Chapter 1. Introduction to Blazor WebAssembly: This chapter introduces Blazor, exploring its key features, advantages, and the underlying concepts that make it a powerful tool for web development.

Chapter 2. Razor Components: This chapter covers how to create, reuse, and compose components to build dynamic user interfaces.

Chapter 3. Routing and Navigation: This chapter explores Routing and Navigation in Blazor WebAssembly, guiding you through the process of configuring client-side routing for single-page applications.

Chapter 4. Razor Class Library: This chapter explores Razor Class Library (RCL) in Blazor, demonstrating how to organize and share UI components and logic across multiple projects.

Chapter 5. State Management: This chapter focuses on state management in Blazor WebAssembly, presenting various techniques for managing and preserving state within your applications.

Chapter 6. REST Services: This chapter covers the integration of RESTful services in Blazor WebAssembly, showcasing how to consume external APIs to retrieve and manipulate data.

Chapter 7. Entity Framework Core: This chapter dives into Entity Framework (EF) Core in Blazor WebAssembly, illustrating how to interact with databases using EF Core for data access.

Chapter 8. Validation in Blazor WebAssembly: This chapter addresses validation in Blazor WebAssembly, discussing how to implement client-side and server-side validation to ensure data integrity and security.

Chapter 9. JavaScript Interop in Blazor: This chapter explores the integration of JavaScript interop in Blazor WebAssembly, allowing you to leverage existing JavaScript libraries and functionality within your Blazor applications.

Chapter 10. Azure Service in Blazor: We shift our focus to Azure services, demonstrating how to leverage various Azure services to enhance the scalability, performance, and security of your Blazor applications.

Chapter 11. Security in Blazor WebAssembly: Finally, the last chapter covers security in Blazor WebAssembly, discussing best practices for securing your applications and protecting sensitive data.

Whether you're a beginner looking to get started with Blazor or an experienced developer seeking to enhance your skills, this book provides you with the knowledge and tools you need to build robust and engaging web applications with Blazor WebAssembly.

Happy coding!

Get a Free eBook

We hope you are enjoying your recently purchased book! Your feedback is incredibly valuable to us, and to all other readers looking for great books.

If you found this book helpful or enjoyable, we would truly appreciate it, if you could take a moment to leave a short review with a 5 star rating on Amazon. It helps us grow, and lets other readers discover our books.

As a thank you, we would love to send you a free digital copy of this book, and a **30%** discount code on your next cart value on our official websites:

www.orangeava.com

www.orangeava.in (For Indian Subcontinent)

☑ **Here's how:**

Leave a review for the book on Amazon.

Take a screenshot of your review, and send an email to **info@orangeava.com** (it can be just the confirmation screen).

Once, we receive your screenshot, we will send you the digital file, within 24 hours.

Thank you so much for your support – it means a lot to us!

Downloading the code bundles and colored images

Please follow the links or scan the QR codes to download the
Code Bundles and Images of the book:

https://github.com/ava-orange-education/Ultimate-Blazor-Web-Assembly-for-Web-Development

The code bundles and images of the book are also hosted on
https://rebrand.ly/153597

In case there's an update to the code, it will be updated on the existing GitHub repository.

Errata

We take immense pride in our work at **Orange Education Pvt Ltd**, and follow best practices to ensure the accuracy of our content to provide an indulging reading experience to our subscribers. Our readers are our mirrors, and we use their inputs to reflect and improve upon human errors, if any, that may have occurred during the publishing processes involved. To let us maintain the quality and help us reach out to any readers who might be having difficulties due to any unforeseen errors, please write to us at :

errata@orangeava.com

Your support, suggestions, and feedback are highly appreciated.

DID YOU KNOW

Did you know that Orange Education Pvt Ltd offers eBook versions of every book published, with PDF and ePub files available? You can upgrade to the eBook version at **www.orangeava.com** and as a print book customer, you are entitled to a discount on the eBook copy. Get in touch with us at: **info@orangeava.com** for more details.

At **www.orangeava.com**, you can also read a collection of free technical articles, sign up for a range of free newsletters, and receive exclusive discounts and offers on AVA™ Books and eBooks.

PIRACY

If you come across any illegal copies of our works in any form on the internet, we would be grateful if you would provide us with the location address or website name. Please contact us at **info@orangeava.com** with a link to the material.

ARE YOU INTERESTED IN AUTHORING WITH US?

If there is a topic that you have expertise in, and you are interested in either writing or contributing to a book, please write to us at **business@orangeava.com**. We are on a journey to help developers and tech professionals to gain insights on the present technological advancements and innovations happening across the globe and build a community that believes Knowledge is best acquired by sharing and learning with others. Please reach out to us to learn what our audience demands and how you can be part of this educational reform. We also welcome ideas from tech experts and help them build learning and development content for their domains.

REVIEWS

Please leave a review. Once you have read and used this book, why not leave a review on the site that you purchased it from? Potential readers can then see and use your unbiased opinion to make purchase decisions. We at Orange Education would love to know what you think about our products, and our authors can learn from your feedback. Thank you!

For more information about Orange Education, please visit **www.orangeava.com**.

Table of Contents

CHAPTER 1
Introduction to Blazor WebAssembly

Introduction

Blazor is a **free and open-source web framework** that enables developers to create web apps using C# and HTML.

It is a web development single-page framework developed by Microsoft to compete with industry-leading platforms like React, Angular, Vuejs, and more. Before Blazor, there were not any alternative options to develop the single-page application using C#.

In all leading JavaScript frameworks, we were developing single-page applications using JavaScript and it was very difficult for a .Net developer to master all technologies.

At the 2017 Microsoft MVP (Most Valuable Professional) Summit, Steve Sanderson (https://github.com/SteveSandersonMS) gave an experimental demo of Blazor. He showed how to create a single-page application using C# instead of JavaScript. It was so exciting for all the .Net developers. Since then, Microsoft and Steve's team started to work on that idea.

They released the first official stable version of Blazor Server in 2018 and Blazor WebAssembly in 2020 with .Net 5.0. Blazor is combination of Browser and Razor.

We will write the UI code in Razor, which is a combination of C# and HTML.

Structure

In this chapter, we will cover the following topics:

- Blazor and Types of Blazor Applications
- Blazor Web App
- Advantages of Blazor WebAssembly
- Disadvantages of Blazor WebAssembly

- Blazor Server vs. Blazor WebAssembly
- New Features in .Net 8.0
- Advantages of .Net 8.0
- Creating Blazor WebAssembly with .Net 8.0 with Visual Studio and VS Code
- Project Structure for Blazor WebAssembly Application

Types of Blazor Applications

There are three types of Blazor Applications:

- Blazor Server
- Blazor WebAssembly
- Blazor Web App (with Blazor 8.0)

Blazor Server

Blazor Server is a type of Blazor application where the UI components are rendered on the server and then sent to the client using SignalR, allowing for fast and responsive user interfaces. It will provide real-time communication between the client and the server.

In the following figure, we can see that Razor Components and DOM will communicate with each other using SignalR.

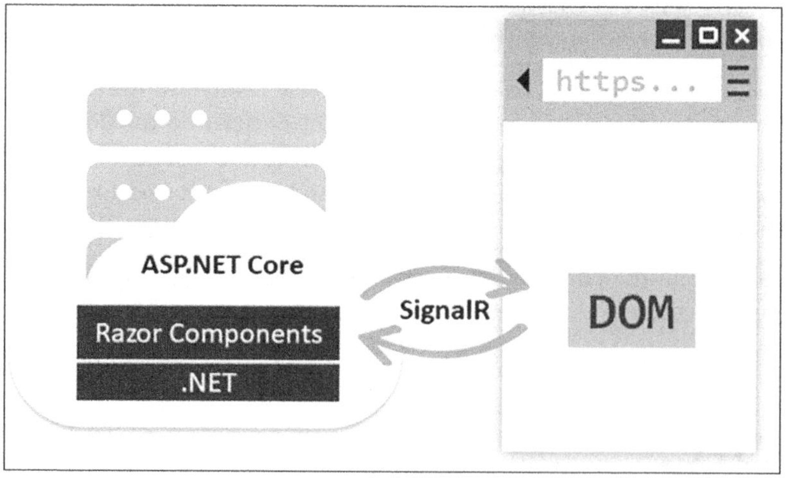

***Figure 1.1**: Communication using SignalR* (Source: Microsoft Website)

As you know, SignalR is a real-time communication library developed by Microsoft that allows bi-directional communication between client and server over HTTP.

It provides a way for server-side code to push content to connected clients instantly as it becomes available, without the need for the client to constantly poll the server for updates. SignalR can be used with various client-side technologies, such as JavaScript, .NET, and Xamarin, making it a useful tool for building real-time web and mobile applications.

Note : *This project type is only available on older version, that is, Blazor 6.0 and 7.0.*

Blazor WebAssembly

It is a true native single-page and open-source framework where C# and Razor component will compile into .Net assemblies and download to the user browser. With the help of WebAssembly, C# code can run directly in the browser. It supports all features of a single-page application.

Thanks to WebAssembly for making this possible.

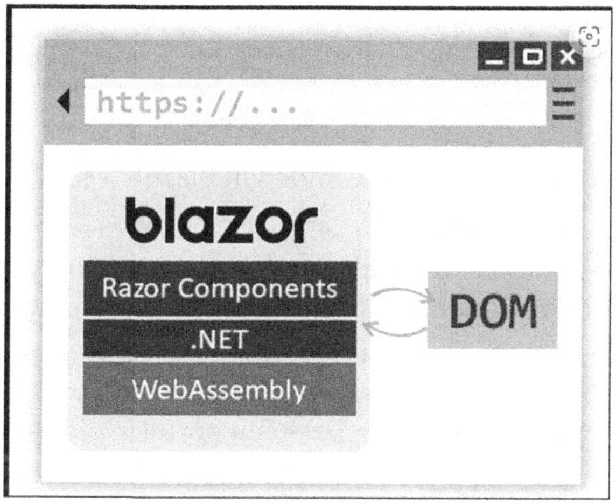

Figure 1.2: *Blazor WebAssembly* (Source: Microsoft Website)

In the preceding figure, we can see that with the help of the WebAssembly, Razor Component and C# will communicate with the DOM element.

In this approach, it will work in the following sequence:

1. Razor Component and C# Compile into .NET assemblies.
2. .Net assemblies and run time downloaded to the browser.
3. Blazor WebAssembly bootstraps the .Net runtime and configures the runtime to load the assemblies for the app.
4. Blazor WebAssembly runtime uses JavaScript interop to handle Document Object Model (DOM) manipulation and browser API calls.

   First, it will download the compiled code on a browser similar to other single-page applications like Angular, React, and so on. After that, it will execute from there.

Blazor Web App

In Blazor 8.0, a new project type called Blazor Web App has been added. This is a combination of Blazor Server and Blazor WebAssembly. We can seamlessly switch between rendering modes or even mix them within the same page.

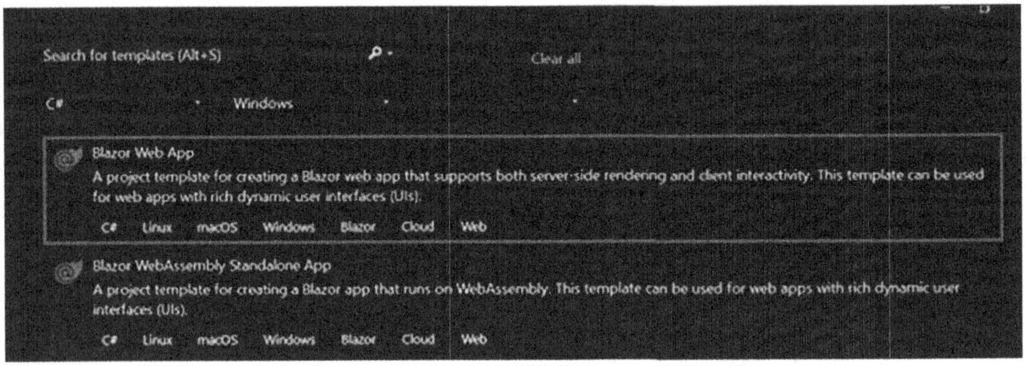

Figure 1.3: *Project Template*

There are four types of rendering mode added in Blazor Web App:

- **Static Server-Side Rendering (SSR)**: This mode renders the entire page as static HTML on the server and sends it to the client. This results in faster initial page loads and improved SEO but lacks interactivity after the initial load.
- **Interactive Server:** Components are rendered on the server and streamed to the client, enabling real-time updates and interactivity without full page reloads. This mode offers a good balance between performance and interactivity.
- **Interactive WebAssembly (WASM):** Components are pre-compiled to WebAssembly and run directly in the browser, providing full client-side interactivity and offline capabilities. However, it has a larger initial download size and might have slightly slower initial rendering compared to other modes.
- **Interactive Auto:** This mode automatically chooses the best render mode based on the component and its usage within the application. It's ideal for applications with mixed requirements for static content and interactive features.

Mode	**Description**	**Advantages**	**Disadvantages**
Static SSR	Pre-rendered HTML	Fastest initial load, good SEO	No client-side interactivity
Interactive Server	Server-side rendering with updates	Real-time updates, good mix of performance and interactivity	Requires constant server connection

Interactive WASM	Client-side rendering with WebAssembly	Full interactivity, offline capabilities	Larger initial download, potential performance overhead
Interactive Auto	Automatic mode selection	Flexible, adapts to component needs	Relies on complex logic for mode selection

***Table 1.1**: Four rendering modes and their differences*

Note: In this book, we are not going to cover all concepts of Blazor Web App. Instead, we will only focus on Blazor WebAssembly.

Is WebAssembly faster than JavaScript?

Yes, it is faster than JavaScript in certain scenarios. In general, WebAssembly (WASM) is faster than JavaScript when it comes to performance-critical tasks, such as mathematical calculations or complex algorithms.

WebAssembly (Wasm) is designed to provide a low-level, efficient way to run code on the web. JavaScript, on the other hand, is a high-level language that needs to be interpreted by the browser's JavaScript engine.

Wasm is designed to be executed by a virtual machine that runs directly on the computer's processor, which makes it faster and more efficient than JavaScript in some cases.

Wasm code is also compiled ahead of time, which means that it can be optimized before it is executed, leading to faster performance.

However, it's important to note that the performance benefits of WebAssembly over JavaScript depend on the specific use case and the type of application you are building.

For some types of applications, JavaScript may be just as fast or even faster than Wasm like DOM manipulation and event handling tasks.

Additionally, Wasm and JavaScript can work together to create high-performance applications. For example, you can use Wasm to implement performance-critical parts of an application, while using JavaScript for other parts that do not require the same level of performance.

Advantages of Blazor WebAssembly

The following are the advantages of Blazor WebAssembly:

- **Improved Performance**: Blazor WebAssembly uses ahead-of-time (AOT) compilation, which allows it to load and run faster than traditional JavaScript-based web applications. It also has smaller file sizes than many JavaScript frameworks, resulting in faster load times.
- **Seamless Integration with .NET:** Since Blazor is built on top of .NET, it offers seamless integration with other .NET technologies such as ASP.NET Core

and Entity Framework Core. Developers can use the same language and tools across the entire stack, making it easier to develop and maintain complex applications.

- **Increased Security:** Blazor WebAssembly offers improved security over traditional JavaScript-based web applications. Since the code runs in a sandboxed environment, it is much harder for malicious code to access sensitive data or perform unauthorized actions.
- **Familiar Development Experience:** Blazor WebAssembly offers a familiar development experience for .NET developers, making it easier for them to transition to building web applications. The syntax is similar to other .NET languages, and the development environment is similar to other Visual Studio tools.
- **Code Reusability:** Since Blazor WebAssembly is built on top of .NET, developers can reuse existing .NET libraries and components in their web applications. This can significantly reduce development time and improve code quality.
- It is supported by all streaming browsers , such as Chrome, Edge, Firefox, Opera, and Safari, along with the ability to run on old (non-WebAssembly) ones using asm.js.
- It will compile into static files, which can be deployed anywhere like an html page.
- Blazor WebAssembly does also support Progressive Web App (PWA).
- It also supports offline behavior, which means you can run the application without the internet. This will save a lot of development time and cost as compared to other JavaScript frameworks like Angular, React, Vue.js, and so on.

Disadvantages of Blazor WebAssembly

Blazor WebAssembly has a few disadvantages:

- The initial page load will be a little bit slower.
- It is restricted to the capabilities of the browser. So performance will vary depending on the browser.
- It will not work on older browsers.
- We need to write a little bit more code since the code will run on the Browser Sandbox.

Blazor Server vs. Blazor WebAssembly

The following table shows the differences between Blazor Server and Blazor WebAssembly.

Features	Blazor Server	Blazor WebAssembly
Offline Mode Support	Does Not support	Support
PWA application	Does Not support	Support
Initial Page Load	Fast	Slow
Static web Deployment	Does Not support	Support
Development time and cost	Less	A little bit more, since we need to create a separate API layer
For Intranet application	It is more suitable	Not suitable
For public-facing large web portal	Not suitable	More suitable

Table 1.2: *Differences between Blazor Server and Blazor WebAssembly*

In this book, we are going to use .Net 8.0. This is the latest framework from Microsoft. As you know, .Net 8.0 is 20% to 30% faster than .Net 6.0 and .Net 7.0.

For more details you can refer Microsoft blog post:

Performance Improvements in .NET 8 - .NET Blog (microsoft.com)

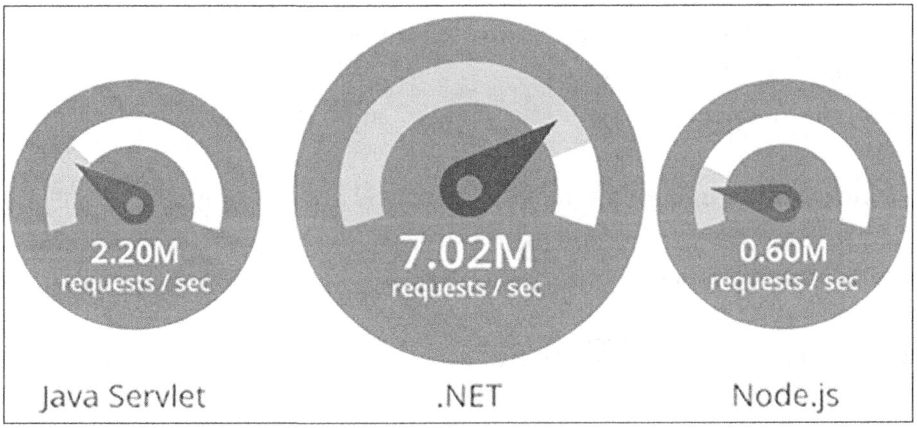

Figure 1.4: *.Net Performance*

Data sourced from official tests available at TechEmpower Round 21:

Round 21 results - TechEmpower Framework Benchmarks

New Features Added to Blazor 8.0

Blazor 8.0 brings several exciting new features, making it a significant upgrade for web development:

Unified Project Template:

Using a single Blazor Web App template, we can create a Blazor Server and WebAssembly project.

Enhanced Render Modes:

- **Static Server-Side Rendering (SSR)**: Pre-render HTML on the server for faster initial loads and SEO benefits.
- **Interactive Server-Side Rendering**: Stream components for real-time updates without full page reloads.
- **Interactive WebAssembly (WASM)**: Utilize WebAssembly for full client-side interactivity and offline capabilities.
- **Interactive Auto**: Automatically choose the best render mode based on component usage.

Other Notable Features:

- **Sections:** Define outlets in your layout for components to fill, fostering modularity.
- **Named Routing:** Route directly to elements using standard URL fragments.
- **Enhanced Navigation and Form Handling:** Avoid full page refreshes for improved user experience.
- **Stream Rendering:** Efficiently handle large datasets or dynamic content updates.
- **QuickGrid Component:** Simplified data grid creation with built-in features.
- **Authentication Components:** Streamlined user authentication and authorization flows.

Benefits of .NET 8.0

Beyond Blazor's enhancements, .NET 8.0 offers broader benefits:

Performance Improvements:

- Dynamic PGO enabled by default for optimized code.
- Faster JIT compiler and performance-focused data structures.
- Kestrel web server optimizations for ASP.NET Core.
- Interpreter-based runtime and garbage collection improvements in Blazor WebAssembly.

Improved Developer Experience:

- Enhanced tooling and diagnostics support.

- Modern C# features like minimal interfaces and parameterless constructors.
- .NET MAUI platform for cross-platform desktop apps.

Cloud-Native Readiness:

- .NET Aspire preview provides opinionated cloud-native stack guidance.
- Improved containerization and deployment support.

Unified Stack with Blazor:

- Develop full-stack web applications with a consistent framework across server and client.
- Combine static, interactive, and WebAssembly rendering modes within a single project.

Overall, .NET 8.0 and Blazor 8.0 offer significant advancements for web development, providing performance gains, modern features, improved developer experience, and a unified approach to building web applications.

In this book, we are covering Blazor WebAssembly with .NET 8.0, so we will only focus on content related to this.

Prerequisite Software for Blazor WebAssembly Application

All the following software are totally free for developers. You can download it from the given URLs:

- Visual Studio 2022 (Any Edition): Visual Studio 2022 Community Edition – Download the Latest Free Version (microsoft.com)
- SQL Server 2019 or any other version: Download Microsoft® SQL Server® 2019 Express from Official Microsoft Download Center
- If you have a low-configuration system, then you can also use VS Code: Download Visual Studio Code - Mac, Linux, Windows

Creating Hello World Blazor Application Using Visual Studio 2022

Here are the steps to create "`Hello World`" project:

Step 1: Install Visual Studio 2022 from the URL mentioned in the previous section.

Step 2: Open Visual Studio 2022 and Select the Blazor WebAssembly Standalone app as given in the following figure.

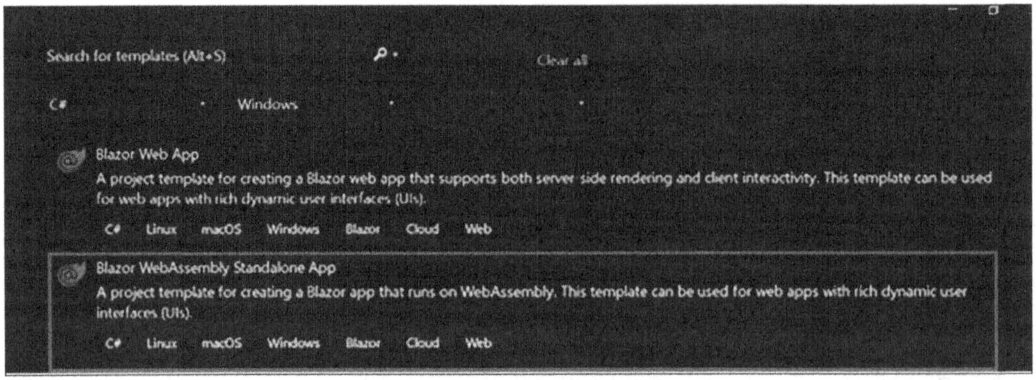

Figure 1.5: *Project Template*

Step 3: Give the Project name as **`HelloWorld`** as follows:

Figure 1.6: *Project Name*

Step 4: Select the Framework as .Net 8.0 and click on the **`Create`** button.

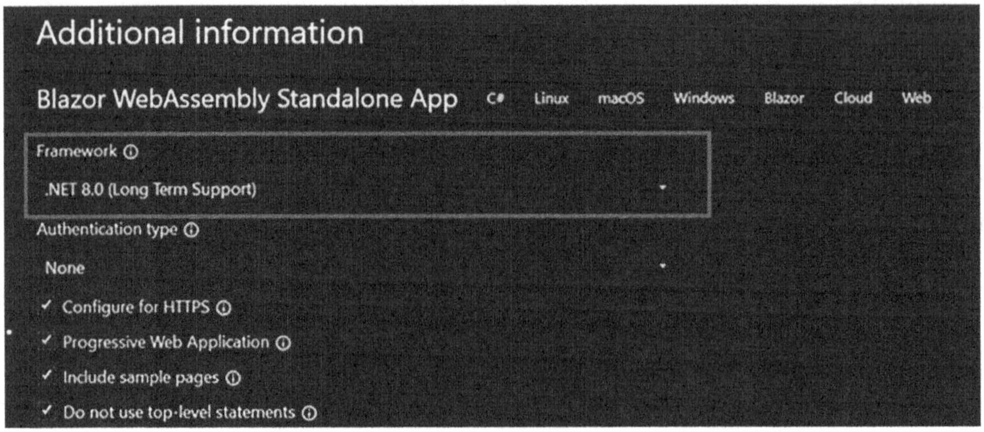

Figure 1.7: *Framework Selection*

Step 5: Now, run the application using F5 or click here on Visual Studio.

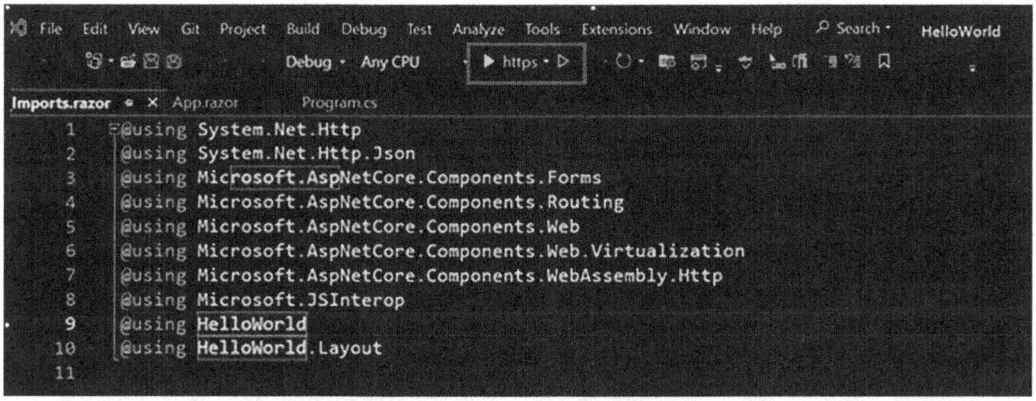

***Figure 1.8**: Blazor App*

You will see the following output:

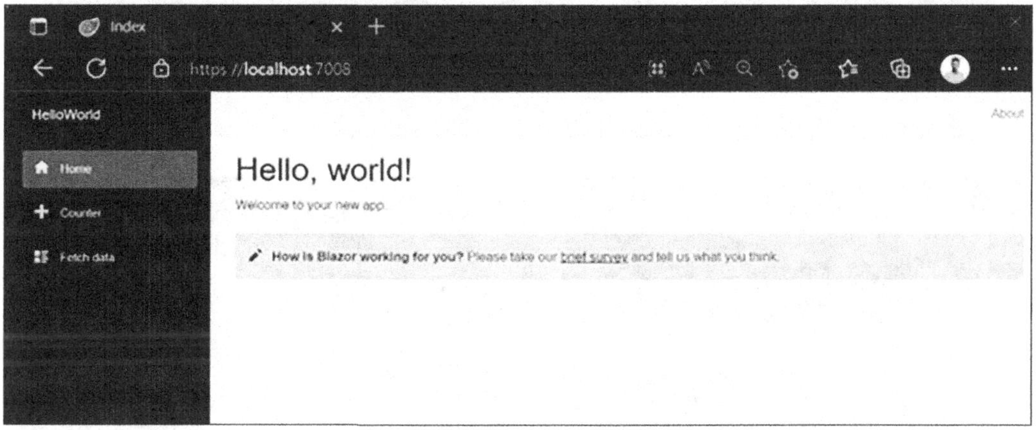

***Figure 1.9**: Output*

Congratulations on creating the Hello world application. As you can see, it is very straightforward to create a Blazor WebAssembly application using Visual Studio 2022.

If you have a low configuration system and you want a very lightweight development experience, then you can choose Visual Studio (VS) Code.

It is a lightweight open-source code editor. It will work on all platforms.

Creating Blazor WebAssembly Using VS Code

The following are the steps to create Blazor WebAssembly using VS Code:

Step 1: Install the VS Code on your system.

Step 2: Open the VS Code in your working folder as follows:

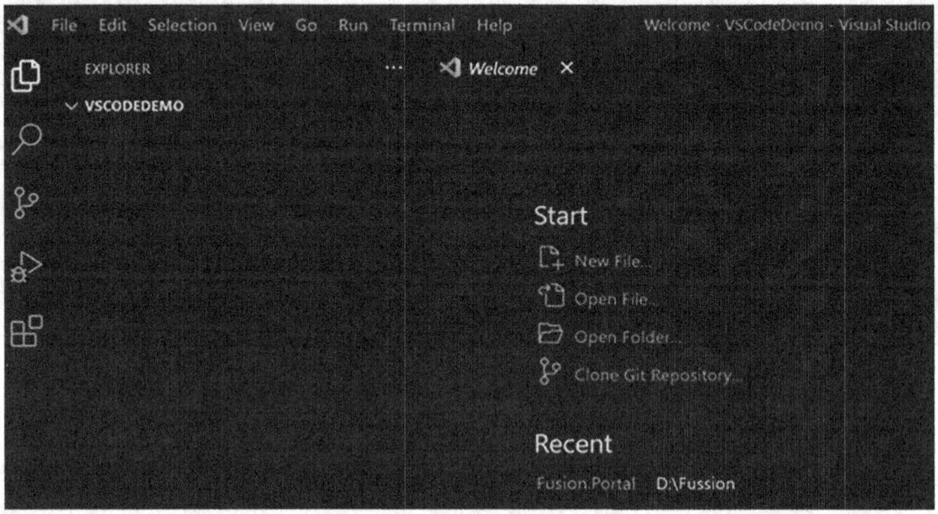

Figure 1.10: VS Code

Step 3: Open the terminal as shown in the following figure:

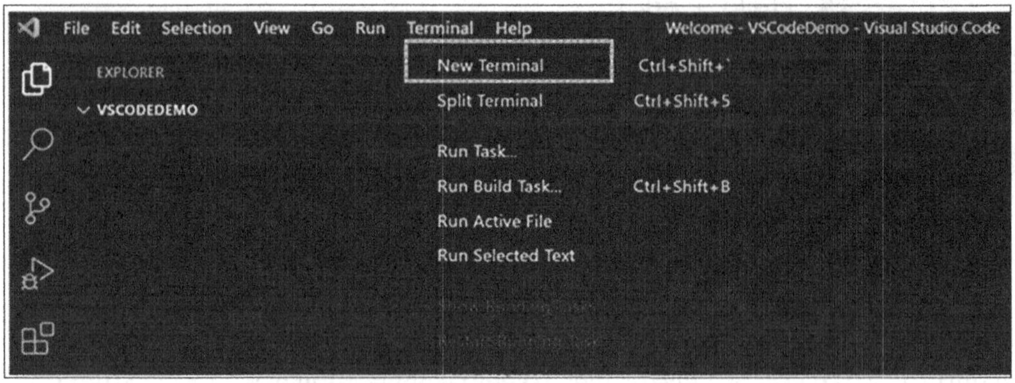

Figure 1.11: *VS Code Terminal*

Step 4: Write the command for creating a Blazor WASM application as follows:

```
dotnet new blazorwasm -n HelloWorld
```

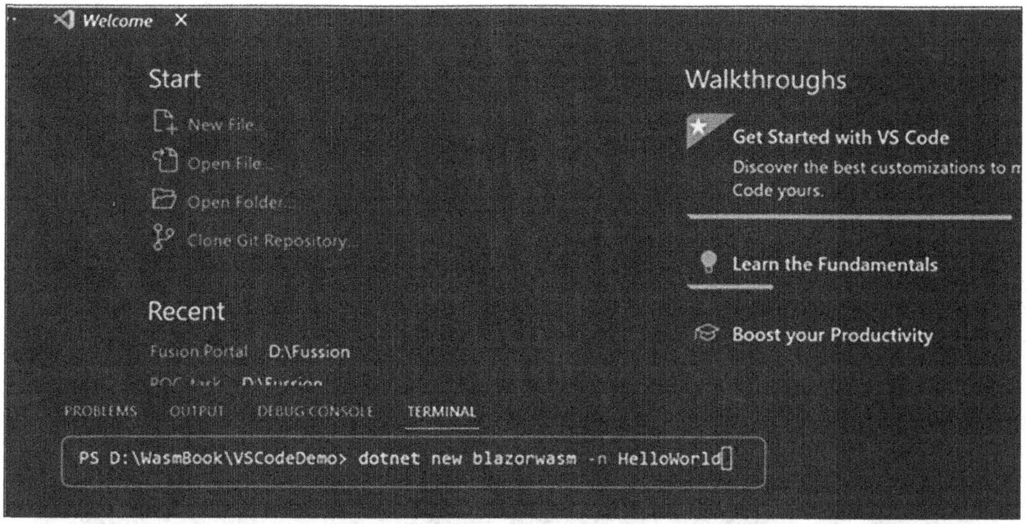

Figure 1.12: VS Code Command

Step 5: Go to the application folder.

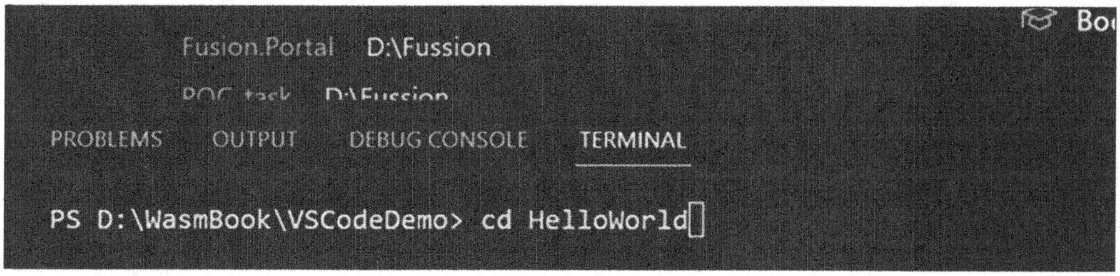

Figure 1.13: VS Code Command

Step 6: Execute the **`dotnet build`** command on the terminal as shown in the following figure:

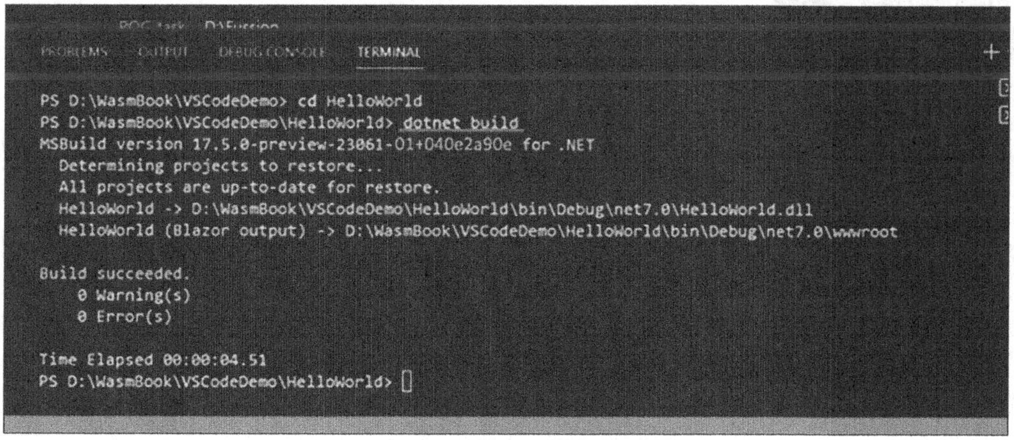

Figure 1.14: VS Code Build

Step 7: Now, execute the **dotnet run** command.

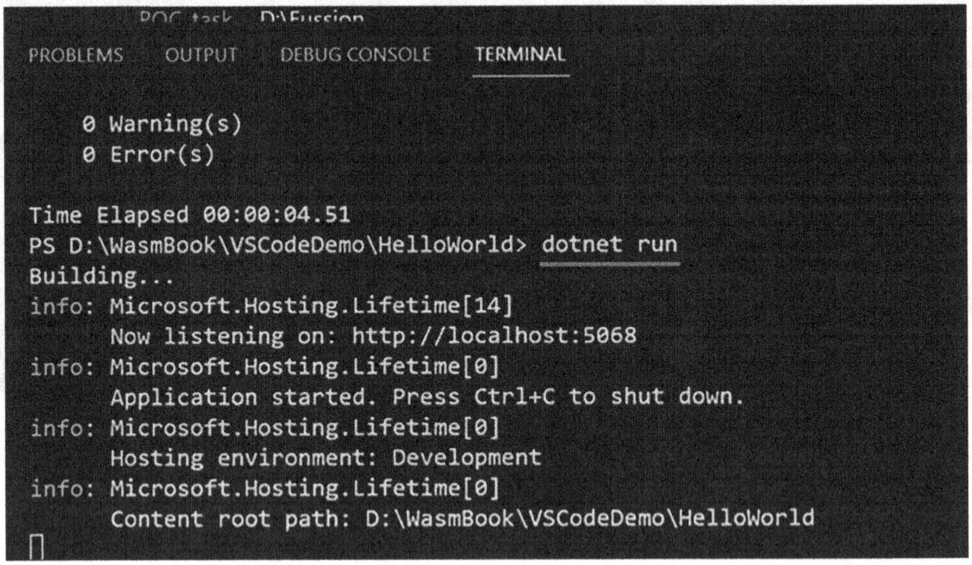

***Figure* 1.15**: VS Code Run

Step 8: If you are not getting the **https port,** then you can run this command on the terminal as follows:

```
dotnet dev-certs https --trust
dotnet watch  run --urls https://localhost:5001
```

Note: *You can provide any port number. For demo purposes, let us give it as* 5001.

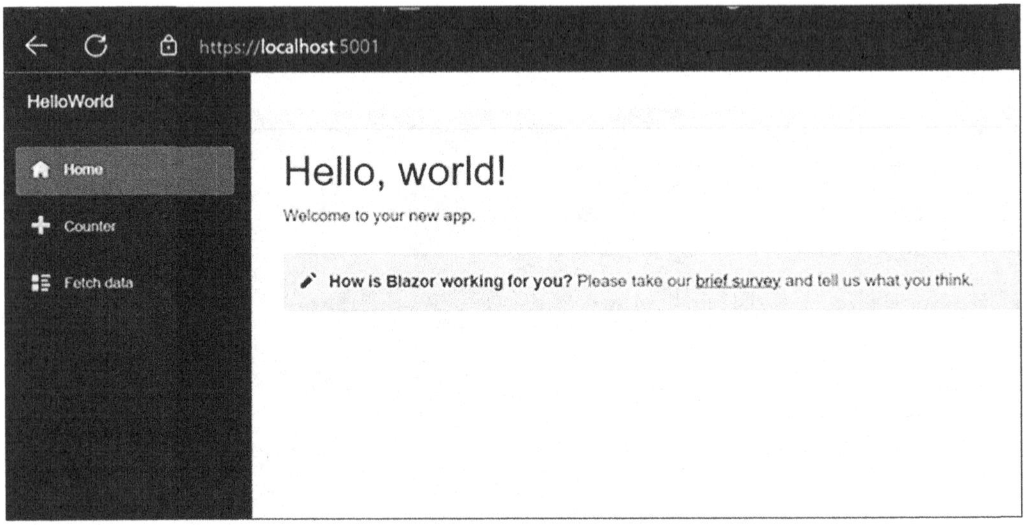

***Figure* 1.16**: VS Code Output

As you can see in both approaches, creating a Blazor application using Visual Studio 2022 is very straightforward. If you are a beginner, then you can choose Visual Studio 2022.

Project Structure in Blazor WebAssembly 8.0 Application

Let's open our Hello World Project in Visual Studio 2022.

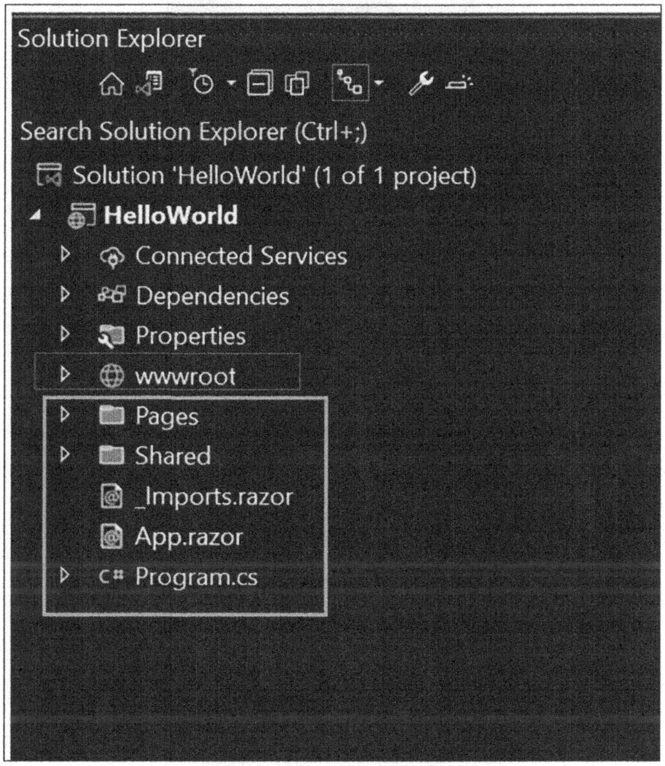

Figure 1.17: *Blazor Project*

As you can see, we have the following folders and files:

- `wwwroot`
- `Pages`
- `Shared`
- `_Imports.razor`
- `App.razor`
- `Program.cs`

Let us look at each one of them:

- `wwwroot Folder`: It is used for storing CSS, JavaScript, Images and Static Content files like html and json data files.

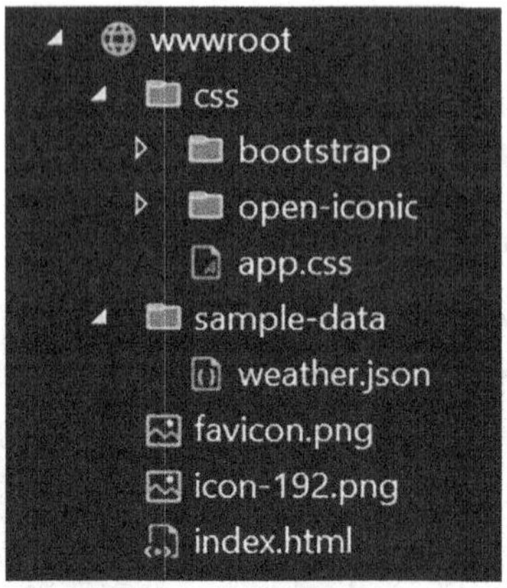

Figure 1.18: *Blazor Project wwwroot*

- `Pages`: It is used for storing razor component files. We will deep dive into this topic in the next chapter.

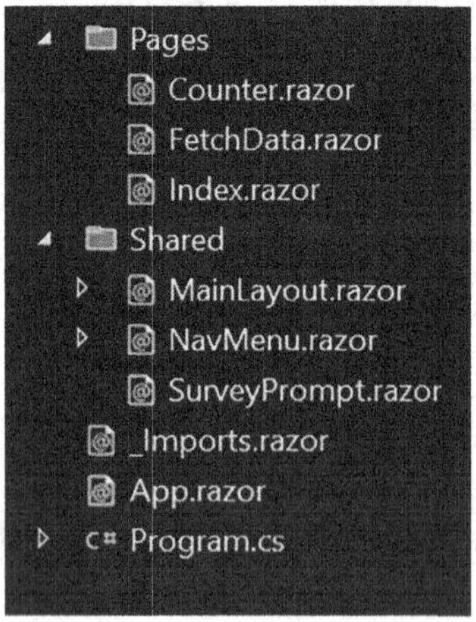

Figure 1.19: *Blazor Project Page*

- `Shared`: It is used for storing shared components, which can be reused in the entire application.

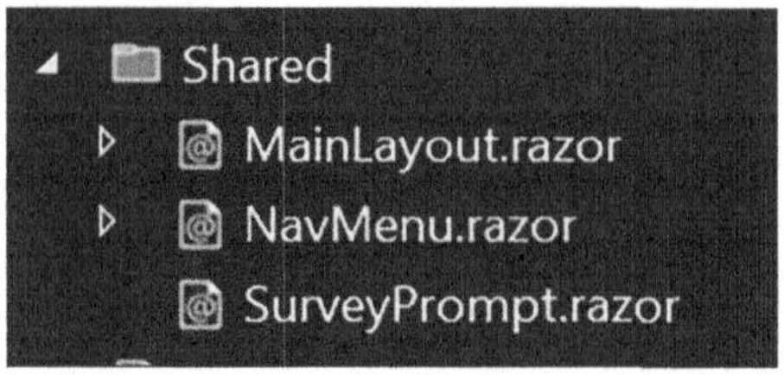

Figure 1.20: *Blazor Shared Folder*

In this folder `MainLayout`, `NavMenu` shared components are present that can be used for the entire application.

- **`_Imports.razor`:** It is used for storing all global namespaces, which can be applied to an entire application.

```
@using System.Net.Http
@using System.Net.Http.Json
@using Microsoft.AspNetCore.Components.Forms
@using Microsoft.AspNetCore.Components.Routing
@using Microsoft.AspNetCore.Components.Web
@using Microsoft.AspNetCore.Components.Web.Virtualization
@using Microsoft.AspNetCore.Components.WebAssembly.Http
@using Microsoft.JSInterop
@using HelloWorld
@using HelloWorld.Shared
```

Figure 1.21: *Blazor Import Razor*

- **`App.Razor`:** It is a special file in the Blazor application, which is used to serve as the root component of the application (refer to *Figure* 1.21). The **`app.razor`** file defines the layout and structure of the application, including the navigation and the content that is displayed on each page. It is responsible for rendering the initial user interface of the application.

  In the Blazor WebAssembly application, the **`app.razor`** file is compiled into a JavaScript file that runs in the user's web browser. In the Blazor Server application, the **`app.razor`** file is compiled into a .NET assembly that runs on the server. It can also be used to define global CSS styles and other resources that are used throughout the application. Overall, the **`app.razor`** file is a key component of a Blazor application, and it is responsible for defining the structure and behavior of the user interface.

```
<Router AppAssembly="@typeof(App).Assembly">
    <Found Context="routeData">
        <RouteView RouteData="@routeData" DefaultLayout="@typeof(MainLayout)" />
        <FocusOnNavigate RouteData="@routeData" Selector="h1" />
    </Found>
    <NotFound>
        <PageTitle>Not found</PageTitle>
        <LayoutView Layout="@typeof(MainLayout)">
            <p role="alert">Sorry, there's nothing at this address.</p>
        </LayoutView>
    </NotFound>
</Router>
```

Figure 1.22: *Blazor App Razor*

- **`Program.cs`:** It is one of the important files of the Blazor application, which contains the entry point of the Blazor application.

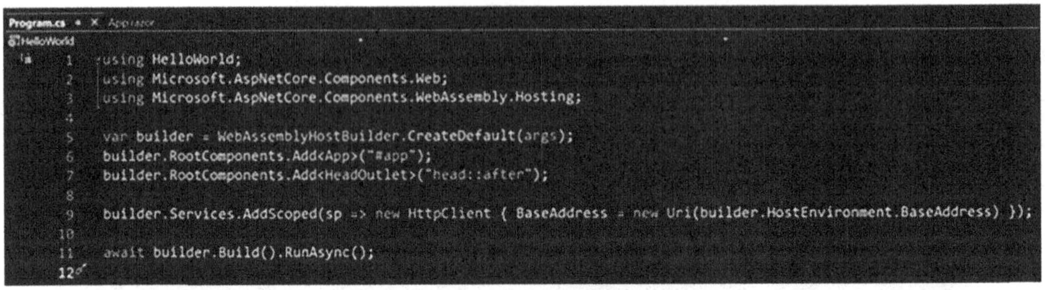

Figure 1.23: *Blazor Program.cs*

It is used to configure the application's hosting environment, services, and middleware. In a Blazor WebAssembly application, the **`program.cs`** file typically contains code to create a new instance of the **`WebAssemblyHostBuilder`** class and configure it with the necessary services and middleware. This includes registering the application's services, configuring the HTTP client, and adding any required middleware components.

The **`program.cs`** file is responsible for setting up the application's hosting environment, which includes defining the server or client hosting mode, configuring the application's logging, and setting up any required authentication or authorization services.

Overall, the **`program.cs`** file plays a key role in configuring and bootstrapping a Blazor application, and it is an essential file to understand while working with Blazor application.

Conclusion

In this chapter, we saw what Blazor is, why we should learn the Blazor web application, and what are the advantages and disadvantages of the Blazor WebAssembly application. We also saw different types of Blazor applications.

Blazor WebAssembly 8.0 is one of the leading, super-fast, and most modern web application development frameworks. It saves 30%–40% development and support time as compared to other competitor single page application(SPA) web development frameworks.

We saw how to create a "**`Hello World`**" Application using Visual Studio 2022 and VS Code. We also saw the project structure of the Blazor WebAssembly application. In the next chapter, we will discuss the basic and advanced concepts on Blazor component.

References

Host and deploy ASP.NET Core Blazor WebAssembly | Microsoft Learn (https://learn.microsoft.com/en-us/aspnet/core/blazor/host-and-deploy/webassembly?view=aspnetcore-7.0)

Multiple Choice Questions

1. Blazor WebAssembly run on?
   a. Client browser
   b. Server
   c. Cloud machine
   d. None
2. What does WASM stand for?
   a. WebAssembly
   b. WebActionScript Markup
   c. WebAsset Scripting Model
   d. WebAPI Service Module
3. Is WebAssembly faster than JavaScript for computationally intensive tasks?
   a. Yes
   b. No
   c. It depends on the specific task
4. Can we run Blazor application on all platforms?
   a. Yes
   b. No
   c. Only on specific platforms
5. Is Blazor open-source project?
   a. Yes
   b. No
   c. Only the documentation is open source

Answers

1. a
2. a
3. c
4. a
5. a

Chapter 2
Razor Components

Introduction

This chapter covers the Blazor component, which is the building block of the Blazor application. We will discuss all the basic and advanced concepts on Blazor component with sample code.

Structure

This chapter covers the following topics:

- Introduction to Blazor component
- Creating a Blazor Component
- Razor Component Lifecycle
- Parameters in Blazor Component
- Data Binding in Blazor Component
- Passing Data from Parent to Child Component
- Passing Data from Child to Parent Component
- Nested Blazor Component
- Code Segregation Approach in Blazor Component
- Styling Component in Blazor

Introduction to Blazor Component

The Blazor component is the building block of the Blazor application. It is a self-contained chunk of user interface (UI), like a login page, popup screen, and so on.

We cannot imagine a Blazor application without components. If you have worked with Angular or React applications, you might already be familiar with component-driven applications.

Blazor is a totally component-driven application, with each component being a combination of Razor, Html, and C# code. Components are self-contained and reusable, encapsulating their own logic and data. They can be composed together to build larger user interfaces.

The main benefits of a component-based application are code sharing across multiple applications, nested UI design, code reusability and a clean application design.

Creating a Blazor Component

The following are the steps to create a Blazor Component:

Step 1: Open Visual Studio 2022 and create a Blazor WebAssembly application.

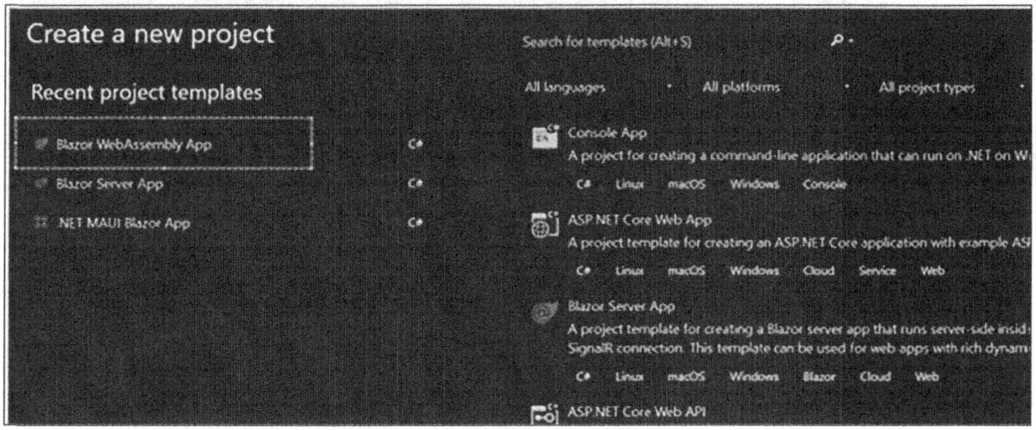

***Figure 2.1**: Project template*

Step 2: Select the framework as .NET 8.0.

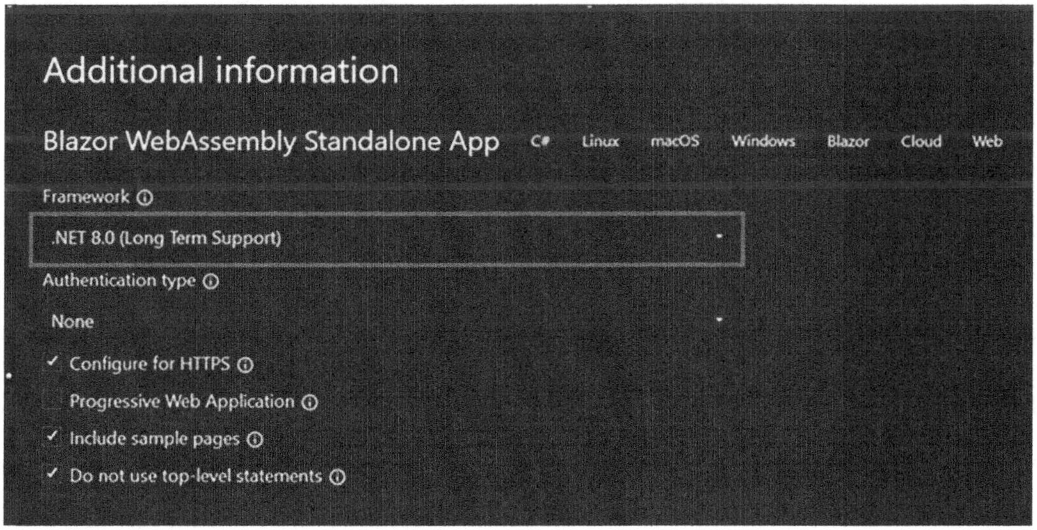

***Figure 2.2**: Project wizard*

Step 3: Create the Blazor application.

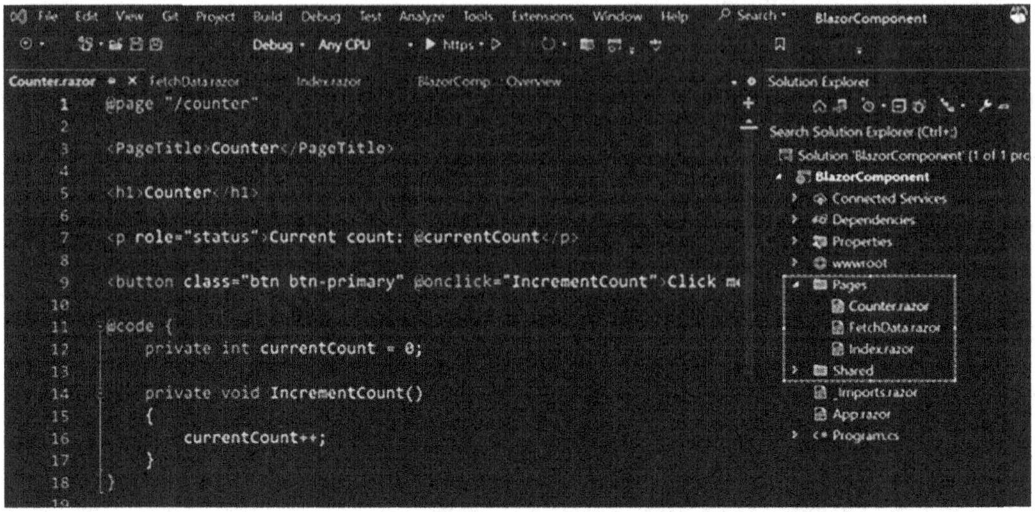

Figure 2.3: *Project Files*

In the following figure, all pages and the shared folder contain components that consist of directive, markup, and logic.

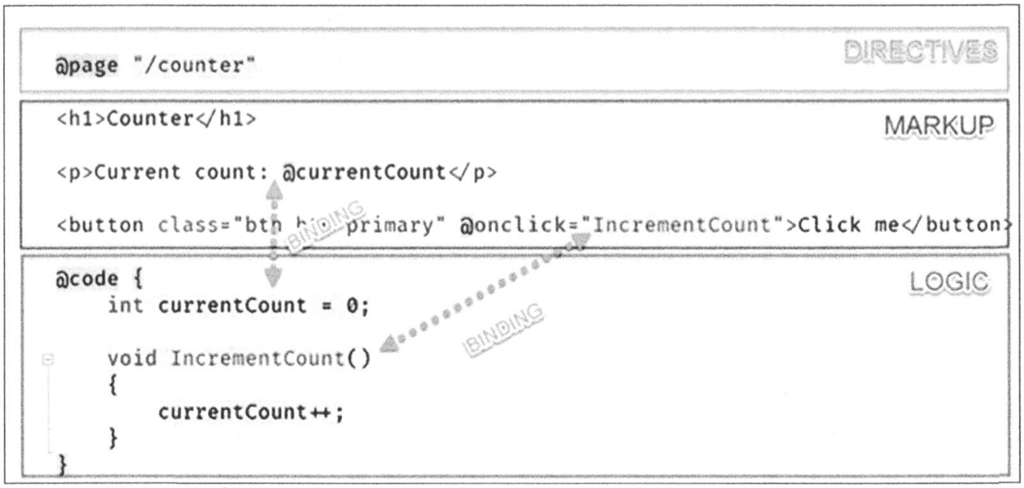

Figure 2.4: *Data binding syntax*

Razor Component Lifecycle

Whenever we create a component, it will derive from `ComponentBase`.

`ComponentBase` implements `Icomponent`, which Blazor uses to locate components throughout the project. `ComponentBase` contains important lifecycle methods.

As you work with components, you will notice that the **`ComponentBase`** class provides a number of virtual methods that can be overridden to hook into various points during the life cycle of a Razor component.

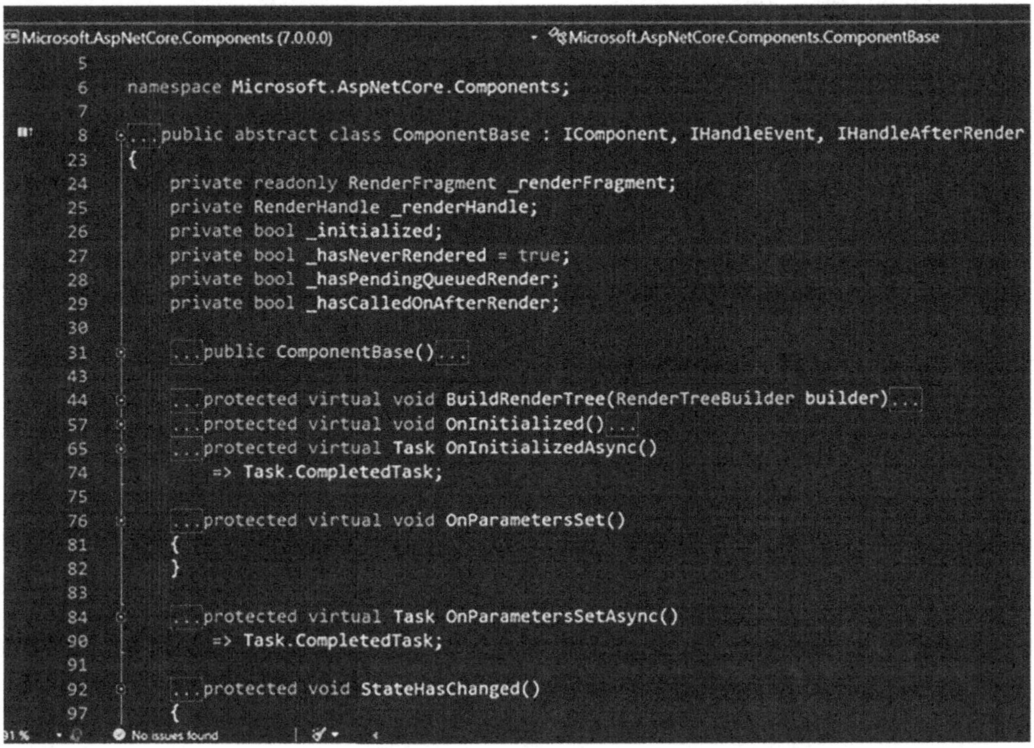

***Figure* 2.5**: *Component lifecycle*

These points include:

- Whenever parameter values are set.
- When the component is initialized.
- Each time the component is rendered.

Let's have a detailed explanation of these points here:

- **When Parameter Values are set**

The first hook in the component life cycle is available when a component's parameters receive their values from the parent component.

The virtual methods that can be overridden at this point are **`OnParametersSet`** and its async method, **`OnParametersSetAsync`**. These methods are called when a component is first initialized and each time new or updated parameters are received from the parent in the render tree.

Let's consider a simple example.

Create the **Parent component**.

```
<!-- Parent Component -->
@page "/home"
<h1>Hello, world!</h1>
Welcome to your new app.
<Counter count=theCount />
<button @onclick=incrementCount>Click</button>
@code {
    int theCount { get; set; } = 1;
    void incrementCount()
    {
        theCount++;
    }
}
```

Create the **Child component**.

```
<!-- Child Component -->
@page "/counter"

<h1>Counter</h1>
<p>@message</p>
@code {
    [Parameter]
    public int count { get; set; } = 0;
    string? message { get; set; }
    protected override void OnParametersSet()
    {
        if (string.IsNullOrEmpty(message))
        {
            message = "Parameters set for the first time";
        }
        else
        {
            message = "Parameter reset to " + count;
        }
        base.OnParametersSet();
    }
}
```

Whenever you run this application, you will see the following output: "**Parameters set for first time**".

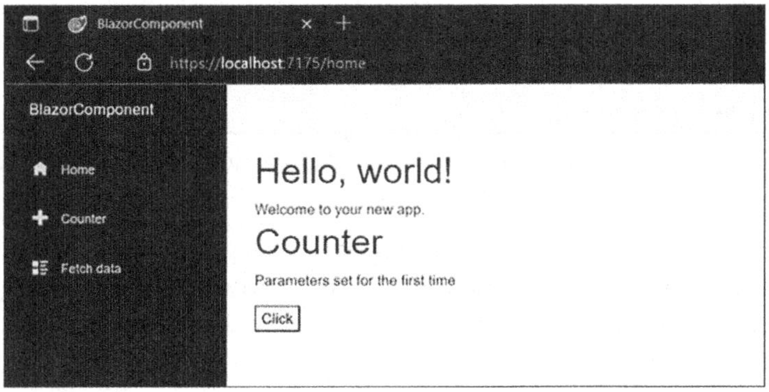

Figure 2.6: *Output*

When you click the **`Click`** button, you will see the message: **`"Parameter reset to 2"`**.

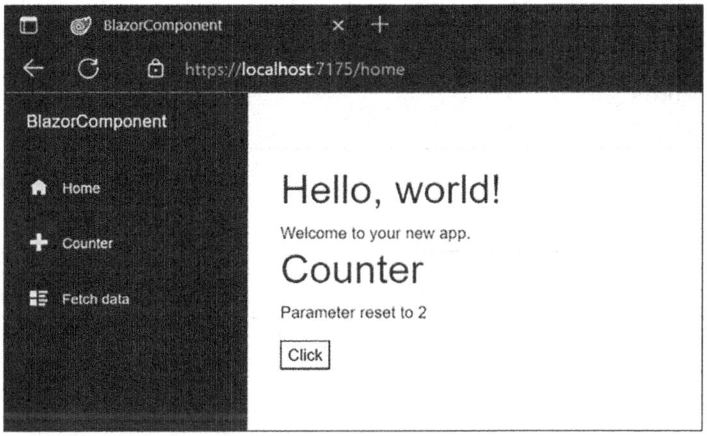

Figure 2.7: *Output*

This demonstrates that the method is called after parameter values are set.

- **When the Component is Initialized**

Once the component has received its initial parameters from its parent in the render tree, the **`OnInitialized`** and **`OnInitializedAsync`** methods are called.

This is the point where you would typically make calls to Web API services to obtain data for the component before it can be rendered.

Here is a simple code snippet that demonstrates this:

```
protected override async Task OnInitializedAsync()
    {
        forecasts = await Http.GetFromJsonAsync<WeatherForecast[]>
("sample-data/weather.json");
    }
```

- **After the Component has been Rendered**

At this point, The **OnAfterRender** and **OnAfterRenderAsync** methods are called after each render of the component.

At this point, element and component references are available, so this phase is ideal for performing the initialization of JavaScript resources that depend on DOM elements.

Both methods take a bool named **firstRender** as an argument. This is set by the framework and is true when the component is rendered for the first time. We can use this flag to prevent one-time initialization being executed unnecessarily when the component is re-rendered.

Here is the code snippet for calling the JavaScript resource **OnAfterRender**:

```
@inject IJSRuntime JS
JSObjectReference module;
protected override void OnAfterRender(bool firstRender)
{
    if(firstRender)
    {
        module = await JS.InvokeAsync<JSObjectReference>("import",
"./js/exampleJsInterop.js");
    }
}
```

Use **OnAfterRenderAsync** to call asynchronous methods.

```
protected override Task OnAfterRenderAsync(bool firstRender)
{
    //...
}
```

- **Prevent Rendering**

In this phase, the **ShouldRender** method is called. This method returns a **bool** that determines whether a component should be re-rendered. The component will still render at least once. We can use this method to suppress UI refreshing.

```
@page "/shouldrendertest"
<h1>Counter</h1>
<p>Current count: @currentCount</p>
<button class="btn btn-primary" @onclick="IncrementCount">Click me</but-
ton>
@code {
    private int currentCount = 0;
    private bool shouldRender;
    protected override bool ShouldRender() => shouldRender;
    private void IncrementCount()
```

```
    {
        currentCount++;
        shouldRender = currentCount % 2 == 0;
    }
}
```

In the following demo, the on-button click counter will increment by 1, but the UI will only refresh on the next click event.

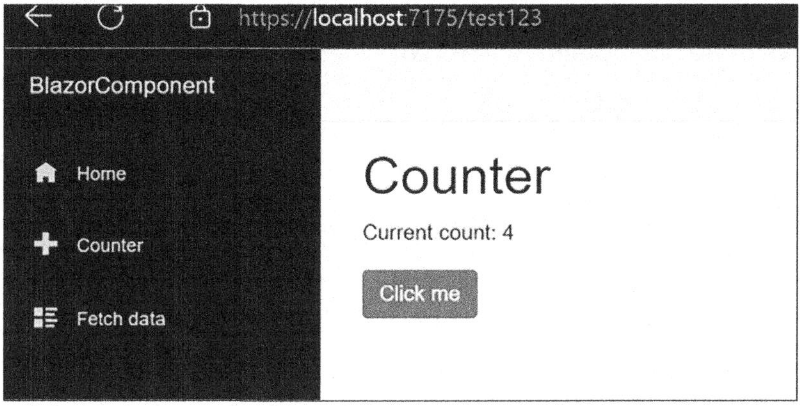

***Figure 2.8**: Output*

`StateHasChanged()`

This method is not a part of the component lifecycle, but it is closely related to it. We use this method to inform the Blazor runtime that the state of the component has changed and that the component needs to be re-rendered.

It is called after any lifecycle method has been called and can also be invoked manually to trigger a re-render.

Let's take one simple example.

```
@code {
    private WeatherForecast[] forecasts;

    protected override async Task OnInitializedAsync()
    {
        var httpClient = new HttpClient();
        forecasts = await httpClient.GetFromJsonAsync<WeatherForecast[]>
("sample-data/weather.json");
        StateHasChanged();
    }
}
```

In the preceding code snippet, we are forcefully refreshing the UI to re-render to fetch the latest data.

Parameters in Blazor Component

In Blazor components, parameters are a way to pass data from a parent component to a child component. Parameters are defined as public properties or fields in the child component and can be assigned values by the parent component when the child component is rendered.

There are two types of parameters in Blazor components, including:

- Non-cascading parameters
- Cascading parameters

Non-cascading Parameters

Non-cascading parameters are explicitly passed from a parent to a child component and can be defined as public properties or fields in the child component.

To pass a non-cascading parameter to a child component, the parent component includes the parameter in the child component's markup using the **`@`** character followed by the name of the parameter, such as: **`<ChildComponent MyParameter="@ myValue" />`**

Let's take a look at an example of non-cascading parameters in our sample project.

Go to the **`SurveyPrompt.razor`** component.

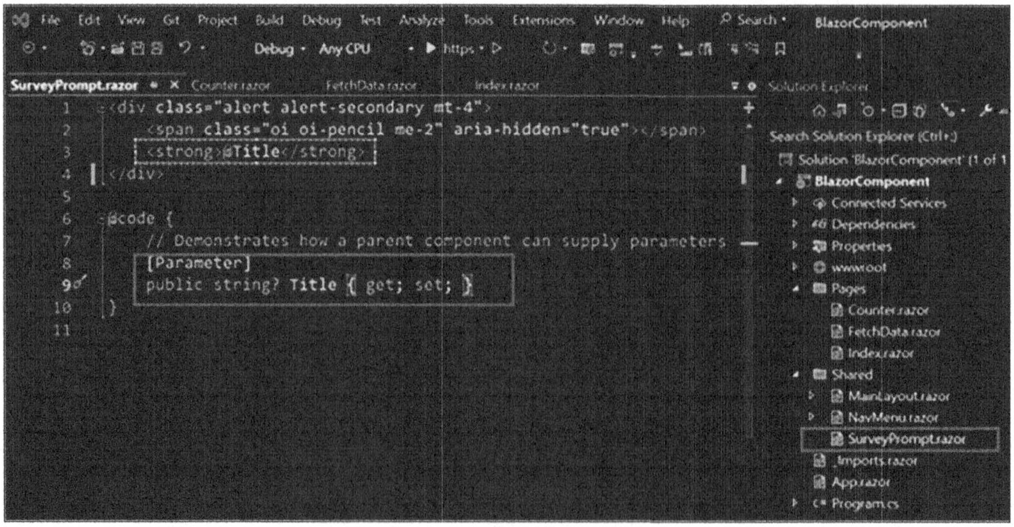

***Figure 2.9**: Non-cascading parameter*

As you see in the preceding figure, Title public Property has been created with the Parameter attribute and has been called on **`@Title`** in Html UI.

This means that whenever the parent component passes a specific title to the child component, it will be read and rendered on the HTML UI using **`@Title`**.

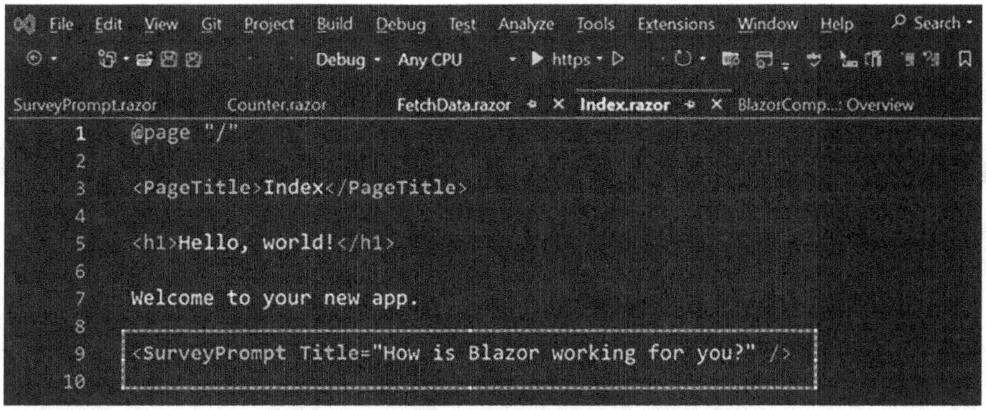

***Figure 2.10**: Parameter passing syntax*

Here **`index.razor`** is the parent component, and we are passing Title as a string to the `Child component`.

To see the output, you can run the application.

***Figure 2.11**: Output*

In the preceding figure, we see that by using the **`@Parameter`** attribute, we are passing Title as a string from the parent component (that is, **`Index.razor`**) to the child component (that is, **`SurveyPrompt.razor`**). We have nested the child component within the parent component.

Cascading Parameters

Cascading parameters allow data to be passed down through a hierarchy of components, without the need to pass the data explicitly from parent to child.

A component can define a cascading parameter using the **`[CascadingParameter]`** attribute. The parent component can then provide a value for the parameter by wrapping the child component in a **`CascadingValue`** component.

Let's create a simple example of cascading parameters by following these steps:

Step 1: Create two child components with cascading parameters as follows:

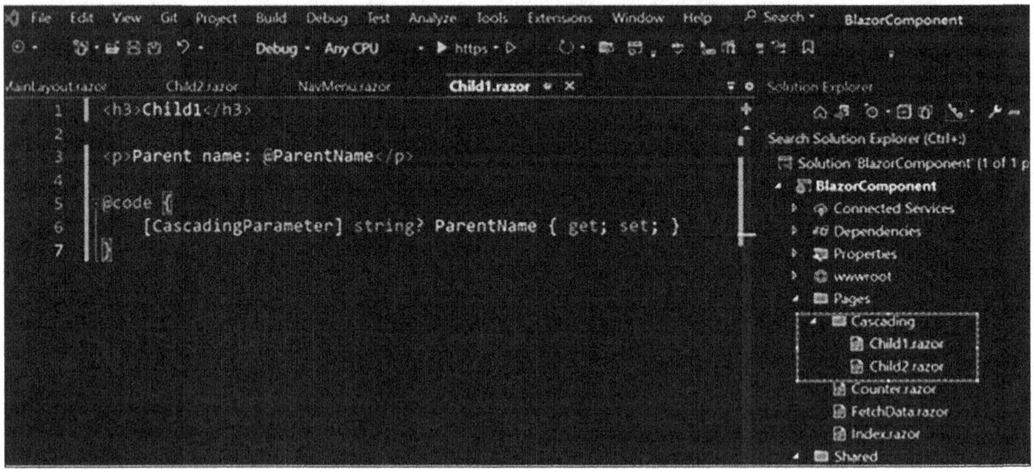

***Figure 2.12**: Cascading parameter*

The complete code snippet for the Child1.razor page is as follows:

```
<h3>Child1</h3>

<p>Parent name: @ParentName</p>

@code {
    [CascadingParameter] string? ParentName { get; set; }
}
```

For Child2.razor component:

```
<h3>Child2</h3>

<p>Parent name: @ParentName</p>

@code {
    [CascadingParameter] string? ParentName { get; set; }
}
```

Step 2: Go to the parent component, that is, **`Index.razor`** and pass the cascading values to all child components as follows:

```
@page "/"
@using BlazorComponent.Pages.Cascading

<PageTitle>Index</PageTitle>

<h1>Demo of Cascading Parameter</h1>
<hr />

<CascadingValue Value="@Name">
    <Child1></Child1>
    <Child2></Child2>
</CascadingValue>

@code {
    String Name = "Index Page";
}
```

Step 3: Run the application.

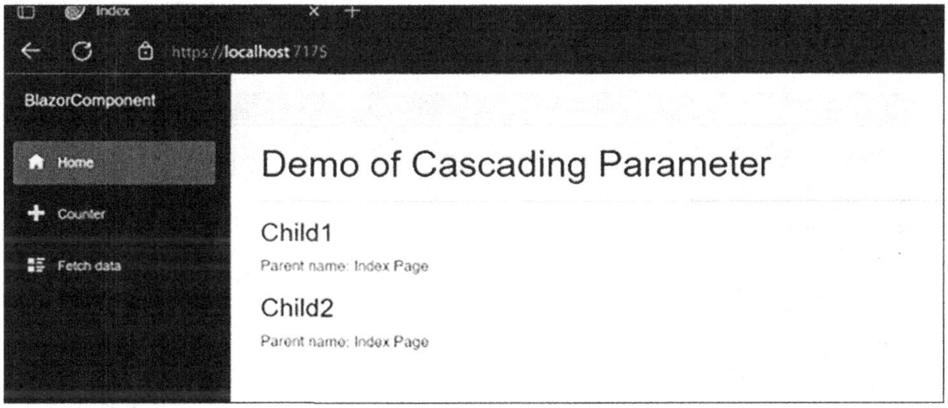

***Figure* 2.13**: *Cascading parameter demo*

In the preceding figure, we can see that we are passing the `"Index Page"` from the parent page with the help of a cascading parameter. This value is then passed to all child components.

Data Binding in Blazor Components

Data binding in the Blazor components is one of the core concepts when working with Blazor applications. We cannot create any Blazor application without data binding. Whether we are creating an entry screen or displaying data on a grid, we need to do data binding.

In Blazor, there are two types of data binding, including:

- One-way data binding
- Two-way data binding

One-Way Data Binding

In this approach, data communication happens in one way. One-way bindings have a unidirectional flow, meaning that the value is updated only one time.

Let's take a simple example to demonstrate one-way data binding.

```
@page "/onewaybinding"
<h1>@Title</h1>

@code {
    private string Title { get; set; } = "This is one way databinding
demo";
}
```

In the preceding code snippet, we are binding the title to **`@Title`**. This binding occurs only once.

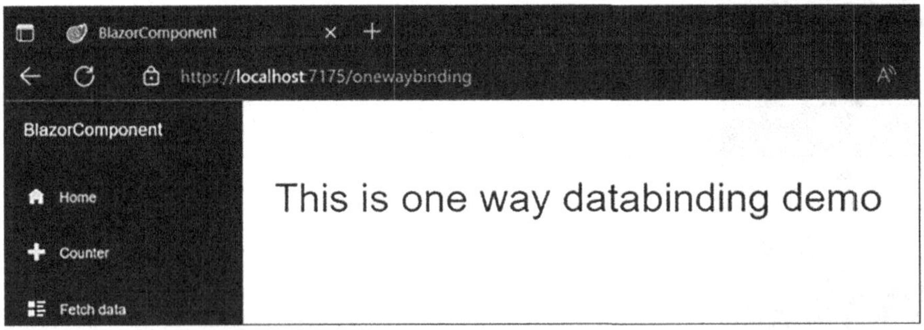

Figure 2.14: *One-way data binding*

We will also see one more example of one-way data binding on Event click.

```
@page "/onewaybinding2"
<h1>@Title</h1>

<button @onclick="UpdateTitle">Update Title</button>

@code {
    private string Title { get; set; } = "Hello, World!";

    private void UpdateTitle()
```

```
    {
        Title = "Hello, Updated text message!";
    }
}
```

In the preceding code snippet, whenever we click a button, the new text will be bound to the Title. So, in this demo, we saw that value will be updated in one direction on `Click Event`.

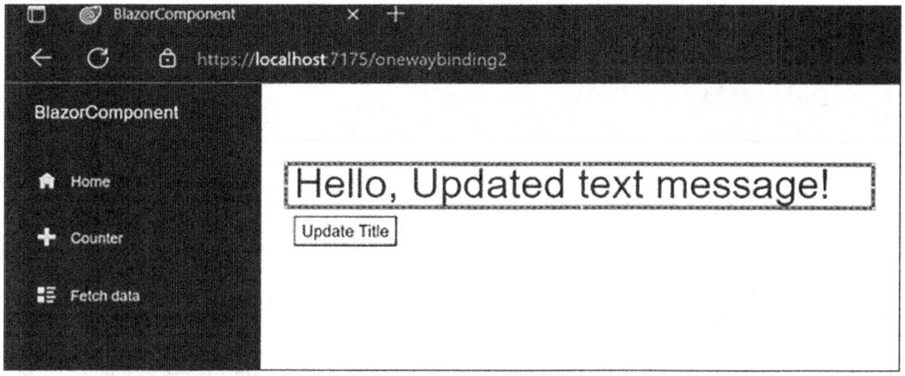

***Figure 2.15**: Output*

One-way data binding

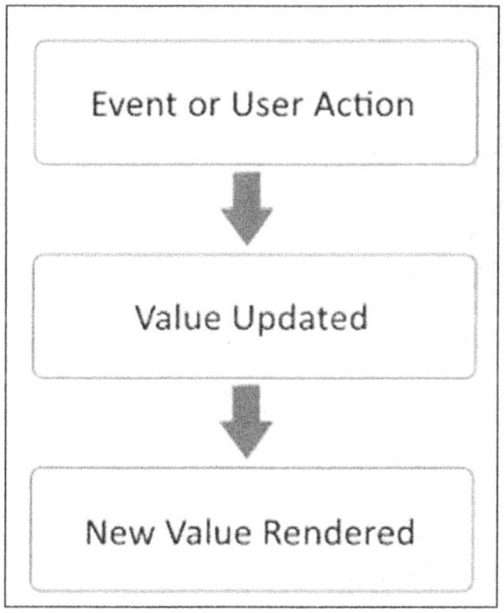

***Figure 2.16**: One-way binding workflow*

Two-Way Data Binding

Two-way data binding has a bidirectional flow, allowing values to be updated from two directions. The most suitable scenario to use two-way data binding is in forms, although we can use it anywhere in the application wherever we need two-way data flow.

Two-way binding is achieved using the **@bind** directive in Blazor.

Let's see the basic demo of two-way data binding.

```
@page "/TwoWayDataBinding"
<h3>TwoWayDataBinding</h3>

<h1>@Title</h1>

<input @bind="@Title" />

@code {
    private string Title { get; set; } = "Hello, World!";
}
```

In the preceding example, we saw that when we update on textbox, it will also update on the HTML UI screen.

***Figure 2.17**: Two-way data binding*

Two-way data binding can be achieved using the following bind attributes:

- `@bind=Property`
- `@bind-Value=Property`
- `@bind-Value:event="onevent"`

We will now take a look at another example of two-way binding on Event.

```
@page "/TwowayBindEvent"
<h3>TwowayBindEvent</h3>

<h1>@Title</h1>
```

```
<input @bind-value="Title" @bind-value:event="oninput" />

@code {
    private string Title { get; set; } = "Hello, World!";
}
```

In the preceding code snippet, we saw that whenever we change any text in the preceding textbox, it will keep updating the UI in real-time using **`@bind-value:event`**

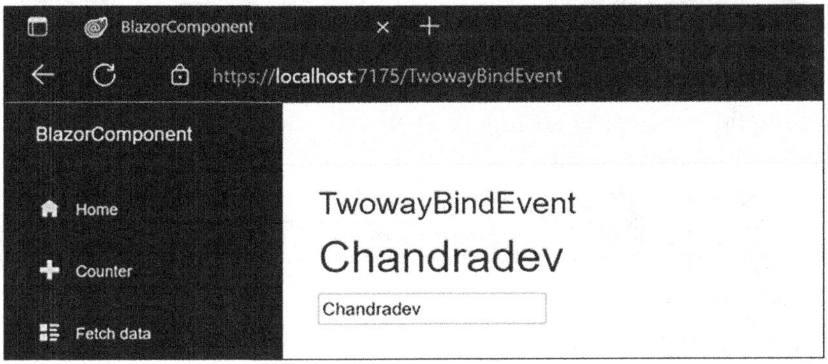

***Figure 2.18**: Output*

Passing Data from Parent to Child Component

As discussed previously, in Blazor, we can pass data from parent to child components using the `@parameter` attribute.

Step 1: Create the Child component with `[Parameter]` attribute.

```
<div class="alert alert-secondary mt-4">
    <span class="oi oi-pencil me-2" aria-hidden="true"></span>
    <strong>@Title</strong>
</div>

@code {
    // Demonstrates how a parent component can supply parameters
    [Parameter]
    public string? Title { get; set; }
}
```

Step 2: Call the child component in the parent component and pass the parameter as follows:

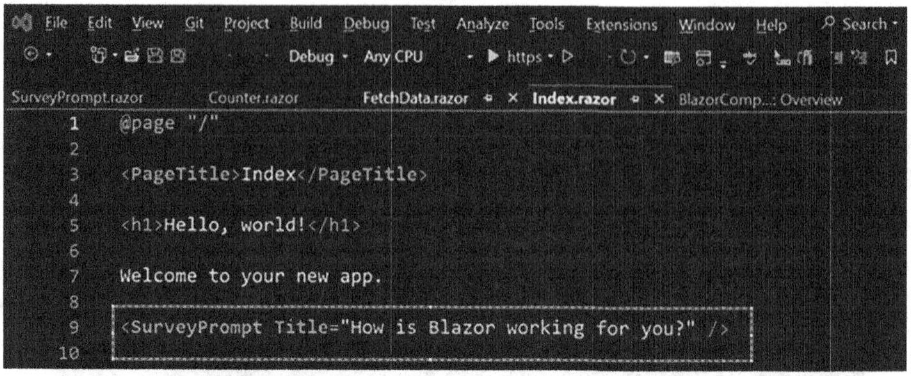

***Figure 2.19**: Parent to child syntax*

In the preceding figure, we are passing the title parameter as a string, and it will render the UI on the parent component.

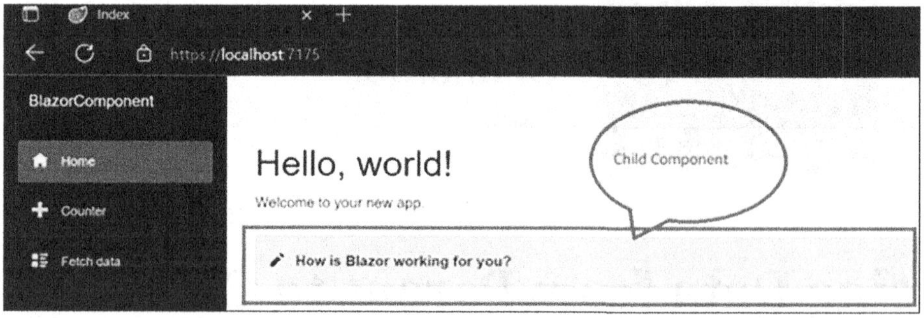

***Figure 2.20**: Output*

Passing Data from Child to Parent Component

We can communicate child components to parent components using **`EventCallback`**.

For this demo, we will create a child component with Textbox as input and a button. Whenever we pass input data into the textbox and click the button, the input text will be displayed on the parent component.

Step 1: Create the child component with **`EventCallback`** as a string.

```
<div>
    <input type="text" @bind="@message" />
    <button @onclick="DisplayMessage">Click Here</button>
</div>

@code {
```

```
    [Parameter]
    public string InputParam { get; set; }
    [Parameter]
    public EventCallback<string> OnClickCallback { get; set; }

    private string message;
    private async Task DisplayMessage()
    {
        await OnClickCallback.InvokeAsync(message);
    }
}
```

Step 2: Create the parent component.

```
@page "/"

<PageTitle>Index</PageTitle>

<SurveyPrompt InputParam="message" OnClickCallback="@ShowMessage" />
<p>@message</p>

@code
{
    private string message;

    private void ShowMessage(string _message)
    {
        message = _message;
    }
}
```

Now, run the application.

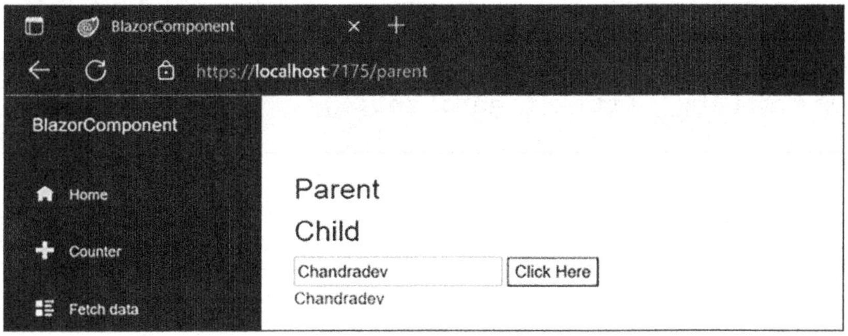

***Figure 2.21**: Output*

In this demo, we have demonstrated that by using **EventCallback**, we can communicate from the child component to the parent component.

Nested Component in Blazor

Creating nested components in Blazor is very simple and straightforward.

We need to create parent and child components, as shown in the following figure.

All the child components need to be nested inside the parent component.

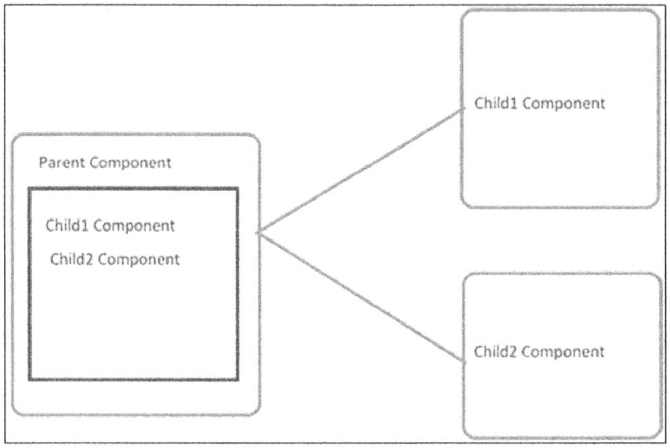

Figure 2.22: *Nested component*

Let's create a simple sample code.

Create two child components.

```
<h3>ChildComp1</h3>

<div class="alert alert-secondary mt-4">
    <strong>@Title</strong>
</div>

@code {
    [Parameter]
    public string? Title { get; set; }
}
```

Child 2 Component:

```
<h3>ChildComp2</h3>

<div class="alert alert-secondary mt-4">
```

```
    <strong>@Title</strong>
</div>

@code {
    [Parameter]
    public string? Title { get; set; }
}
```

Create the nested parent component.

```
@page "/nested"
<h3>Nested Demo</h3>
<hr />
<div>
    <ChildComp1 Title="This is Child1 Component"></ChildComp1>
    <ChildComp2 Title="This is Child2 Component"></ChildComp2>
</div>
```

Now, run the application, and the output will be as follows:

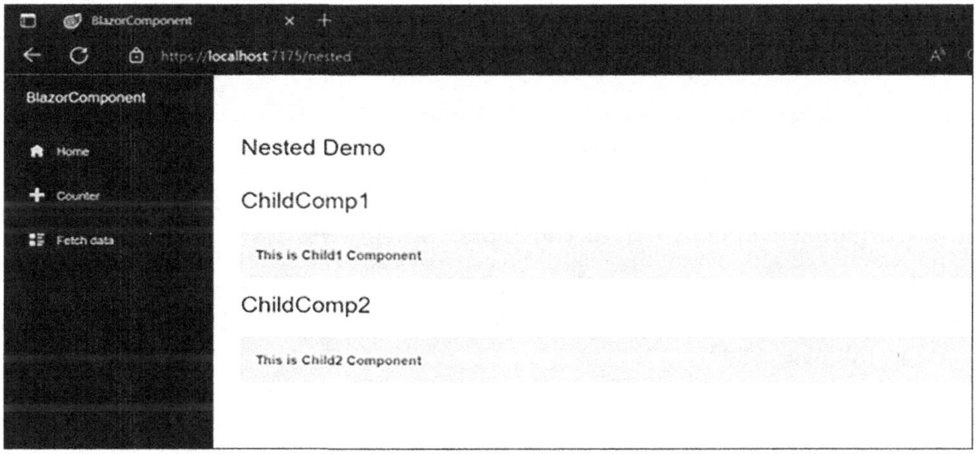

Figure 2.23: *Output*

Code Segregation Approach in Blazor Component

In Blazor, we can write C# and Razor code using the following two approaches:

- Inline approach
- Code-behind approach

Inline Approach

Let's take the example of the inline approach.

```
@page "/statehaschanged"
<h3>StateChanged</h3>
<p>Current count: @currentCount</p>
<button class="btn btn-primary" @onclick="IncrementCount">Click me</
button>

@code {
    private int currentCount = 0;

    private async Task IncrementCount()
    {
        currentCount++;
        StateHasChanged();
    }
}
```

In this code snippet, we can see that C# code and Razor code are present in the same file. By default, blazor supports the inline code approach. However, if the application is growing and creating enterprise-level applications, this approach is not recommended.

Code-Behind Approach

Using this approach, we write Razor code and C# code in two separate files. So, it will look more organized and cleaner. As the application grows, it will be easier to maintain the code.

In this approach, create the razor component, for example, `Hello.Razor,` and write the code as follows:

```
@page "/hello"
<h3>This is Code behind razor page demo</h3>
<p>Message from C# Code Block: @msg</p>
<button @onclick="SayHello">Click Here</button>
```

Create the C# partial class as **Hello.Razor.cs.**

```
namespace BlazorComponent.Pages.CodeSeperation
{
    public partial class Hello
    {
        public string msg = string.Empty;
        private void SayHello()
```

```
        {
            msg = "Hello Blazor";
        }
    }
```

By segregating the Razor and C# code behind two files, the code looks neater and cleaner as compared to the inline approach.

***Figure 2.24**: Output*

Styling Component in Blazor

Whenever working on a Blazor application, we receive a requirement to write CSS classes.

There are various approaches to writing CSS classes in Blazor, such as:

- Shared/Global CSS
- Embedded CSS
- External CSS
- Isolated CSS

Shared/Global CSS

To implement this approach, we need to write a **`CSS`** class on **`app.css`** in Blazor WebAssembly and **`/wwwroot/css/site.css`** in Blazor Server.

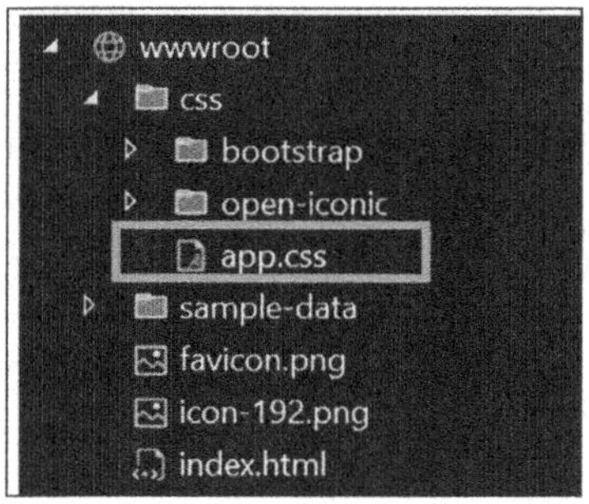

***Figure 2.25:** CSS file path*

Embedded CSS

In this approach, we write the CSS class in the Razor component itself, which is also known as inline **CSS** class.

```
@page "/mystyle"
<h3>Inline Style Demo</h3>

<p class="parastyle"> This is test message</p>

<style>
    .parastyle
    {
        background-color:green;
        font-size:22px;
    }
</style>
```

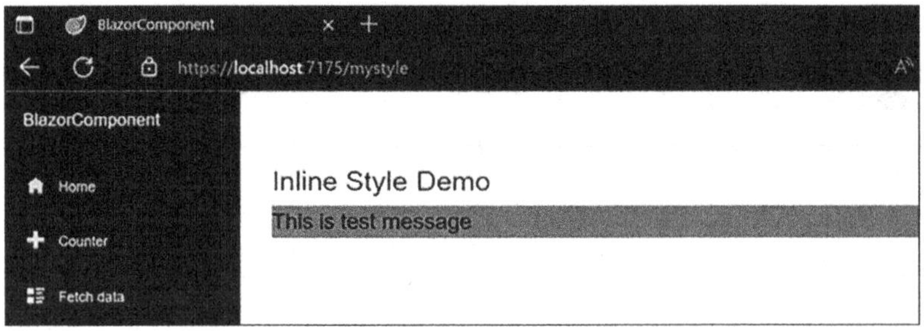

***Figure 2.26**: Output*

External CSS

In this approach, we store all CSS classes in external CSS files and use them in our components. This is very similar to the Asp.net WebForm approach.

```
<link href="/css/external-css-file.css" rel="stylesheet" />
<h3 class="external-style">ExternalCssStyle.</h3>
```

Isolated CSS

In this approach, we create an isolated CSS class file with the component name and write the CSS class there. This CSS class will only apply to the specific component. So all unnecessary CSS classes will not get loaded on the browser. This can improve the performance of the page load.

```
<YourComponent>.razor.css
```

***Figure 2.27**: Isolated CSS*

Write the CSS class as follows:

```
.parastyle {
    background-color: green;
    font-size: 22px;
}

h1 {
    color: red;
    font-style: italic;
    text-shadow: 2px 2px gray;
}
```

Now, run the application, and you will see the output as follows:

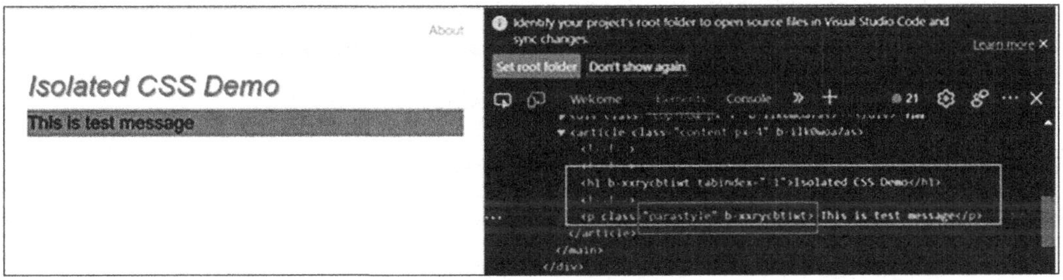

***Figure 2.28**: Output*

In this approach, CSS classes are applied at runtime of the application.

Conclusion

In this chapter, we covered all the basic concepts related to components, which are essential while developing a Blazor WebAssembly application.

In the upcoming chapters, we will be using these component concepts. If you have a clear understanding of these basic concepts, it will be much easier to develop complex Blazor projects.

References

ASP.NET Core Razor components | Microsoft Learn

For Source Code

https://github.com/ava-orange-education/Practical-Web-Development-with-Blazor-and-.Net-8

Multiple Choice Questions

1. What is a Blazor component?

   a. A reusable piece of UI that can be rendered on a web page

   b. Class that contains all of the logic for a web page

   c. An interface for defining the structure of a web page

2. What are the two types of Blazor components?

   a. Razor components and code-behind components

   b. Server-side components and client-side components

   c. Class components and function components

3. What is the syntax for defining a Blazor component?

   a. `@component MyComponent { ... }`

   b. `<MyComponent> ... </MyComponent>`

   c. `@code { ... }`

4. What is the purpose of the @code block in a Blazor component?

   a. To define the HTML markup for the component

   b. To define the CSS styles for the component

   c. To write the C# code that controls the behavior of the component

5. What is the difference between a Razor component and a code-behind component?

   a. Razor components use HTML markup and C# code in the same file, while code-behind components separate the HTML markup and C# code into different files.

   b. Razor components are rendered on the client side, while code-behind components are rendered on the server side.

   c. Razor components are used for simple UI elements, while code-behind components are used for more complex UI elements.

6. What is the purpose of the @inherits directive in a code-behind component?

   a. To specify which class the component should inherit from

   b. To specify which HTML element the component should render as

   c. To specify which CSS styles should be applied to the component

7. How can you pass data from a parent component to a child component in Blazor?

   a. Using the `@parameter` directive

   b. Using the `@inject` directive

   c. Using the `@component` directive

8. What is the purpose of the `@on{EventName}` directive in a Blazor component?

   a. To specify a method that should be called when a certain event occurs

   b. To specify a CSS class that should be applied when a certain event occurs

   c. To specify a data binding that should be updated when a certain event occurs

9. What is the difference between a local parameter and a `CascadingParameter` in Blazor?

   a. A local parameter is passed directly to a child component, while a `CascadingParameter` is passed through a chain of parent components.

   b. A local parameter is defined in the same component as it is used, while a `CascadingParameter` is defined in a parent component.

   c. A local parameter can only be used once in a component, while a `CascadingParameter` can be used multiple times.

10. How can you handle user input in a Blazor component?

    a. Using the `@on{EventName}` directive to specify a method to handle the event

    b. Using the `@bind` directive to create a two-way data binding between a property and a form field

    c. Using the `@code` block to write JavaScript code that handles the user input.

Answers

1. a
2. a
3. b
4. c
5. a
6. a
7. a
8. a
9. a
10. a or b

CHAPTER 3
Routing and Navigation

Introduction

This chapter will cover routing and navigation in the Blazor application, which is a very important concept while developing any web application. We will discuss all the basic and advanced concepts of Routing and Navigation with sample code.

Structure

This chapter covers the following topics:

- Introduction to Routing and Navigation
- Router Components
- Route Parameter
- Route Constraints
- Optional Parameters
- Route Overloading
- Navigation in Blazor
- Forcing a Page Reload

Introduction to Routing and Navigation

Routing and Navigation is an essential part of any web application framework. Without this, we cannot develop any web application. Routing is the concept of navigating from one page to another on a website. Routing in Blazor involves mapping URLs to components or pages in your application.

Navigation in Blazor refers to the process of programmatically navigating between different components or pages within the application.

Now, we will see how routing works in the Blazor application.

Router Components

Whenever we type any page URL in a browser such as:

https://localhost:7224/counter

The preceding URL will go to the **router component** of the **app.razor** file, which will scan all the razor pages in the current assembly.

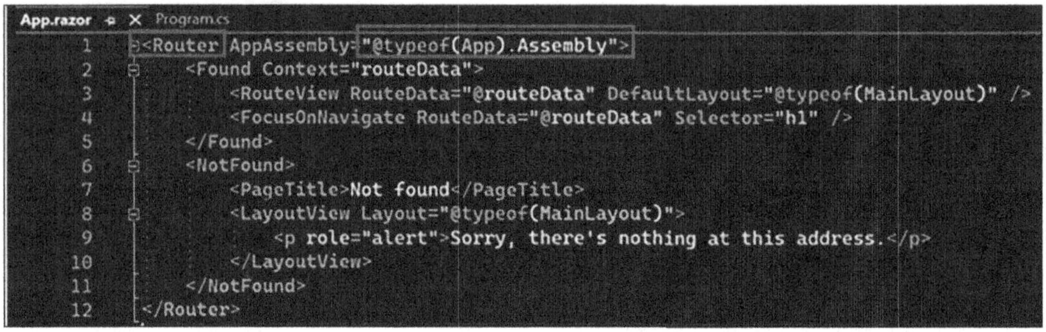

Figure 3.1: *Route Component*

If it is found in the assembly, then **`RouteView`** will render the given component with the Default page Layout; in the preceding case, it will render Counter Component.

If you enter:

https://localhost:7224/counter123

It will search for **`Conter123`** in the assembly file, which is unavailable in the application. In this scenario, it will go to the **`NotFound`** Section and display the following message:

`Sorry, there's nothing at this address.`

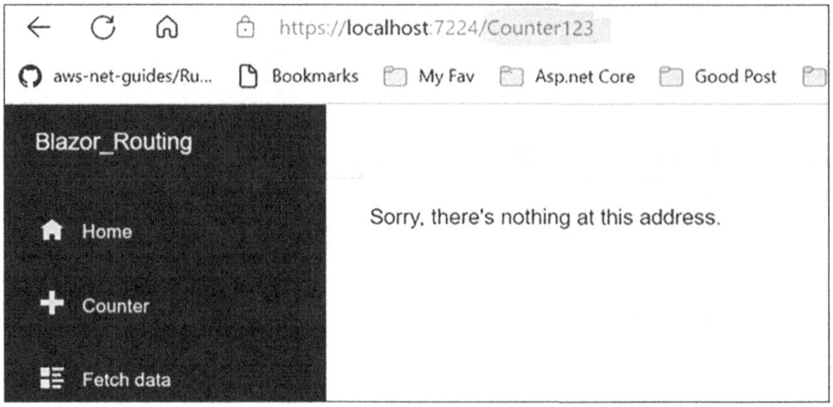

Figure 3.2: *Not Found*

Route Parameter in Blazor

Route parameters are placeholders for values you want to pass to a specific component via the URL. The placeholder is represented in a route template within curly braces such as `{ Id }`.

The parameter name must match a public property within the component that is decorated with the `[Parameter]` attribute

Let's see the basic demo code snippet for the route parameter:

```
@page "/users/{userId}"

<h3>User Details</h3>

<p>User ID: @userId</p>

@code {
    [Parameter]
    public string? userId { get; set; }
}
```

In the previous code snippet, we see there are public properties of **`UserId`** as a parameter and within curly braces: **`{ UserId }`**.

Whenever we pass **`UserId`** on the browser, it will read the route parameter value and display it on the page, as shown in the following screenshot:

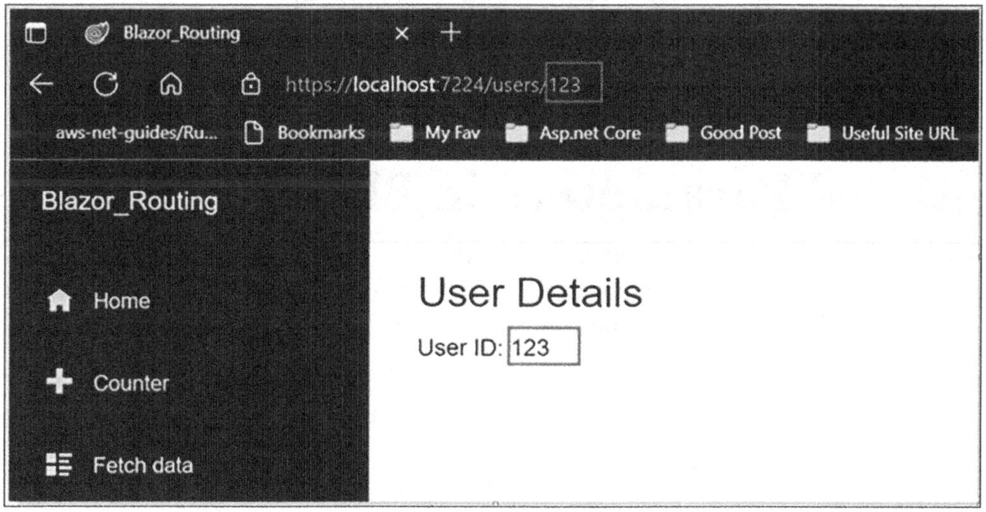

***Figure 3.3**: Found Path*

The key points of route parameters are as follows:

- By default, all route data values are strings.
- Route parameters are placeholders for values. Blazor will bind the parameter value to the public property automatically.

If you want to work with different data types, you must apply a constraint to the parameter in the route template. You can do this by adding a colon, followed by the data type that you want to work with:

```
@page "/details/{id:int}"
<h1>Details</h1>
@code{
    [Parameter] public int Id { get; set; }
}
```

There are a large number of constraints, but Blazor Supports only supports the following constraints.

Constraints	**Descriptions**	**Example**
`bool`	Matches a Boolean value	`{isActive:bool}`
`int`	Matches a 32-bit integer value	`{id:int}`
`datetime`	Matches a DateTime value	`{dob:datetime}`
`decimal`	Matches a decimal value	`{price:decimal}`
`double`	Matches a 64-bit floating-point value	`{latitude:double}`
`float`	Matches a 32-bit floating-point value	`{x:float}`
`long`	Matches a 64-bit integer value	`{y:long}`
`guid`	Matches a GUID value	`{id:guid}`

Table 3.1: *Constraints*

Optional Parameters in Blazor

In Blazor, you can define optional route parameters by specifying a default value for the parameter, or by using a nullable data type. This allows you to have routes that can match with or without a specific parameter value.

To define an optional route parameter in Blazor, you must provide a default value for the parameter in the **`@page`** directive of a Blazor component. Here's an example using a nullable data type:

```
@page "/users/{userId:int?}"

<h3>User Details</h3>

@if (userId.HasValue)
{
    <p>User ID: @userId.Value</p>
}
else
{
    <p>No user ID provided</p>
}

@code {
    [Parameter]
    public int? userId { get; set; }
}
```

In the preceding example, the **@page** directive specifies a route pattern **/users/{userId:int?}**.

The **int?** indicates that the **userId** parameter is of type int, and it is optional (**?** denotes optional).

It will not be mandatory to pass it as a parameter. **UserId** is an optional parameter.

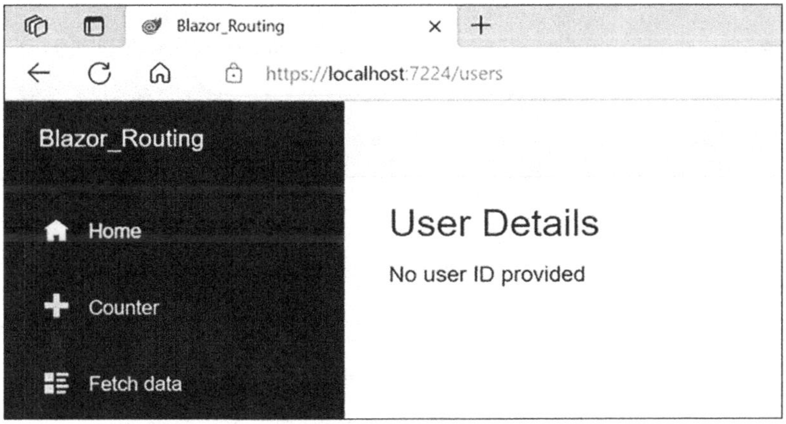

Figure 3.4: *Not Found Path*

Route Overloading

Blazor does not support route overloading in the same way as some traditional server-side frameworks. Route overloading typically refers to defining multiple routes with the same URL pattern but different HTTP verbs or other parameters to differentiate them.

In Blazor, the **@page** directive is used to define a route for a specific component.

The route pattern specified in the **@page** directive determines when the component is rendered based on the URL.

To achieve similar functionality as route overloading, you can use parameterized routes and handle the differentiation within the component itself.

Here is the code snippet for route overloading:

```
@page "/users/{userId:int}"
@page "/users"

<h3>User Details</h3>

@if (userId.HasValue)
{
    <h4>User Details</h4>
    <p>User ID: @userId.Value</p>
}
else
{
    <h4>All Users</h4>
    <!-- Display all users -->
}

@code {
    [Parameter]
    public int? userId { get; set; }
}
```

Here are two **@page** directives: **"/users/{userId:int}"** and **"/users"**.

The first directive matches URLs like **/users/123**, where **userId** is an integer.

The second directive matches the base URL **/users.**

When a user navigates to **/users/123**, the component will display the user details for the provided **userId**.

If a user navigates to /users (without a specific **userId**), the component will render the section displaying all users.

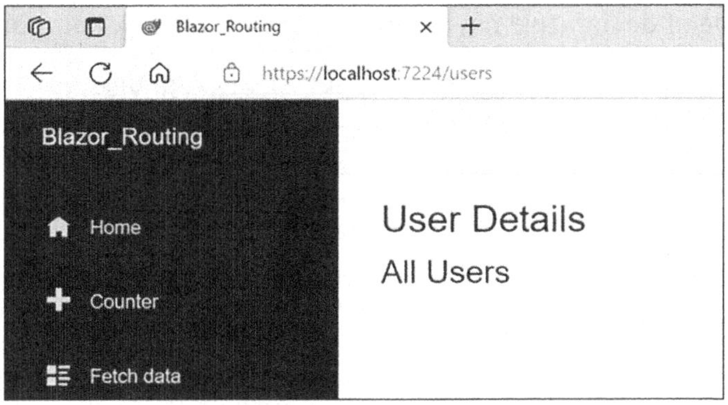

Figure 3.5: *Route Overload*

Navigation in Blazor

In Blazor, navigation refers to the process of moving between different pages or components within a web application. Blazor provides several ways to perform navigation, including programmatic navigation and declarative navigation.

- **Programmatic navigation:** Programmatic navigation allows you to navigate to different pages or components in response to user actions or events. To perform programmatic navigation in Blazor, you can use the **`NavigationManager`** service, which provides methods for navigating within your application. Here's an example of programmatic navigation using the **`NavigationManager`** service:

```
@inject NavigationManager NavigationManager

<button @onclick="NavigateToPage">Go to Another Page</button>

@code {
    private void NavigateToPage()
    {
        NavigationManager.NavigateTo("/anotherpage");
    }
}
```

In this example, when the button is clicked, the **`NavigateToPage`** method is executed, which uses the **`NavigationManager`** to navigate to the **`/anotherpage`** URL. You can provide relative or absolute URLs depending on your navigation needs.

- **Declarative navigation:** Declarative navigation allows you to define navigation links directly in your Blazor markup using the NavLink component. The NavLink component renders an anchor tag (**`<a>`**) that automatically applies an active CSS class when the associated URL is the current active URL.

Here's an example of declarative navigation using the NavLink component:

```
<NavLink href="/users" class="nav-link">Users</NavLink>
<NavLink href="/products" class="nav-link">Products</NavLink>
```

In this example, two NavLink components are used to create navigation links for the **"Users"** and **"Products"** pages. When the associated link is clicked, Blazor handles the navigation automatically.

```
<a href="/users">Users</a>
<a href="/products">Products</a>
```

Forcing a Page Reload

In Blazor, you can force a page reload by utilizing the **NavigationManager** service and its Reload method. The **Reload** method is responsible for reloading the current page, effectively refreshing the entire Blazor application.

```
@inject NavigationManager NavigationManager

<button @onclick="ReloadPage">Reload Page</button>

@code {
    private void ReloadPage()
    {
        NavigationManager.Reload();
    }
}
```

When the button is clicked, the **ReloadPage** method is executed, which in turn calls the Reload method of the **NavigationManager** service. This will reload the current page and refresh the entire Blazor application.

Please note that forcing a page reload in Blazor should be used sparingly, as it disrupts the normal flow of the application and may result in data loss or inconsistencies. It is generally recommended to rely on Blazor's built-in mechanisms for handling state and updating components rather than relying on full page reloads.

Conclusion

In this chapter, we saw all the concepts of routing and navigation of Blazor, which is common in Blazor Server and Blazor WebAssembly. These concepts are very important while working on the Blazor project. We also provided code snippets to illustrate each concept. In the next chapter, we will discuss Razor class library and its implementation.

References

- ASP.NET Core Blazor routing and navigation | Microsoft Learn
- For source code:

  https://github.com/ava-orange-education/Practical-Web-Development-with-Blazor-and-.Net-8

Multiple Choice Questions

1. Which directive is used to define the route pattern for a Blazor component?
   a. `@route`
   b. `@url`
   c. `@page`
   d. `@nav`
2. How can you perform programmatic navigation in Blazor?
   a. Using the `<NavLink>` component
   b. Using the `NavigationManager` service
   c. Using the `@route` directive
   d. Using the `BlazorNavigation` class
3. Which attribute is used to specify a route parameter in Blazor?
   a. `[Route]`
   b. `[NavParameter]`
   c. `[Parameter]`
   d. `[RouteParam]`
4. How can you pass route parameters during navigation in Blazor?
   a. By using the `@route` directive
   b. By calling the `NavigateTo` method with the parameter value
   c. By using the `NavLink` component with the parameter value
   d. By appending the parameter value to the URL

5. How can you access the current URL in a Blazor component?
    a. By using the `@url` directive
    b. By injecting the `NavigationManager` service
    c. By calling the `GetCurrentUrl` method
    d. By using the `@page` directive

Answers

1. c
2. b
3. c
4. b
5. b

CHAPTER 4
Razor Class Library

Introduction

This chapter will focus on one of the cool features of Blazor, that is code reusability. Using Razor Class Library, we can use our Razor component in all Blazor type projects, including Blazor Server, WASM, and MAUI Hybrid.

If we have a requirement to develop a product that should work in all environments, then we can take advantage of Razor Class Library. It will save 70% of development time and money. We will also learn the advantages of Razor Class Library.

Structure

This chapter covers the following topics:

- Introduction to Razor Class Library
- Creating Razor Class Library Project
- Sharing Code with Multiple Applications
- Integrating Bootstrap in Razor Class Library
- Creating NuGet Package of RCL
- Advantages of Razor Class Library

Introduction to Razor Class Library

A Razor Class Library (RCL) in Blazor is a reusable component library that contains Razor components, pages, and other supporting files. It allows you to package and distribute UI components and resources that multiple Blazor applications can consume.

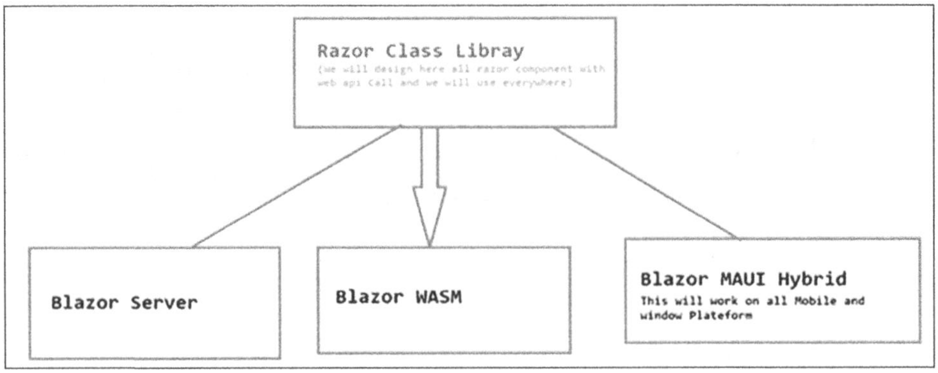

Figure 4.1: *Razor Class Library*

Creating RCL and Sharing Code with Multiple Application

We will create a simple POC project for the Class library using Syncfusion Blazor Control and use it in Blazor Server, Blazor WASM, and MAUI Blazor Hybrid application. Here is the step-by-step process:

Step 1: Open the Visual Studio Project template and select Razor Class Library:

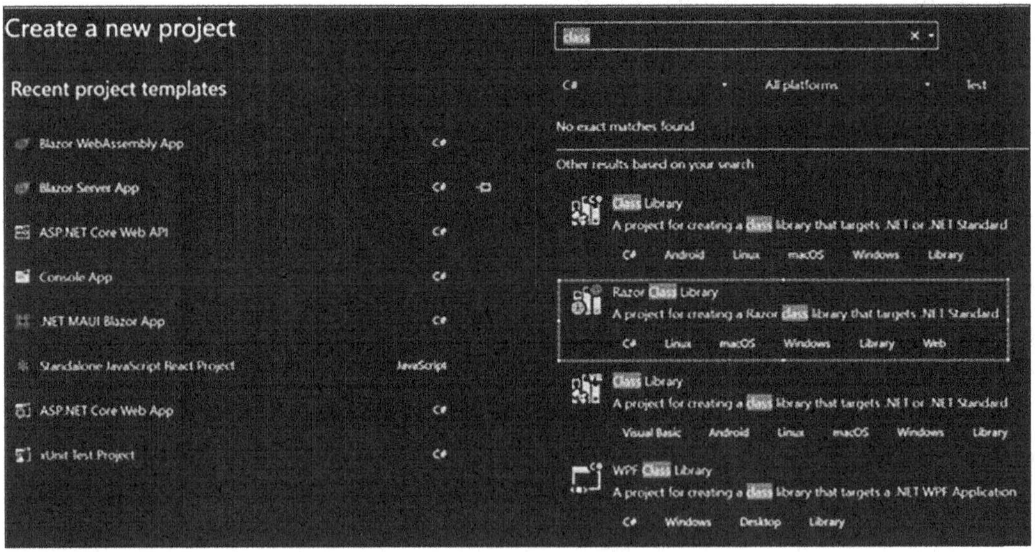

Figure 4.2: *Class Library*

Step 2: Give the Project Name as "**`RazorClassDemo`**":

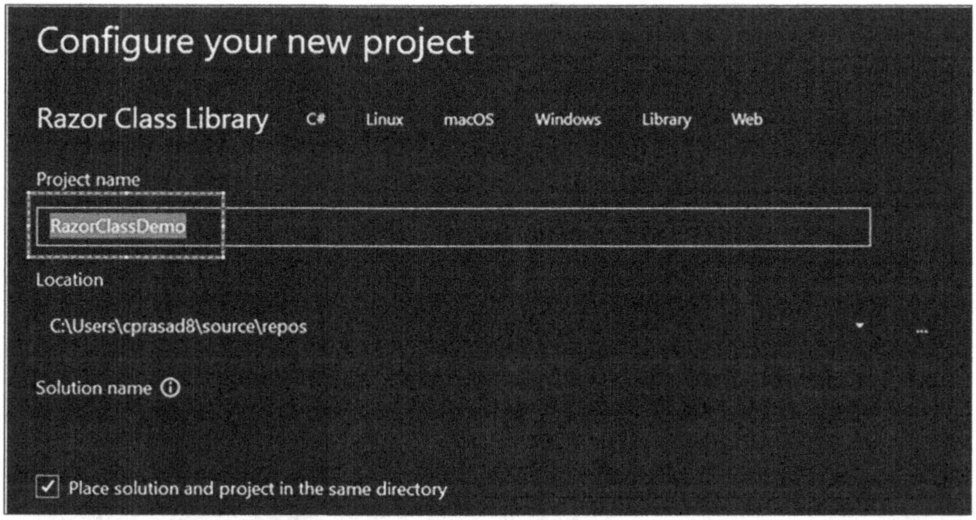

Figure 4.3: *Project Name*

Step 3: In the **`RazorClassDemo`**, add the **`syncfusion`** Controls using **`NuGet`** Package Manager, as shown in *Figure 4.4*:

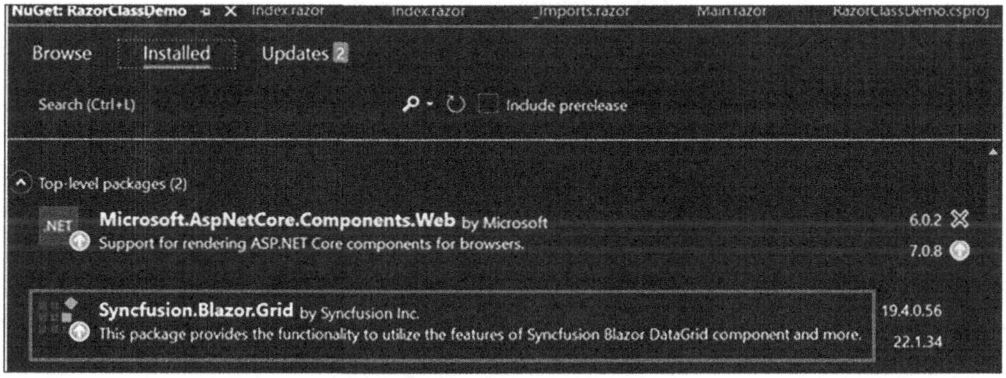

Figure 4.4: *Syncfusion Grid*

Note: `Syncfusion` *is a very popular Blazor Control provider. You can create a very interactive and rich Blazor project using this library.*

For more details about this, please refer to the following URL:

Blazor DataGrid Example | Grid Overview | Syncfusion Demos

Step 4: Create the reusable Orders Component, as shown in *Figure 4.5*:

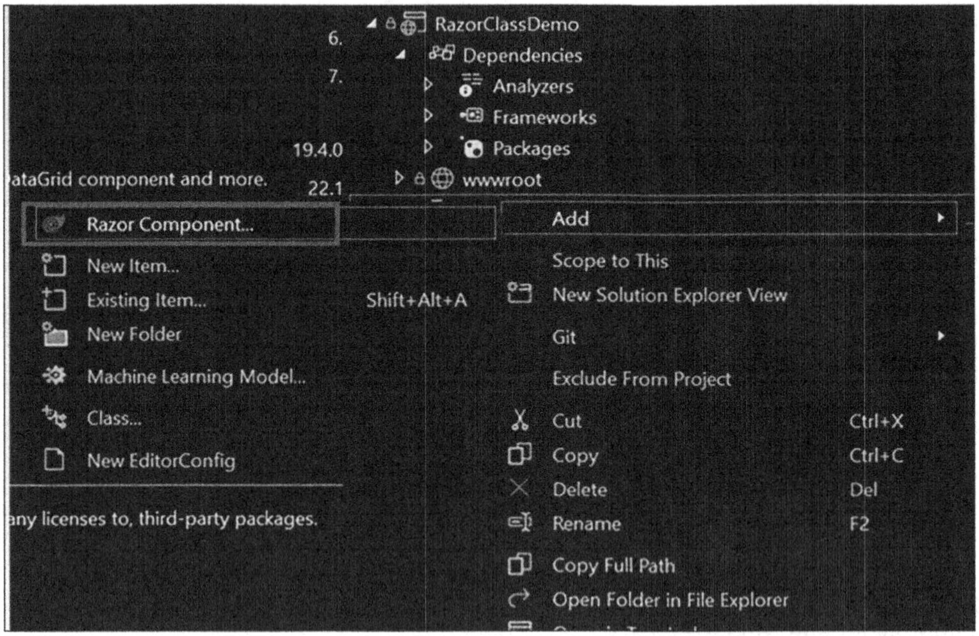

Figure 4.5: *Razor Component*

Step 5: Write the code for populating the **Syncfusion** grid, as shown in the following code:

```
@using Syncfusion.Blazor
@using Syncfusion.Blazor.Grids

<div class="my-component">
    <b>Syncfusion Blazor Grid Demo</b> <br />
    <SfGrid DataSource="@Orders" />
</div>

@code {
     public List<Order> Orders { get; set; }

    protected override void OnInitialized()
    {
        Orders = Enumerable.Range(1, 5).Select(x => new Order()
        {
            OrderID = 0 + x,
            CustomerID = (new string[] { "ALFKI", "ANANTR", "ANTON",
"BLONP", "BOLID" })[new Random().Next(5)],
        }).ToList();
    }
```

```
    public class Order
    {
        public int? OrderID { get; set; }
        public string? CustomerID { get; set; }

    }
}
```

Step 6: Now create Blazor Server, Blazor WebAssembly, and Blazor MAUI Hybrid as separate standalone project as follows:

Blazor Server:

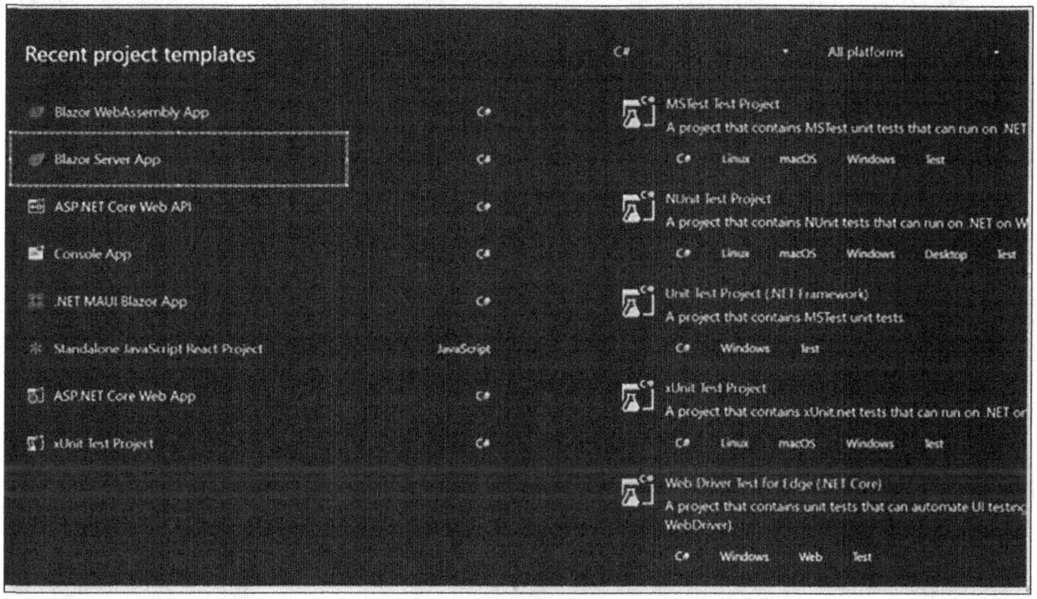

Figure 4.6: Blazor Server App

Blazor WebAssembly App:

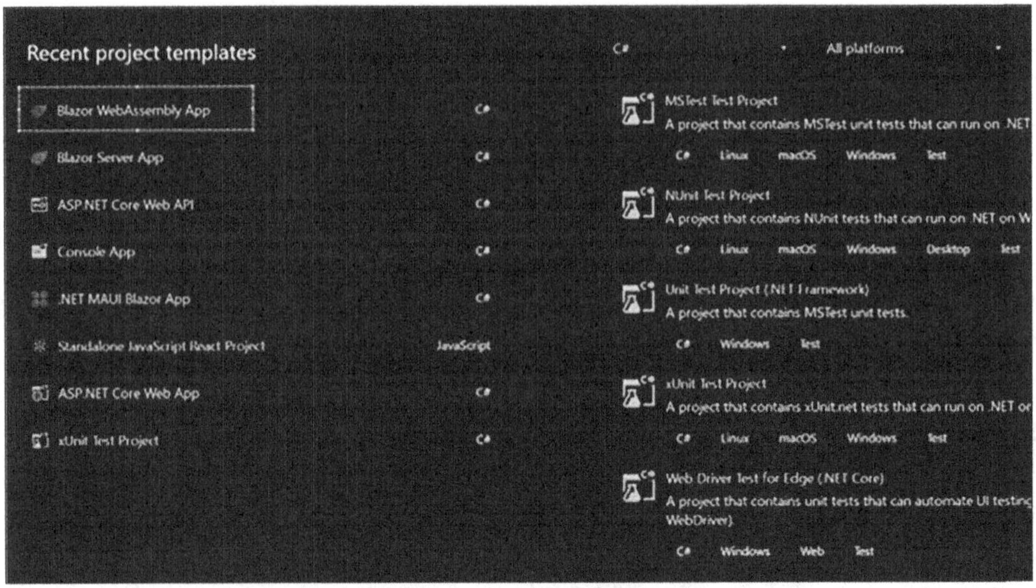

Figure 4.7: *Blazor WebAssembly*

Blazor MAUI Hybrid App:

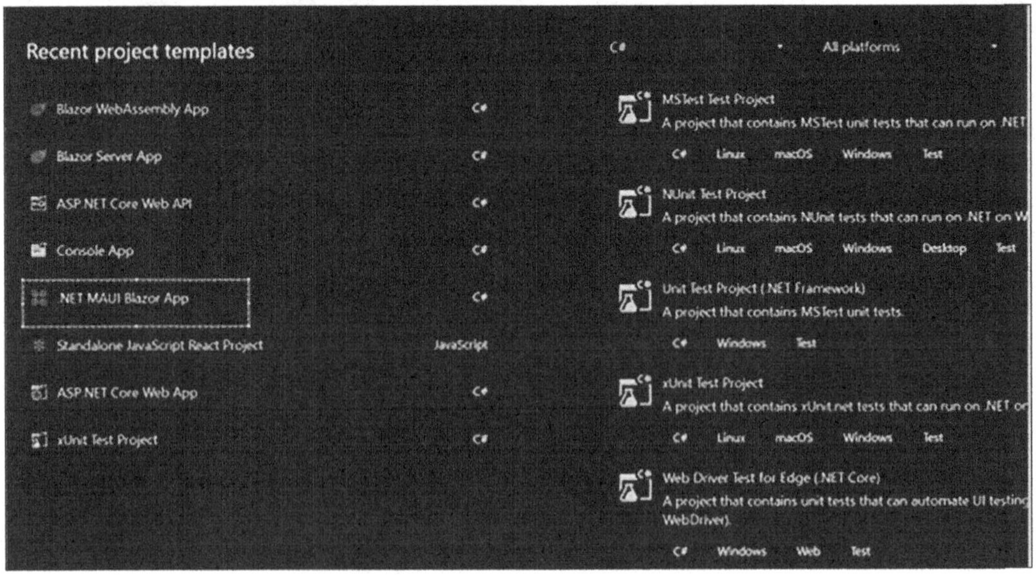

Figure 4.8: *MAUI Blazor App*

Now that we have created all the required projects, we are going to consume the Razor Class Library Orders Components.

Step 7: Add the project references as Razor Class Library in all projects, including Blazor WebAssembly, Blazor Server, and Blazor MAUI Hybrid.

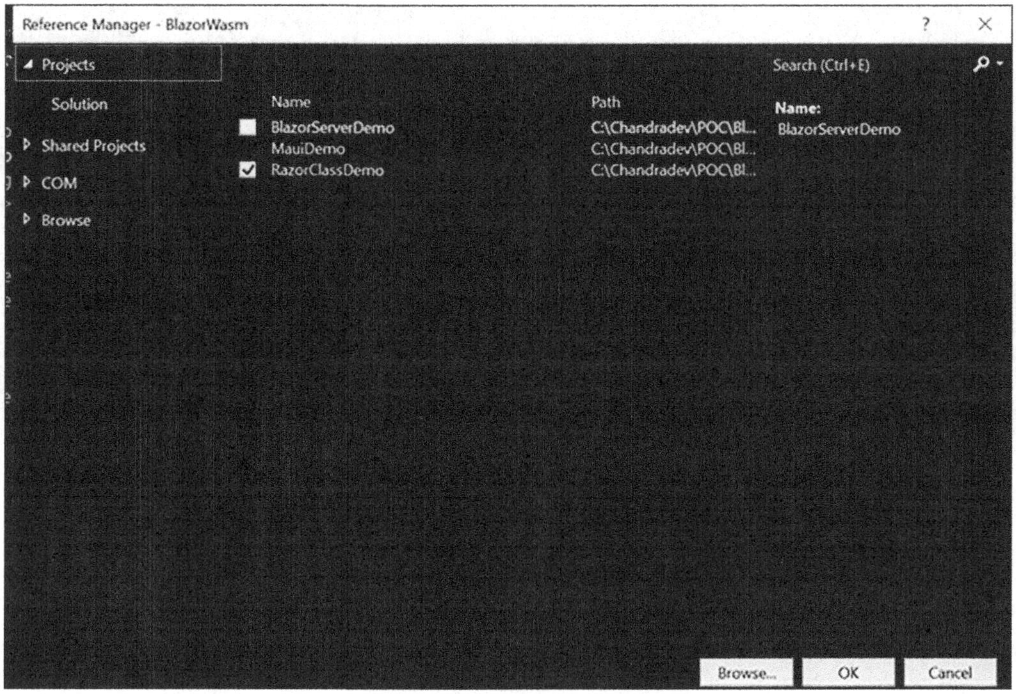

***Figure 4.9**: Project Reference*

Step 8: For Blazor WebAssembly, go to **`Program.cs`** file and register the **`Syncfusion`** Control, as shown in *Figure 4.10*:

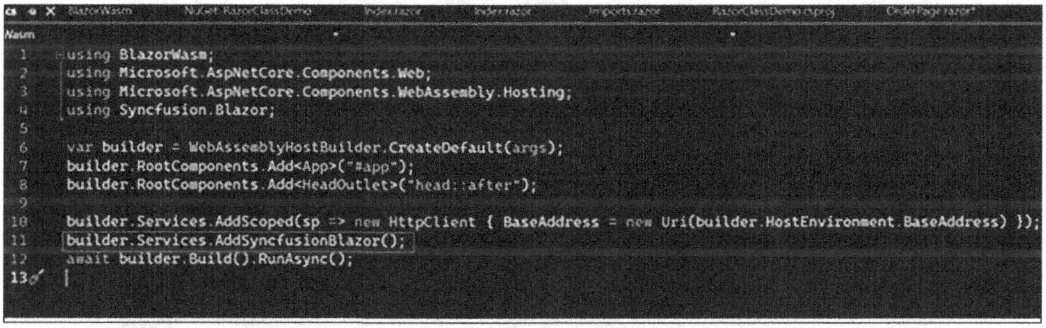

***Figure 4.10**: Program.cs*

Add the CSS and JavaScript file in **`index.html`** page as follows:

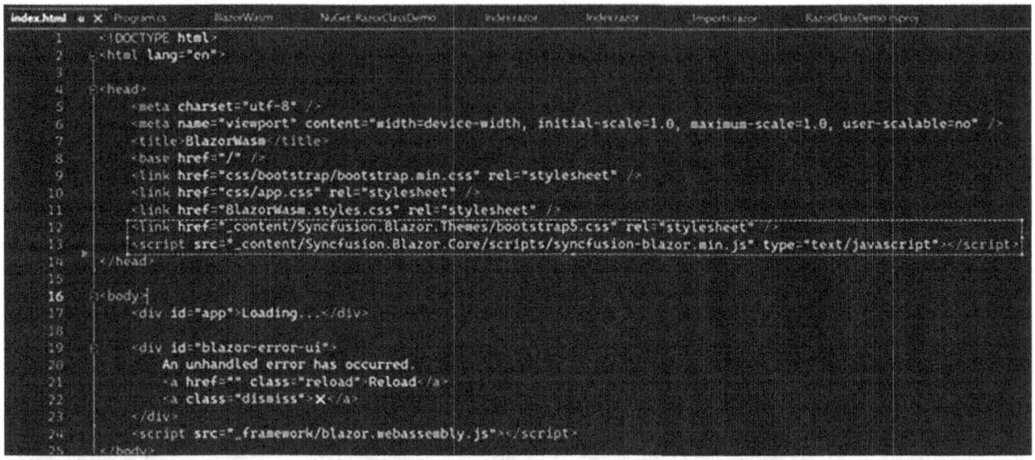

Figure 4.11: *Index.html*

```
<link href="_content/Syncfusion.Blazor.Themes/bootstrap5.css"
rel="stylesheet" />
    <script src="_content/Syncfusion.Blazor.Core/scripts/
syncfusion-blazor.min.js" type="text/javascript"></script>
```

File Change for Blazor Server Application:

Program.cs file:

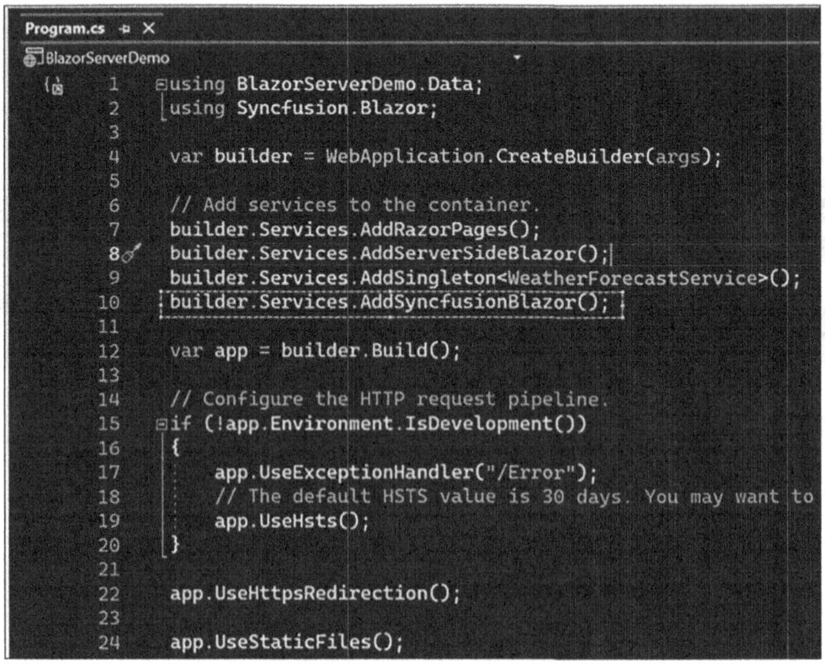

Figure 4.12: *Program.cs*

In **Layout.html** page:

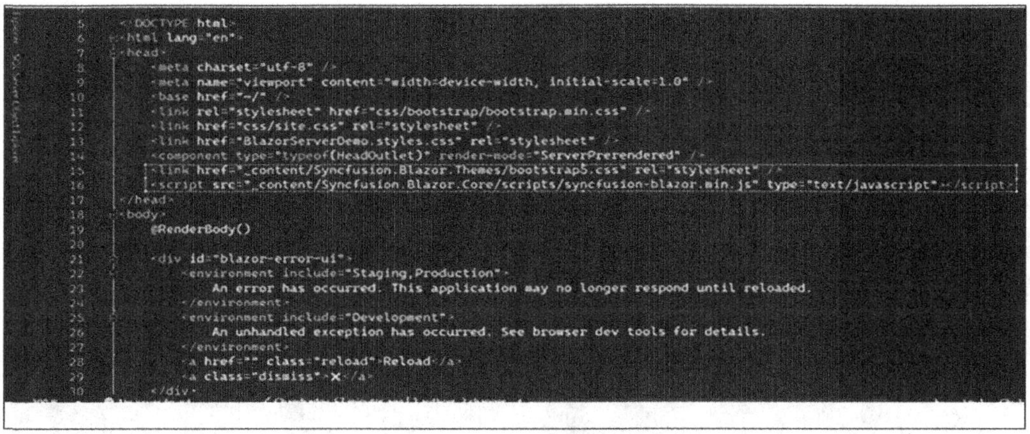

Figure 4.13: *Layout.html*

```
<link href="_content/Syncfusion.Blazor.Themes/bootstrap5.css"
rel="stylesheet" />
    <script src="_content/Syncfusion.Blazor.Core/scripts/
syncfusion-blazor.min.js" type="text/javascript"></script>
```

File Changes for Blazor Hybrid MAUI App

MauiProgram.cs:

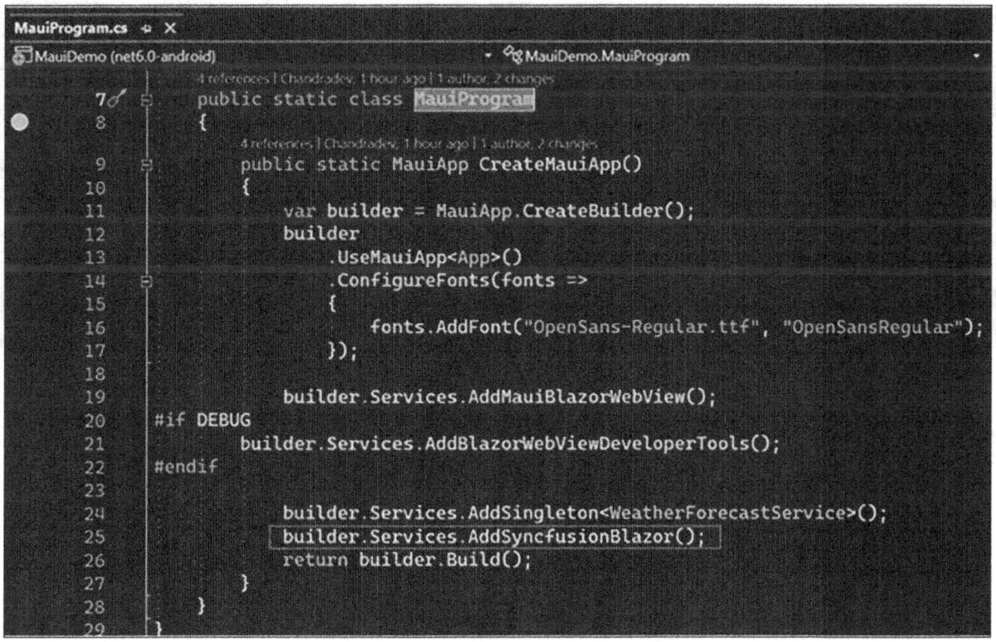

Figure 4.14: *MauiProgram.cs*

In **Index.html** page:

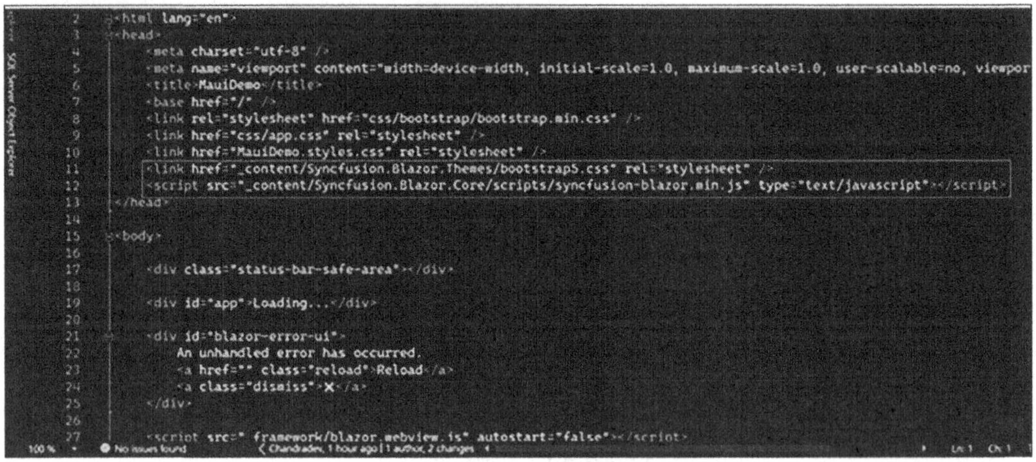

Figure 4.15: *Index.html*

Step 9: Go to **`Index.razor`** page of all projects and call Razor Class Library component as follows:

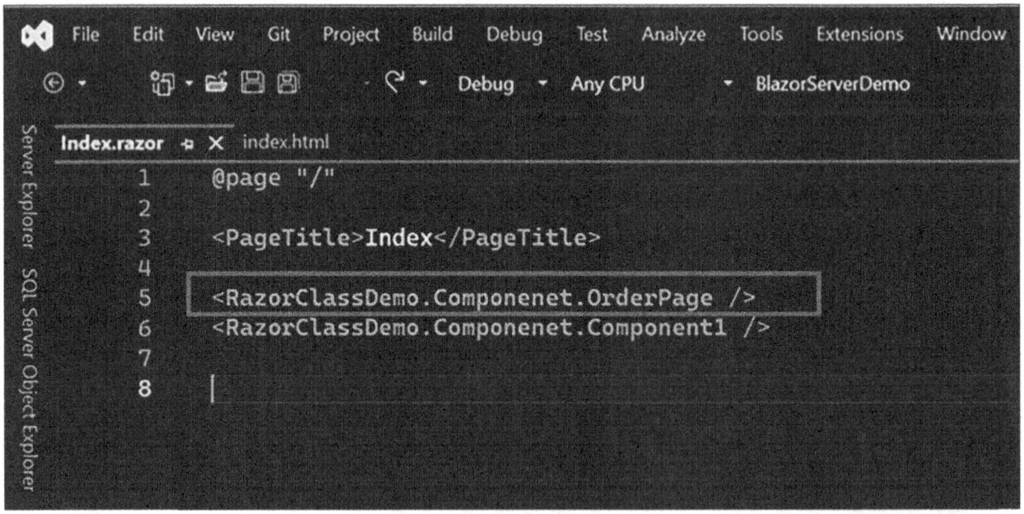

Figure 4.16: *Index.razor*

Step 10: Now run the Blazor Server application.

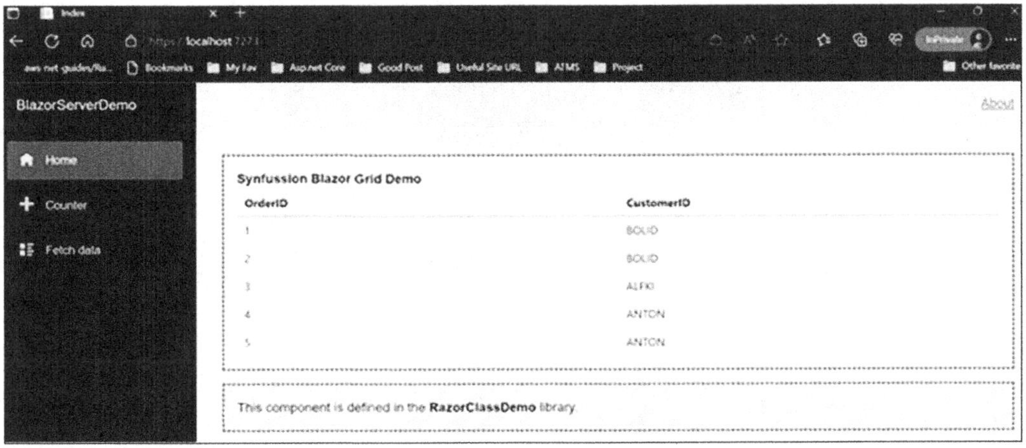

Figure 4.17: Output

Step 11: Now run the Blazor WebAssembly application.

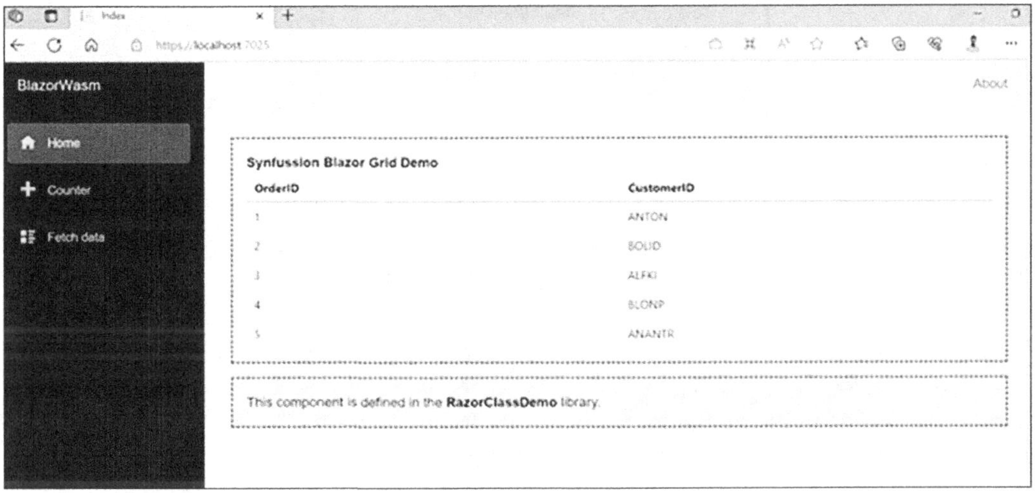

Figure 4.18: Output

Step 12: Run the Blazor MAUI Hybrid App.

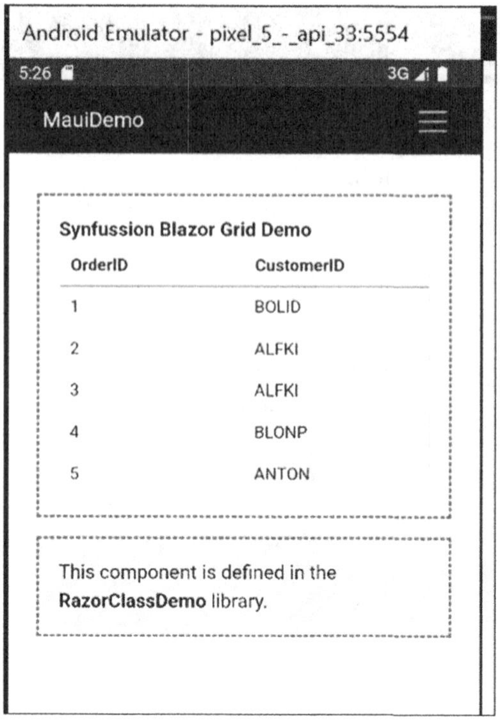

Figure 4.19: *MAUI Output*

In this demo, we saw that by using Razor Class Library (RCL), we can easily create a similar look and feel of the UI for all applications using a single code base.

Creating NuGet Package of RCL

We can also create NuGet Package from our Razor Class Library by following these steps:

Step 1: Go to the Razor Class Library project **`properties >> Package >> General`** and configure the input as follows:

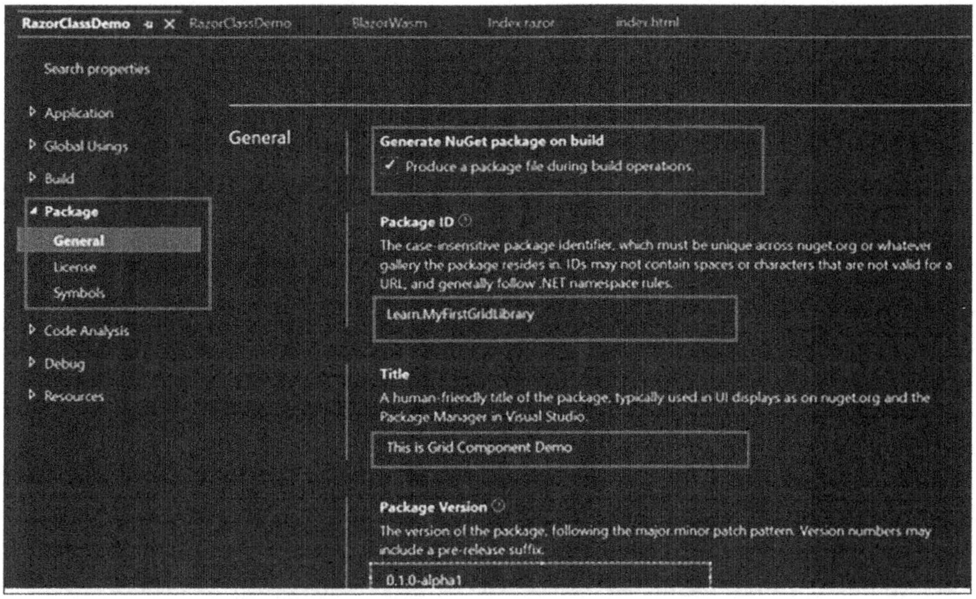

***Figure 4.20**: Package*

Step 2: Build the application and go to **RazorClassDemo\bin\Debug** folder.

You will see a `NuGet` package file.

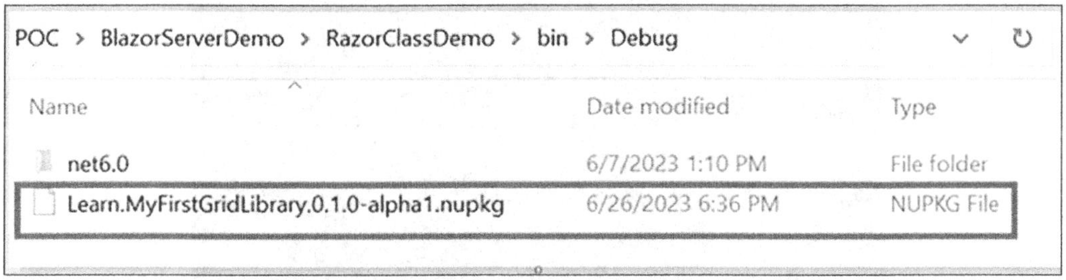

***Figure 4.21**: Debug*

Step 3: Create Blazor WebAssembly application and add this package as follows:

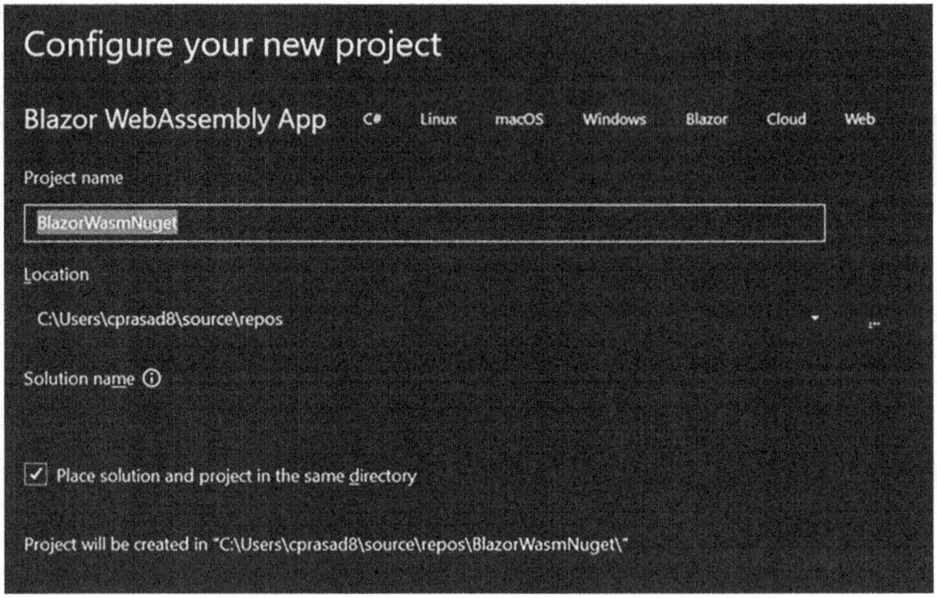

Figure 4.22: *Blazor WASM*

Step 4: Go to the **`NuGet`** of project:

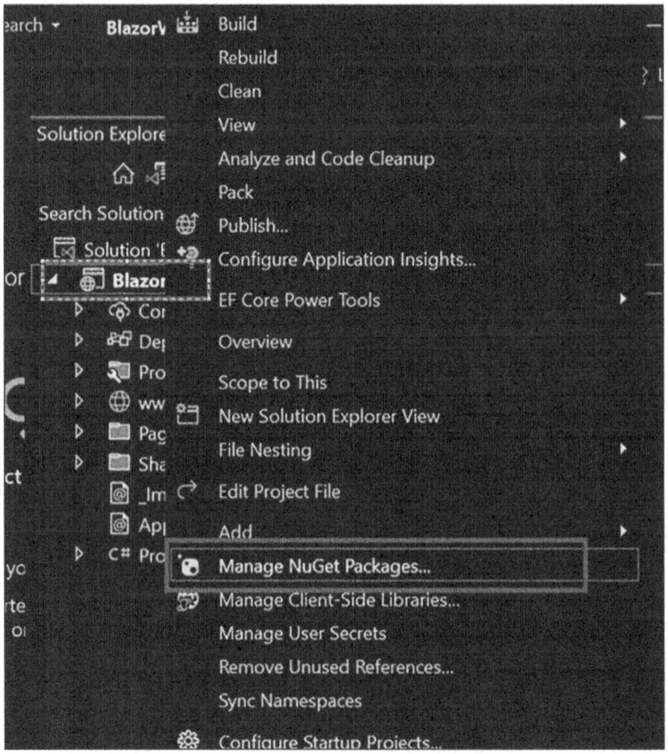

Figure 4.23: *NuGet Package*

Step 5: Add the **`NuGet`** package on our application as follows:

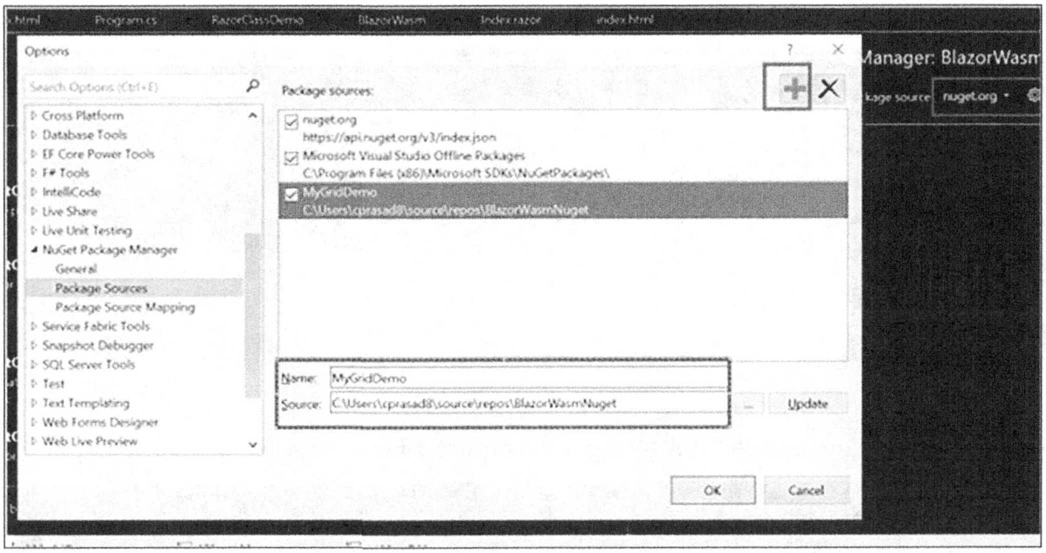

Figure 4.24: *NuGet Package*

In the preceding figure, the Source is the path of the **`NuGet`** package on our local system. We have kept the **`NuGet`** package on a given folder path.

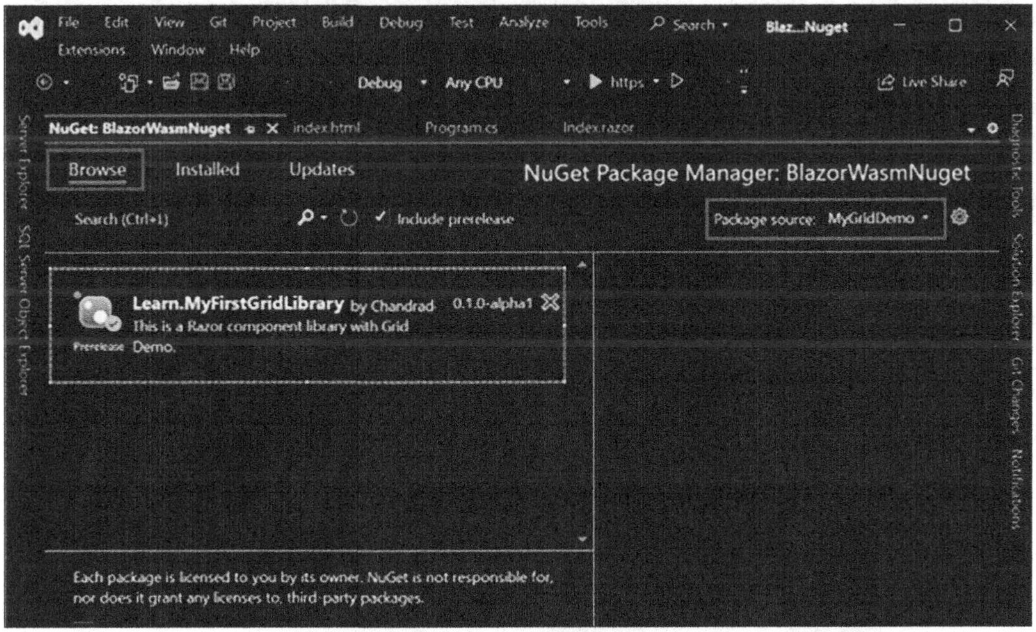

Figure 4.25: *NuGet Package*

Step 6: Install the preceding NuGet package in the Blazor WebAssembly application.

Step 7: Now, configure all the required dependencies in Blazor application.

In **Program.cs** file

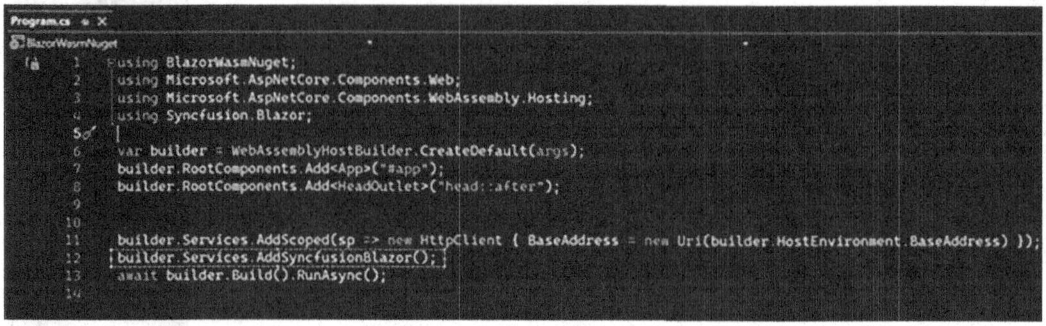

Figure 4.26: *Program.cs*

In **Index.html** page, add the Bootstrap and required JavaScript file as follows:

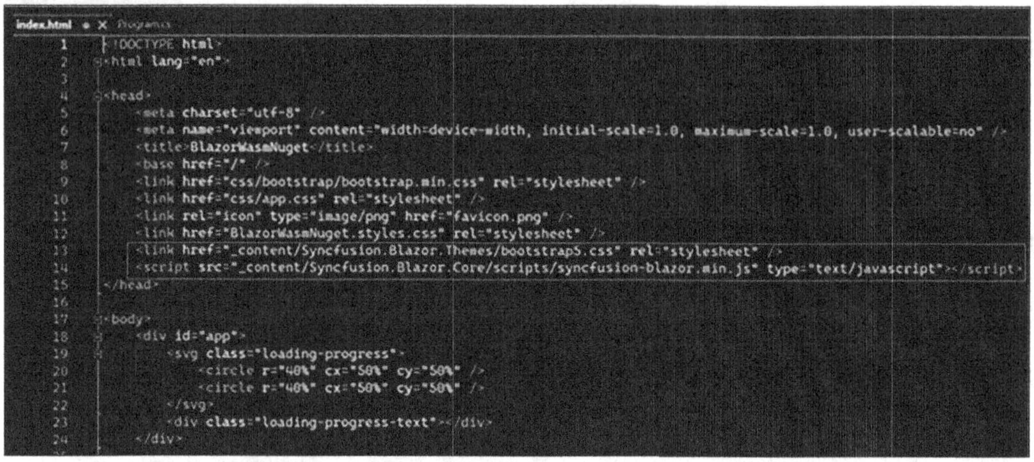

Figure 4.27: *Index.html*

Step 8: Go to the **Index.razor** file and call the **`OrderPage`** component as follows:

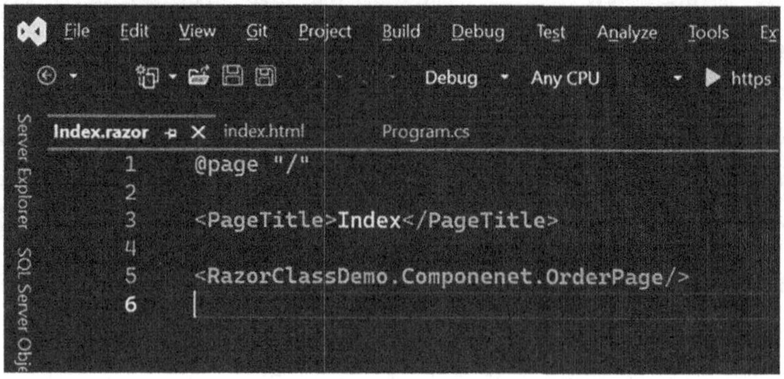

Figure 4.28: *Page Route*

Step 9: Run the application:

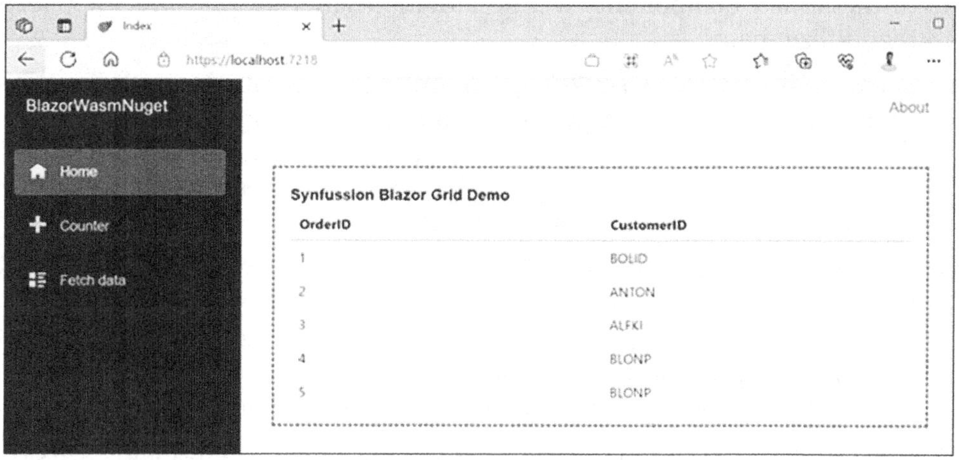

Figure 4.29: *Output*

In the preceding demo, we saw that using NuGet Package, we are able to call Razor Class Library Components in any project.

Advantages of Razor Class Library

Razor Class Library (RCL) in Blazor offers several advantages for organizing and distributing reusable components and resources. Here are some key advantages of using a RCL in Blazor:

- **Reusability:** RCL allows you to create a collection of reusable UI components, pages, and supporting files in a single library. These components can be easily shared and reused across multiple Blazor applications. It promotes code reuse, reduces duplication, and improves development efficiency.
- **Modular Development:** RCL enables modular development by encapsulating related components and resources into a self-contained library. This modular approach simplifies project organization and promotes the separation of concerns. Developers can focus on building and maintaining individual components without worrying about the larger application context.
- **Versioning and Updates:** RCL provides versioning capabilities, allowing you to manage and distribute updates to the library independently from the consuming applications. This makes it easier to maintain and evolve the library over time while ensuring backward compatibility. Developers can update the library in one place, and the changes can be propagated to all applications that use it.
- **Consistent User Interface:** By using RCL, you can maintain a consistent user interface across different applications. The library enforces consistent styling,

behavior, and functionality, ensuring a unified user experience. Changes made to the library components will be automatically reflected in all applications that utilize them.

- **Separation of Concerns:** RCL promotes the separation of UI concerns by encapsulating the UI components and associated logic in a separate library. This separation allows for better organization, code maintainability, and testability. Developers can focus on specific areas of development, such as UI, business logic, or data access, independently.
- **Packaging and Distribution:** RCL provides a convenient way to package and distribute your reusable components and resources. The library can be published as a NuGet package or shared via other distribution mechanisms. This simplifies the process of sharing components with other developers or teams, making collaborating and leveraging each other's work easier.

Using a Razor Class Library in Blazor brings modularity, reusability, versioning, and distribution advantages to your application development. It promotes efficient development practices, code sharing, and consistency across applications, leading to faster development cycles and improved software quality.

Conclusion

In this chapter, we saw how to create a Razor Class Library in real time project. Using the Razor Class library, we can create reusable and optimized code. We can also create NuGet packages and consume them in multiple projects. These are cool and nice features to optimize any project's cost and development time.

We also understood how to register external third-party controls such as Blazor `syncfusion` with Bootstrap and JavaScript. In the next chapter, we will explore the state management in Blazor WebAssembly.

References

Share assets across web and native clients using a Razor Class Library (RCL) | Microsoft Learn

For Source Code

https://github.com/ava-orange-education/Practical-Web-Development-with-Blazor-and-.Net-8

Multiple Choice Questions

1. What is a Razor Class Library (RCL) in Blazor?
    a. A library containing only Razor components
    b. A library containing only C# code
    c. A library containing both Razor components and C# code
    d. A library used exclusively for CSS stylesheets
2. Which of the following statements about RCL in Blazor is true?
    a. RCLs cannot be shared across different Blazor applications
    b. RCLs can contain reusable UI components and pages
    c. RCLs are exclusively used for server-side Blazor applications
    d. RCLs cannot contain code-behind files
3. What is the purpose of using a RCL in Blazor?
    a. To create standalone Blazor applications
    b. To encapsulate and share UI components and pages across multiple Blazor applications
    c. To improve the performance of Blazor applications
    d. To restrict access to code for security purposes
4. Which file extension is typically used for Razor component files within a RCL?
    a. .cs
    b. .js
    c. .razor
    d. .html
5. How can you reference a RCL in a Blazor application?
    a. By adding it as a reference in the Blazor application's project file
    b. By copying the RCL's files directly into the Blazor application's folder structure

c. By creating a symbolic link to the RCL's folder

d. By embedding the RCL's files into the Blazor application's assembly

Answers

1. c
2. b
3. b
4. c
5. a

CHAPTER 5
State Management

Introduction

State Management is a key concept in any web application. Without state management, we cannot develop modern interactive web applications.

As you know, in any web application, whenever a user is logged in, we need to maintain all information about their profile throughout the entire application until they logs off. In this scenario, we need to use state management.

Another scenario is when we create a survey page that contains multiple pages, and on each page, the user will keep filling in input until the survey is completed. In this scenario, we need to preserve the state of the object.

Structure

This chapter covers the following topics:

- State Management in Blazor WebAssembly
- Type of State Management
- State Management with Code Snippet
- Tips and Tricks While Using State Management

State Management in Blazor WebAssembly

State Management is the process of preserving the state of the user and object while navigating from one page to another page.

Since Blazor WebAssembly applications are client-side web applications, they run entirely in the browser and don't have a server-side state like traditional server-rendered web applications.

So, we will discuss only the client-side state management approach.

State management in Blazor WebAssembly can be achieved using various techniques, including:

- Component Parameters
- Cascading Values and Parameters
- Services
- Local Storage or Session Storage
- Server Side

Component Parameters

This is one of the simple approaches to passing data from parent to child components. In this approach, the child component will receive data from the parent component.

For this approach, create the razor **child** component as shown in the following code:

```
@page "/child"

<p>@Message</p>

@code {
    [Parameter]
    public string Message { get; set; }
```

Create the Parent Component as follows:

```
@page "/parent"

<ChildComp Message="@message" />

@code {
    private string message = "Hello from parent!";}
```

Now run the application, and it will show output as follows:

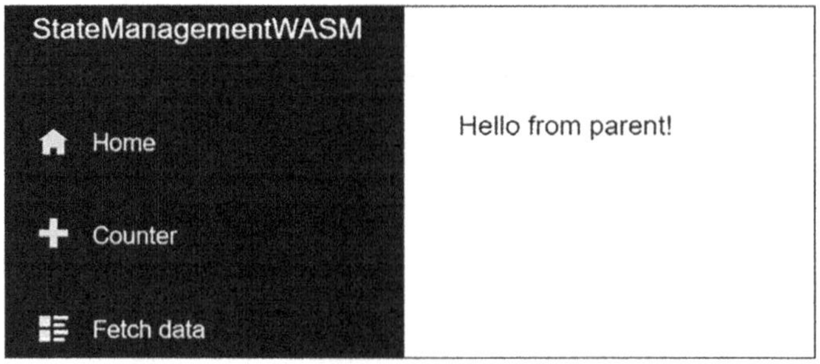

Figure 5.1: *Component parameter demo*

Cascading Values and Parameters

Blazor provides a mechanism called cascading values and parameters that allow data to be passed down the component tree implicitly. A parent component can define a value or parameter that its child components can consume without explicitly passing it as a parameter.

For this approach, create the Child Component as follows:

```
@page "/cascadingchild"

<p>@Message</p>

@code {
    [CascadingParameter]
    public string? Message { get; set; }
```

Create the **parent** component as follows:

```
@page "/cascadingparent"

<CascadingValue Value="@message">
    <CascadingChild />
</CascadingValue>

@code {
    private string message = "Hello from parent Cascading Demo!";}
```

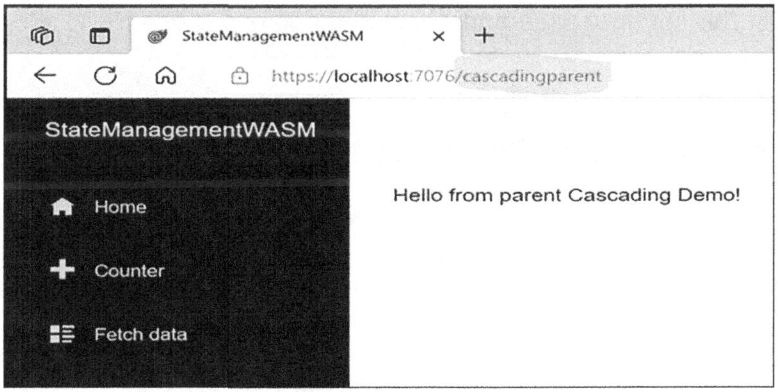

Figure 5.2*: Cascading value and parameter demo*

Services

Services in Blazor WebAssembly are singleton objects that can be registered and injected into components. Services can hold application state and provide data and functionality to multiple components. By injecting the same service instance into multiple components, they can share and manipulate the same state.

Step 1: For this approach, create the variable properties that we want to maintain the state for. In this case, we are maintaining the state for the **`CounterCount`** variable. So, we will create the class as follows:

```
namespace StateManagement.Pages.Service
{
    public class CounterState
    {
        public int CounterCount { get; set; }
    }}
```

Step 2: Inject the service into a program file as follows:

```
builder.Services.AddScoped<CounterState>();
```

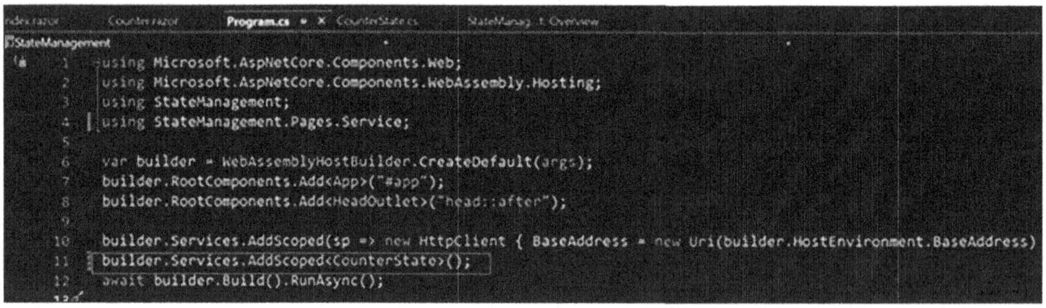

Figure 5.3: *Dependency injection*

Step 3: Go to the counter page and inject the **`CounterState`** Service and use it as shown here:

```
@page "/counter"
@using StateManagement.Pages.Service
@inject CounterState State;

<PageTitle>Counter</PageTitle>

<h1>Counter</h1>

<p>Current count: @State.CounterCount</p>

<button class="btn btn-primary" @onclick="IncrementCount">Click me</
button>

@code {
```

```
    private int currentCount = 0;

    private void IncrementCount()
    {
        State.CounterCount++;
    }
}
```

In the preceding code, we saw that we are injecting the service and creating an instance as represented here:

```
@inject CounterState State;
```

And we are holding the value as follows:

```
State.CounterCount++;
```

Now if we will run the code, we will see output, as shown in the following figure:

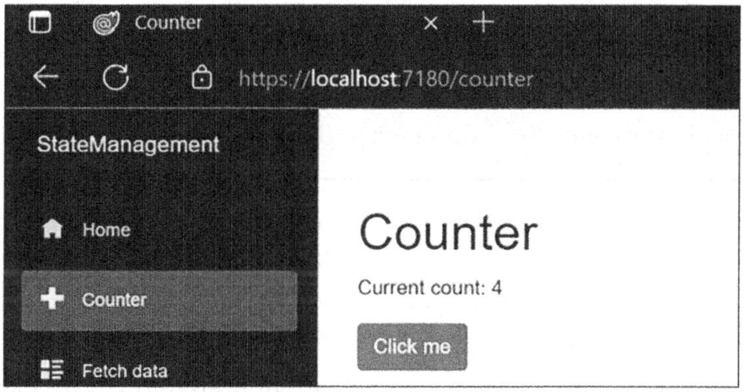

Figure 5.4: *Output*

Now click another tab and come to the same page, you will not lose the state.

Local Storage or Session Storage

Local Storage and Session Storage are two web storage mechanisms provided by modern web browsers to store data locally on a user's device.

They are a part of the Web Storage API, which allows web applications to store data within the user's browser for future retrieval.

Both Local Storage and Session Storage provide a way to persist data between page reloads and browser sessions without the need for server-side storage.

However, they have some key differences in terms of scope and lifespan, such as:

Local Storage:

- **Scope**: Data stored in local storage is accessible across all tabs and windows from the same origin (domain).
- **Lifespan**: The data persists even after the browser is closed and is stored until explicitly removed by the user or cleared by the website/application.
- **Usage**: Local storage is typically used for long-term storage of data, such as user preferences, settings, or cached data that should be available across multiple sessions.

Session Storage:

- **Scope**: Data stored in session storage is limited to the current tab or window. It is not accessible from other tabs or windows of the same origin.
- **Lifespan**: The data is retained as long as the tab or window is open. Once the user closes the tab or window, the session storage is cleared, and the data is lost.
- **Usage**: Session storage is suitable for temporary storage of data that should only last for the duration of the user's visit to the website. It is often used to store state information during a user session, which can be useful for preserving data between page reloads or navigations within the same tab.

When to use Local Storage or Session Storage depends on your specific use case, such as:

- Use local storage when storing data that should be available across multiple sessions and accessible from different tabs or windows within the same origin.
- Use session storage when you need to store temporary data that is specific to the current tab or window and should not persist beyond the current session.
- Both local storage and session storage are limited in terms of capacity (usually around 5-10 MB), and they are accessible only on the client-side, so sensitive data or critical information should not be stored in them. For such data, server-side storage with proper security measures is more appropriate.

Now, let us see the example of local storage in Blazor WebAssembly.

For this demo, we are going to use **`Blazored.LocalStorage`** and **`Blazored.SessionStorage`** NuGet package. It is very popular NuGet package in Blazor community.

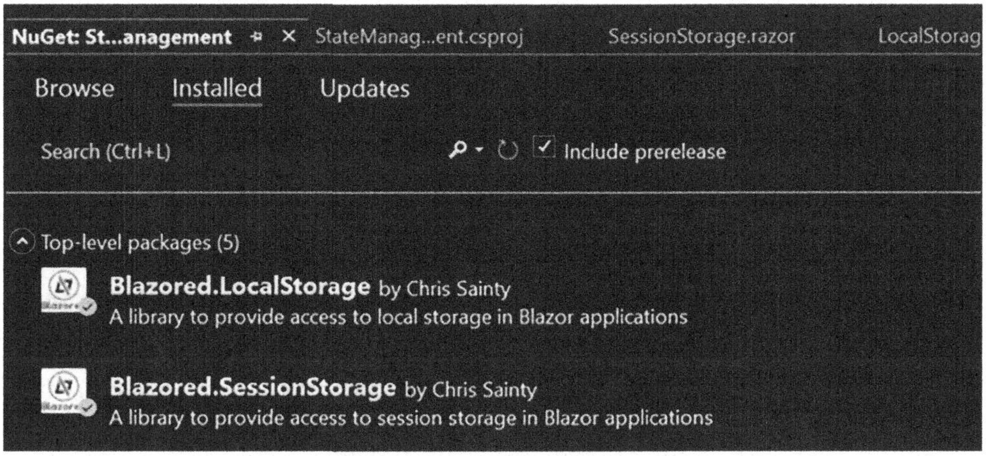

***Figure 5.5**: NuGet package*

After this, we need to register for the **program.cs** file as follows:

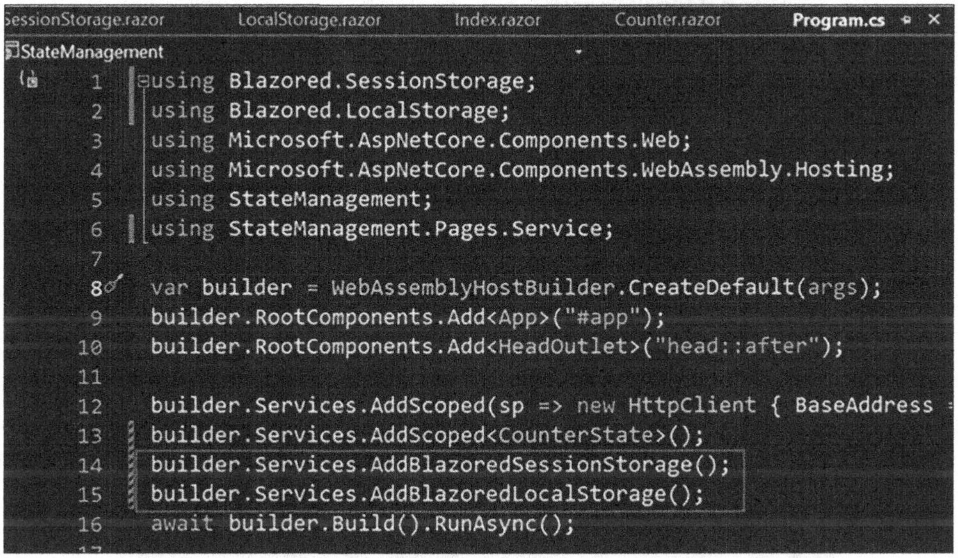

***Figure 5.6**: Adding NuGet package in program.cs file*

Now create the new Razor Component and write the code as follows:

```
@page "/localstorage"
<h3>Local Storage</h3>
@inject Blazored.LocalStorage.ILocalStorageService localStorage
<b>@Name</b>

@code {
    public string? Name { get; set; }
```

```
    protected override async Task OnInitializedAsync()
    {
        await localStorage.SetItemAsync("name", "Chandradev");
        Name = await localStorage.GetItemAsync<string>("name");
    }

}
```

In the preceding code snippet, we are creating an instance of **IlocalStorageService**, that is, **localStorage** using dependency injection.

We are saving the value in localstorage using **localStorage.SetItemAsync** method and reading a value from localstorage using **localStorage.GetItemAsync**:

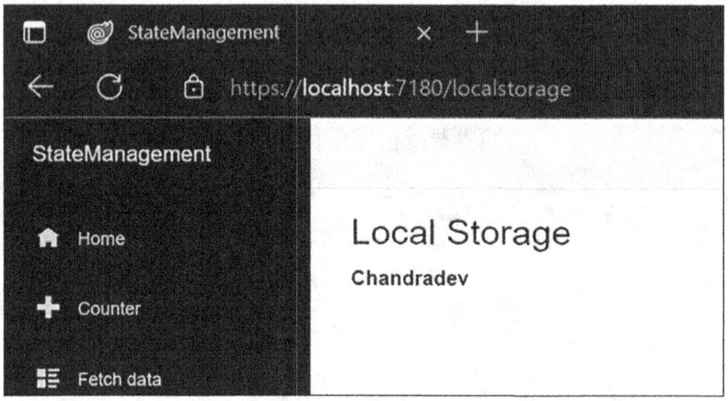

Figure 5.7: *Local Storage demo*

If you will see it on a browser using **F12**, you can see the localstorage value, as shown in *Figure* 5.8.

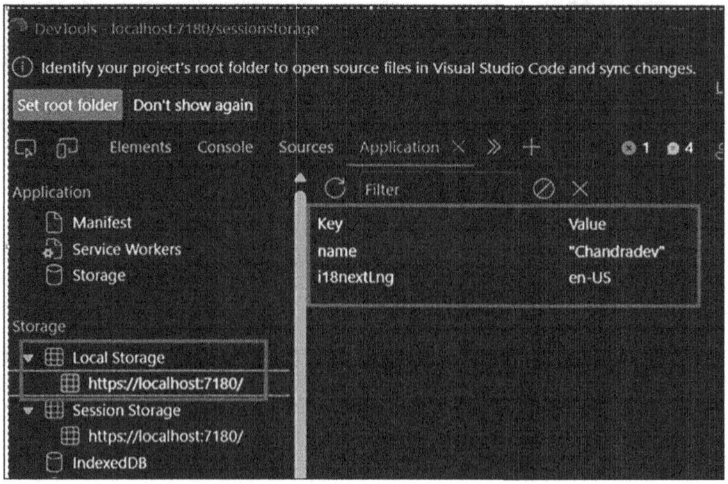

Figure 5.8: *Local Storage in browser*

Now, let us see **SessionStorage** code snippet:

For this also, all the processes will be the same as local storage. Now, we will create new Razor component and write the code as follows:

```
@page "/sessionstorage"
<h3>Session Storage</h3>
@inject Blazored.SessionStorage.ISessionStorageService sessionStorage
<b>@Name</b>

@code {
    public string? Name { get; set; }
    protected override async Task OnInitializedAsync()
    {
        await sessionStorage.SetItemAsync("name", "Chandradev");
        Name = await sessionStorage.GetItemAsync<string>("name");
    }
```

In the preceding code snippet, **sessionStorage.SetItemAsync** is used for saving data in session storage, and **sessionStorage.GetItemAsync** is used for reading data from session storage.

***Figure 5.9**: Session Storage demo*

If you will see it on a browser using **F12**, you can see the session value, as shown in *Figure 5.10*:

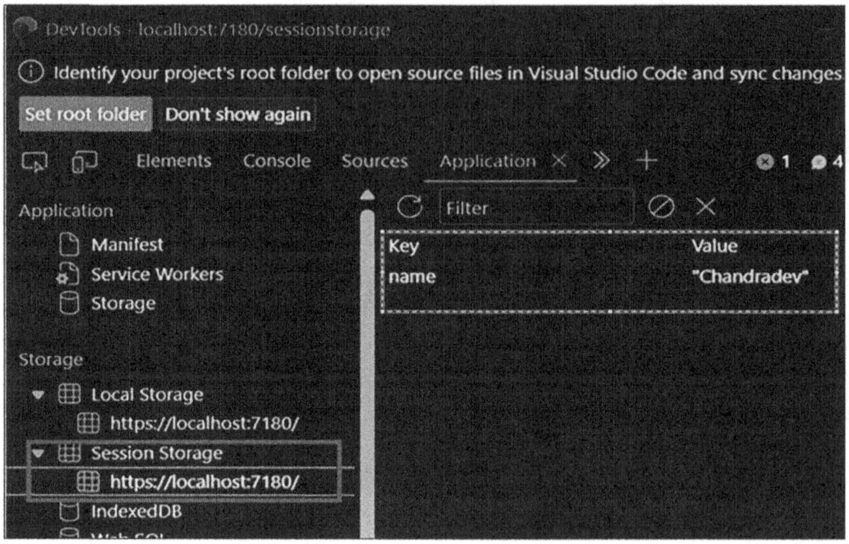

***Figure* 5.10**: *Session Storage in browser*

Server-Side State Management

In this approach, we will save the state in the database or cloud storage with the help of web API. However, this is not the best approach to use in Blazor WebAssembly. It would make an extremely slow application since we are constantly calling the database.

It is the least used approach in Blazor WebAssembly.

Tips and Tricks for Choosing State Management in Blazor WebAssembly

So far, we have seen that there are various approaches to maintaining state management in Blazor WebAssembly. We can decide to use each one depending on our scenario:

Component State:

- Use for a simple and isolated state that is specific to a particular component.
- Ideal for local UI state that doesn't need to be shared across components.
- Suitable for managing state with limited scope and not requiring communication between components.

Cascading Parameters:

- Utilize when passing data from a parent component down to its descendants.
- Useful for scenarios where multiple components require access to the same data.
- Avoid excessive nesting of cascading parameters as it can lead to unnecessary complexity.

Services and Dependency Injection:

- Choose for managing application-wide state or data that needs to be shared across different components.
- Helpful for decoupling state management logic from the components, promoting cleaner code organization.
- Use for state that requires complex business logic, data fetching, or communication with external services.

Local Storage and Session Storage:

- Opt for browser storage when persisting data across page reloads or browser sessions.
- Ideal for saving user preferences, settings, or cached data to provide a better user experience.
- Avoid using it for sensitive data or large amounts of data due to storage limitations.
- If you are saving sensitive data, then please use it as an encrypted format.

Server-Side versus Client-Side State:

- Choose server-side state management for applications with complex business logic or when the state needs to be shared among multiple clients. It can be achieved using the web API method. We will store data in some database.
- Opt for client-side state management for applications that require fast, responsive UI updates without frequent server communication.

Scalability:

- Evaluate how well the state management solution scales as your application grows.
- Ensure it remains maintainable and efficient as the complexity of your app increases.

Performance Considerations:

- Consider the performance implications of the state management approach you choose.
- Avoid over-engineering state management for simple applications to maintain optimal performance.

Testing and Debugging:

- The chosen state management approach is testable and facilitates debugging.
- Tools like Blazor DevTools can aid in monitoring state changes and debugging Blazor applications.

Conclusion

In this chapter, we explored various approaches for maintaining the state in Blazor WebAssembly. We can choose depending on our scenario and use case.

We also learned the tips and tricks to decide the state management approach in Blazor **`WebAssemblyapplication`**. In the next chapter, we will discuss REST services using Asp.net.

References

ASP.NET Core Blazor state management | Microsoft Learn

For Source Code

https://github.com/ava-orange-education/Practical-Web-Development-with-Blazor-and-.Net-8

Multiple Choice Questions

1. Which of the following options is NOT a state management approach in Blazor WebAssembly?
   a. Component State
   b. Cascading Parameters
   c. Local Storage
   d. Blazor Server
2. Which state management approach is recommended for simple applications with limited shared state requirements?
   a. Blazor Fluxor
   b. Server-Side State Management
   c. Component State
   d. Cascading Parameters
3. In Blazor WebAssembly, where is the state managed when using Blazor Server hosting model?
   a. On the server
   b. On the client's browser

   c. In a centralized database
   d. In local storage
4. Which one is a good approach to store sensitive data in state management?
   a. Local Storage on browser
   b. Session Storage on browser
   c. Encrypted Local Storage or Session Storage
   d. Cookies

Answers

1. d
2. c
3. a
4. c

CHAPTER 6
REST Services

Introduction

Blazor WebAssembly is a client-side web framework that enables us to build interactive web applications using C# and .NET in the browser.

While Blazor WebAssembly is primarily designed to work with RESTful services like other client-side JavaScript SPA frameworks, we can use the HttpClient class provided by .NET to communicate with RESTful services from Blazor WebAssembly. This chapter will dive deep into creating REST Service using Asp.net core. We will also learn how to call REST service in Blazor WebAssembly with complete code snippets.

Structure

This chapter covers the following topics:

- How to Create REST Service using Asp.net Core
- Web API Controller
- HttpClient
- Configuring and Injecting HttpClient
- CRUD Operation in Blazor WebAssembly

Creating REST Service Using Asp.net Core

A Representational State Transfer (REST) service is a type of web service architecture that follows the principles of RESTful design. It is an architectural style for designing networked applications, particularly web services, that rely on a stateless, client-server communication model.

REST services are based on standard HTTP methods, such as GET, POST, PUT, DELETE, and so on, and use simple, human-readable formats, including JSON or XML, to exchange data between clients and servers.

There are so many approaches to creating a REST Service. However, we will only focus on Asp.net Web API Core. This is one of the best and highly performed backend API services.

How to create REST Service using Asp.net core in Blazor?

For creating Web API core REST service, we can create a Standalone Web API core service or a Shared Web API core service in Blazor WebAssembly.

Standalone Web API Core Service

If we choose this approach, we can deploy Web API service on any server as a standalone. We can use this service on multiple applications that have been deployed on other servers.

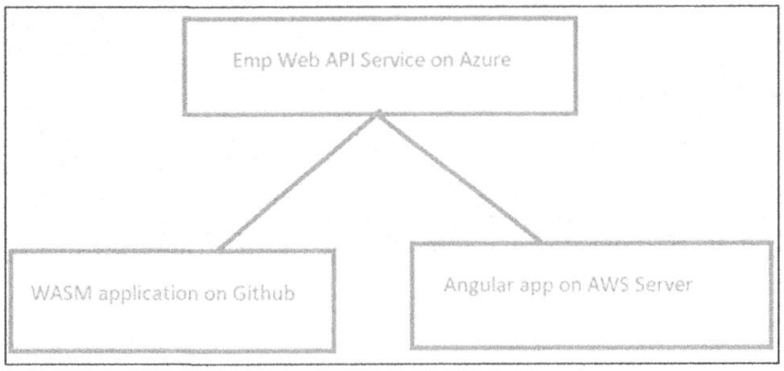

Figure 6.1: *Web API Service*

Note: *In the preceding image, we have created an Emp Web API service and deployed it on Azure. If we have used this service on Blazor WebAssembly or angular application, which has been deployed on GitHub or AWS, it will be a more scalable approach.*

Now we will see, how to create a Standalone Web API Service:

Step 1: Create the project using Visual Studio as follows:

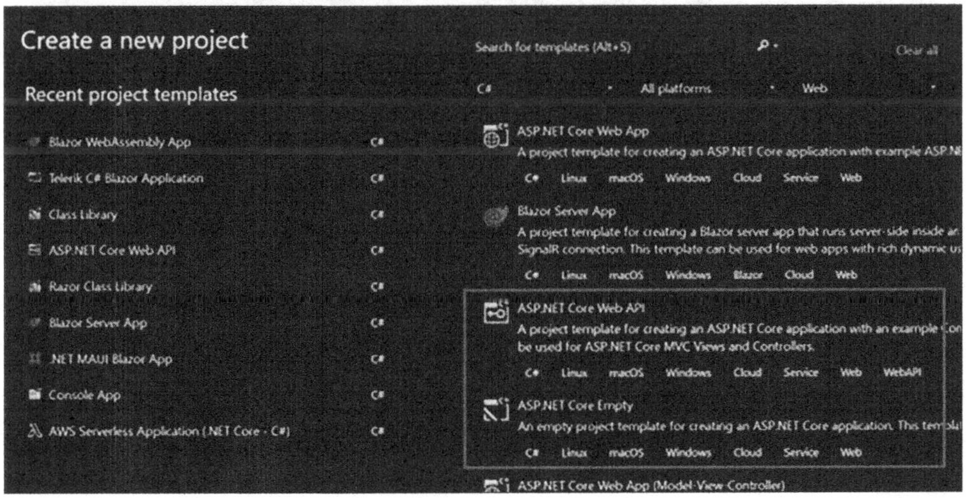

Figure 6.2: *Web API Project*

Step 2: Give the project name as follows:

***Figure 6.3**: EmpService*

Step 3: Select the **`framework`**

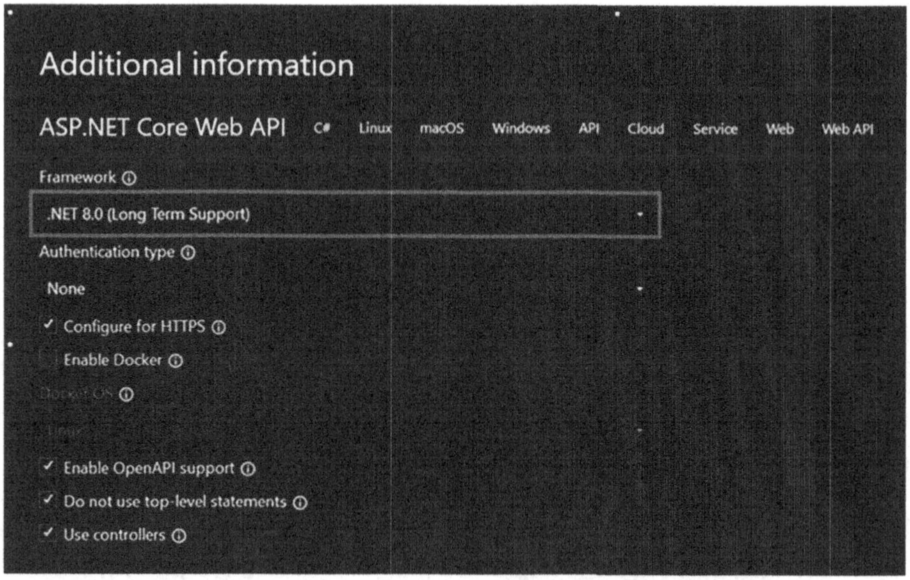

***Figure 6.4**: Framework*

Step 4: Now go to the Controllers folder and add a new **`EmpController`** as follows:

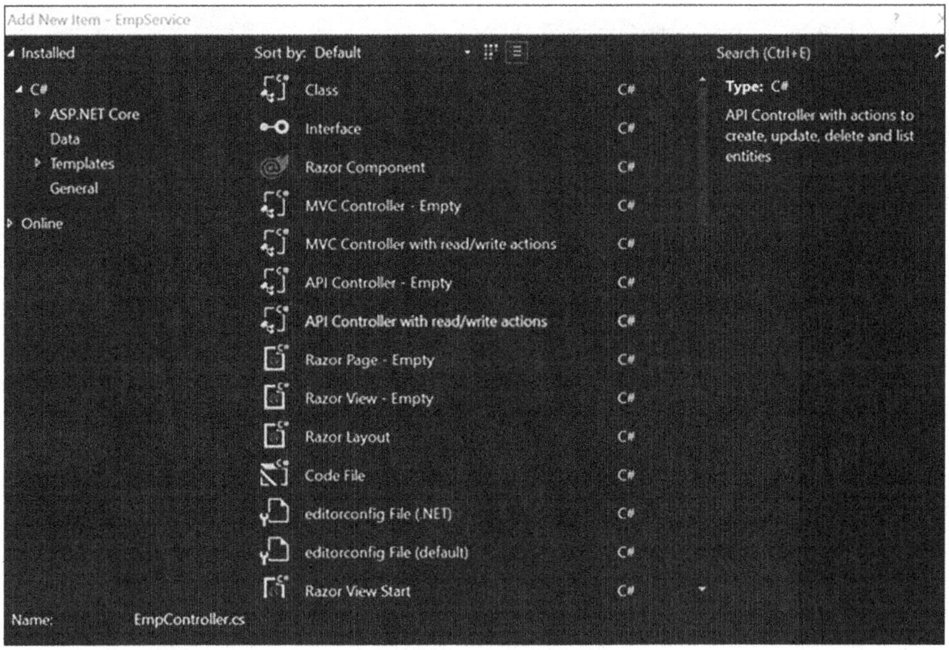

***Figure 6.5**: EmpController*

Now basic **EmpController** scaffolding code will be created as follows:

```
using Microsoft.AspNetCore.Mvc;

namespace EmpService.Controllers
{
    [Route("api/[controller]")]
    [ApiController]
    public class EmpController : ControllerBase
    {
        // GET: api/<EmpController>
        [HttpGet]
        public IEnumerable<string> Get()
        {
            return new string[] { "value1", "value2" };
        }
        // GET api/<EmpController>/5
        [HttpGet("{id}")]
        public string Get(int id)
        {
            return "value";
        }
```

```
        // POST api/<EmpController>
        [HttpPost]
        public void Post([FromBody] string value)
        {
        }

        // PUT api/<EmpController>/5
        [HttpPut("{id}")]
        public void Put(int id, [FromBody] string value)
        {
        }

        // DELETE api/<EmpController>/5
        [HttpDelete("{id}")]
        public void Delete(int id)
        {
        }
    }
}
```

Now run the application using **F5** and go to the home controller. The output will be as follows:

***Figure 6.6**: Output*

This API endpoint we can consume anywhere in any application.

Shared Web API Core in Blazor WebAssembly

In this approach, ASP.NET Web API Core service will be created with Blazor WebAssembly application. We can use this service within Blazor WebAssembly and Blazor Server approach. If we have a simple requirement and need more re-usabilities, then this will be a good approach. You can use this project template up to Blazor WebAssembly 7.0.

For creating the Web API Core service with Blazor WebAssembly, we have to select **`Asp.net Core Hosted`**, as shown in *Figure 6.7*:

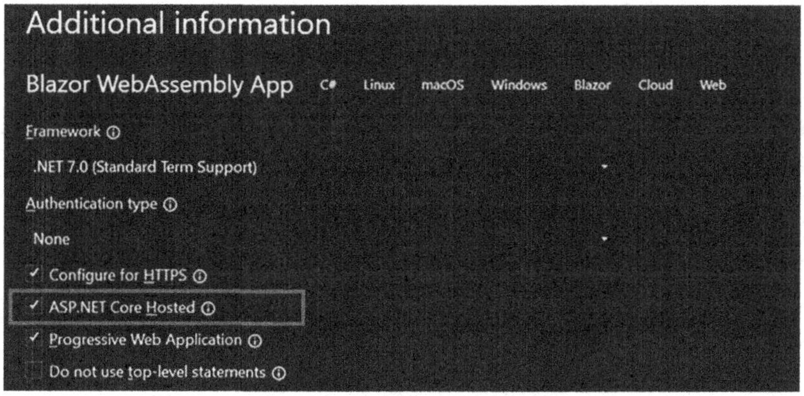

***Figure 6.7**: Asp.net core hosted*

When you click on next, the project will be created as shown in the following screenshot. It will contains Blazor UI Layer, Web API Layer, and Shared Model:

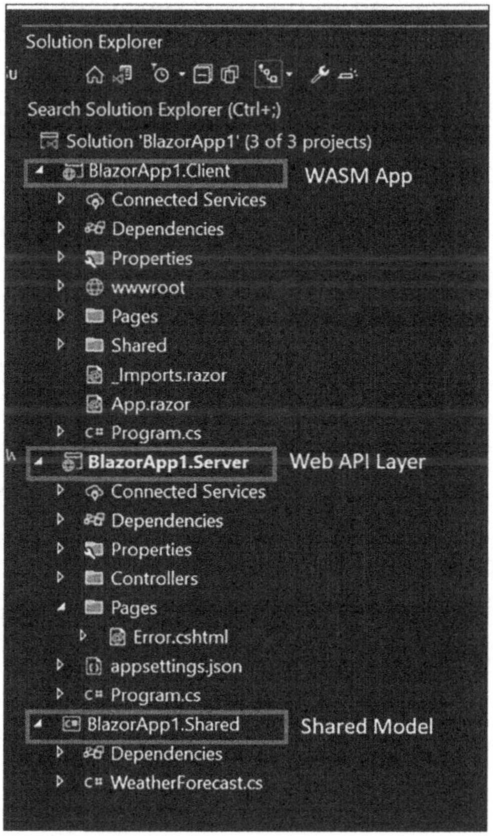

***Figure 6.8**: Asp.net core hosted*

In this approach, we can share the Model in Web API and Blazor WebAssembly and Blazor Server application. It is a good architecture for simple applications.

Now, we will see when to use Standalone and Shared Web API approach.

Standalone Web API Approach:

- **Complexity and Scalability:** If your Web API is a complex system with its own requirements, business logic, and data access layers, it might be better to create it as a standalone project. This approach allows you to manage the Web API independently and gives you more flexibility in terms of scalability and code organization.
- **Separation of Concerns:** A standalone Web API project ensures a clear separation of concerns between the client (Blazor WebAssembly) and the server (Web API). This can make the codebase more maintainable and easier to understand for developers working on different application parts.

Shared Web API Project in Blazor WebAssembly:

- **Simplified Development and Deployment:** If your Web API logic is relatively simple and closely related to the functionality of your Blazor WebAssembly application, creating a shared project can simplify development and deployment. You can avoid the overhead of maintaining two separate projects and reference the shared Web API project in both the client and server parts of your application.
- **Code Reuse:** When both your Blazor WebAssembly and Blazor Server projects require the same API endpoints and data models, having a shared Web API project enables code reuse. Any changes or improvements made to the shared Web API project will reflect in both hosting models, reducing duplication and ensuring consistency.
- **Consistency in API Definition**: Creating a shared Web API project helps ensure that the API endpoints, request/response models, and overall API contract remain consistent across the application, regardless of the hosting model.

Note: *If you are using .Net 8.0, then you will not get* ***Shared Web API Core in Blazor WebAssembly*** *project template. This project template has been removed now. You can create standalone projects for Blazor WebAssembly and Web API Project, but code will be the same.*

.Net 8.0 Web API Project:

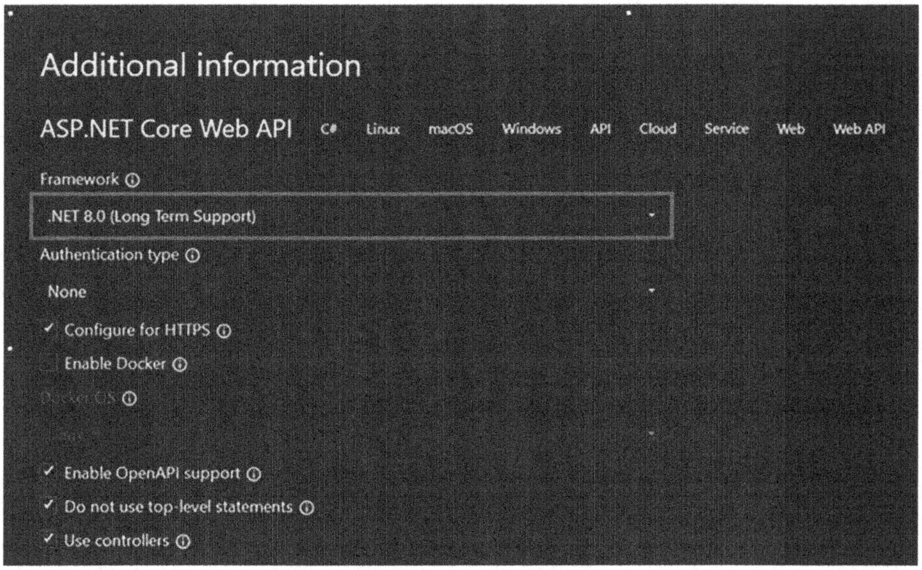

Figure 6.9: Web API project template in .Net 8.0

Blazor WebAssembly 8.0 Project:

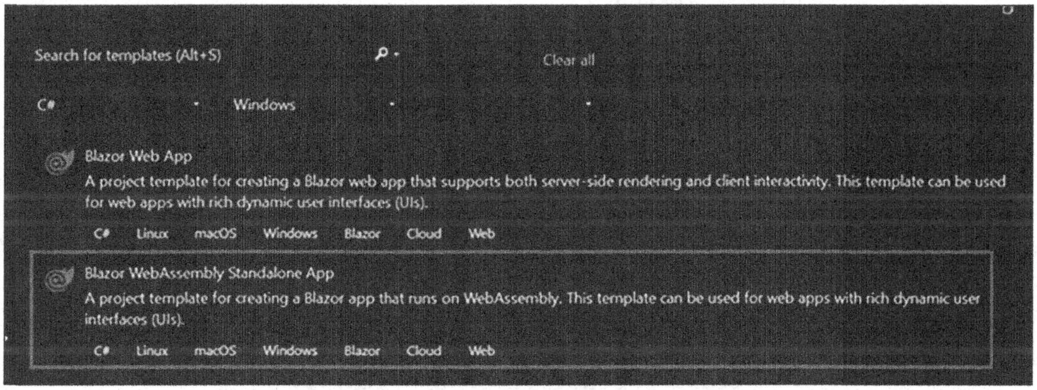

Figure 6.10: Blazor WASM project template in .Net 8.0

HttpClient in Blazor WebAssembly

In Blazor WebAssembly, the HttpClient class is a fundamental component for making HTTP requests to APIs or services from the client-side code. It allows your Blazor WebAssembly application to communicate with backend servers, Web APIs, or other HTTP-based resources. You can use HttpClient to send HTTP requests and process the responses asynchronously.

To use **`HttpClient`** into your component, you need to inject **`HttpClient`** at the top of the page, as follows:

```
@page "/fetchdata"
@using BlazorApp1.Shared
@inject HttpClient Http

<PageTitle>Weather forecast</PageTitle>

<h1>Weather forecast</h1>

<p>This component demonstrates fetching data from the server.</p>

@if (forecasts == null)
{
    <p><em>Loading...</em></p>
}
else
{
    <table class="table">
        <thead>
            <tr>
                <th>Date</th>
                <th>Temp. (C)</th>
                <th>Temp. (F)</th>
                <th>Summary</th>
            </tr>
        </thead>
        <tbody>
            @foreach (var forecast in forecasts)
            {
                <tr>
                    <td>@forecast.Date.ToShortDateString()</td>
                    <td>@forecast.TemperatureC</td>
                    <td>@forecast.TemperatureF</td>
                    <td>@forecast.Summary</td>
                </tr>
            }
        </tbody>
    </table>
}

@code {
    private WeatherForecast[]? forecasts;

    protected override async Task OnInitializedAsync()
```

```
    {
        forecasts = await Http.GetFromJsonAsync<WeatherFore-
cast[]>("WeatherForecast");
    }
}
```

In the preceding code snippet, we have injected **HttpClient** at the top of the page, and then we are calling any API service using **Http.GetFromJsonAsync** method.

If you go to the definition of **Http.GetFromJsonAsync** method, you will see the sets of Json Extension methods that are created by Microsoft for insert, update, and delete operations with REST Service.

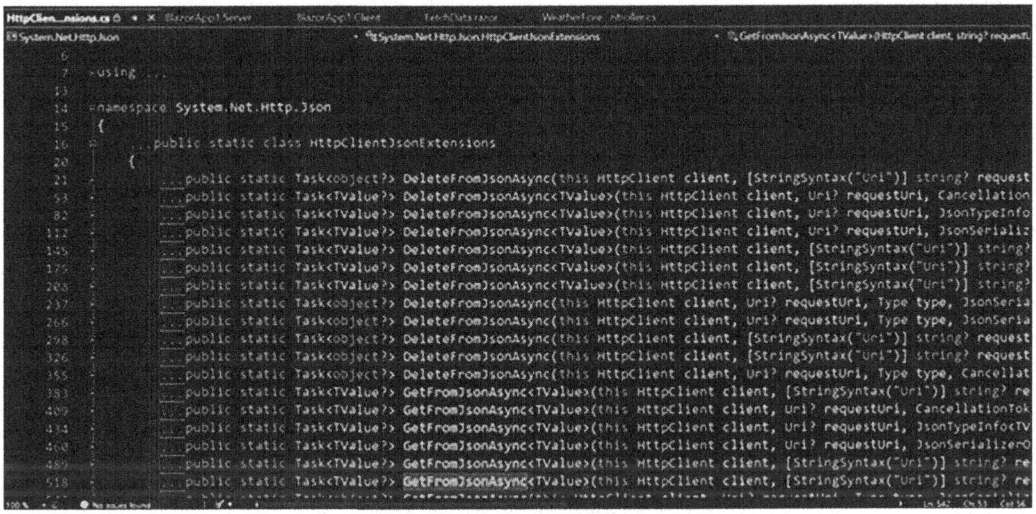

Figure 6.11: *httpClient*

We will write a summary of all Json Extension methods along with when to utilize each one:

- `GetFromJsonAsync`
- `PostAsJsonAsync`
- `PutAsJsonAsync`
- `DeleteFromJsonAsync`
- `PatchAsJsonAsync`

`GetFromJsonAsync`

This method makes a GET request to the specified **requestUri** and attempts to serialize the response into the type represented by the T parameter or the Type parameter. You can see an example of this in the **FetchData** component in the standard Blazor WebAssembly project templates.

PostAsJsonAsync

This method is used to send a POST request with JSON data as the payload. It's typically used for creating new resources on the server.

PutAsJsonAsync

Similar to the **PostAsJsonAsync** method, but it is used for updating existing resources on the server using a PUT request

DeleteFromJsonAsync

Similar to the **GetFromJsonAsync** method, but it would be used to send a **DELETE** request and potentially receive a JSON response. This is useful for deleting resources on the server.

PatchAsJsonAsync

This method sends a PATCH request with JSON data as the payload. It's often used for updating a resource partially instead of replacing the whole resource.

CRUD Operation in Blazor WebAssembly

Here are the code snippets for CRUD operation using **HttpClient** Json Extension Method.

Assuming you have a **TodoItem** class model:

```
public class TodoItem
{
    public int Id { get; set; }
    public string Title { get; set; }
    public bool IsCompleted { get; set; }
}
```

And you have an **HttpClient** instance named **HttpClient** that's configured to communicate with your API.

Create (POST):

```
public async Task CreateTodoItemAsync(TodoItem newItem)
{
    HttpResponseMessage response = await httpClient.PostAsJsonAsync
("api/todo", newItem);

    if (response.IsSuccessStatusCode)
    {
        // Item created successfully
```

```
        // You might want to handle the response or update your local data
    }
    else
    {
        // Handle error cases
    }
}
```

Read (GET):

```
public async Task<List<TodoItem>> GetTodoItemsAsync()
{
    List<TodoItem> items = await httpClient.GetFromJsonAsync<List
<TodoItem>>("api/todo");
    return items;
}
```

Update (PUT or PATCH):

Using **PUT**:

```
public async Task UpdateTodoItemAsync(TodoItem updatedItem)
{
    HttpResponseMessage response = await httpClient.PutAsJsonAsync
($"api/todo/{updatedItem.Id}", updatedItem);

    if (response.IsSuccessStatusCode)
    {
        // Item updated successfully
        // You might want to handle the response or update your local data
    }
    else
    {
        // Handle error cases
    }
}
```

Using **Patch** (it is used for partial update):

```
public async Task UpdateTodoItemStatusAsync(int itemId, bool isComplet-
ed)
{
    var patchDocument = new { IsCompleted = isCompleted };

    HttpResponseMessage response = await httpClient.PatchAsJsonAsync($"
api/todo/{itemId}", patchDocument);
```

```
    if (response.IsSuccessStatusCode)
    {
        // Item updated successfully
        // You might want to handle the response or update your local data
    }
    else
    {
        // Handle error cases
    }
}
```

Delete (DELETE):

```
public async Task DeleteTodoItemAsync(int itemId)
{
    HttpResponseMessage response = await httpClient.DeleteFromJsonAsync
($"api/todo/{itemId}");

    if (response.IsSuccessStatusCode)
    {
        // Item deleted successfully
        // You might want to handle the response or update your local data
    }
    else
    {
        // Handle error cases
    }}
```

Conclusion

In this chapter, we understood REST Service and how to create it using Asp.net Core. We also learned how to call REST service in Blazor WebAssembly with complete code snippets. It is one of the important concepts while working with any Blazor application.

In the next chapter, we will explore more details about REST Service Call with Entity Framework Core.

References

Call a web API from an ASP.NET Core Blazor app | Microsoft Learn

https://learn.microsoft.com/en-us/aspnet/core/blazor/call-web-api?view=aspnetcore-7.0&pivots=webassembly

Multiple Choice Questions

1. What does REST stand for in the context of web services?
   a. Representational Entity State Transfer
   b. Remote Execution and State Transfer
   c. Representational State Transfer
   d. Remote Entity Service Transfer
2. How does Blazor communicate with RESTful services?
   a. Using WebSockets
   b. Using gRPC
   c. Using JSON-RPC
   d. Using HTTP requests
3. Which HTTP methods are commonly used when interacting with RESTful services in Blazor?
   a. GET, POST, PUT, DELETE
   b. READ, CREATE, UPDATE, DELETE
   c. FETCH, ADD, MODIFY, REMOVE
   d. QUERY, INSERT, UPDATE, DELETE
4. In Blazor, which component lifecycle method is commonly used to make REST API calls?
   a. `OnInit()`
   b. `OnInitialized()`
   c. `OnRender()`
   d. `OnLoad()`

Answers

1. c
2. d
3. a
4. b

Chapter 7
Entity Framework Core

Introduction

Nowadays while working with any Blazor Application, you will see Backend API Service with Entity Framework Core or EF Core. This is a very popular and productive ORM from Microsoft. It is one of the alternate and popular options for creating a Backend service. Before EF Core, we were using Ado.net.

EF Core is a very vast topic. It will be very difficult to include all the concepts in a single chapter.

Structure

This chapter covers the following topics:

- EF Core 8.0
- Reasons to Use EF Core
- When Not to Use EF Core
- EF Core Supported Application Types
- Entity Framework Core Approaches
- Supported Databases
- CRUD Operation with EF Core in Blazor WebAssembly

EF Core 8.0

Entity Framework (EF) Core 8.0 is a lightweight, extensible, open-source, and cross-platform version of the popular Entity Framework data access technology.

It provides an object-relational mapping (ORM) framework that allows developers to work with databases using .NET objects.

It has introduced many cool features in EF 8.0, significantly enhancing developer productivity. It is a highly performed and efficient ORM as compared to other competitors in the market.

For more details, please refer the following URL:

What's New in EF Core 8 | Microsoft Learn (https://learn.microsoft.com/en-us/ef/core/what-is-new/ef-core-8.0/whatsnew)

Reasons to Use EF Core

Here are some reasons why you might consider using EF Core in your project:

- **Simplified Data Access**

EF Core simplifies the process of interacting with databases by allowing you to work with database objects as regular .NET objects. This means you can use C# or VB.NET classes to represent database tables, and EF Core will handle the translation between these objects and the actual database queries.

- **Developer Productivity**

EF Core can speed up the development process by eliminating the need to write a lot of repetitive data access code. It offers a higher-level, more abstract way to perform CRUD (Create, Read, Update, Delete) operations on the database.

- **Cross-Platform Support**

EF Core is designed to work on multiple platforms, including Windows, Linux, and macOS. This makes it suitable for building applications that need to run on different operating systems.

- **Database Provider Flexibility**

EF Core supports multiple database providers, including SQL Server, SQLite, MySQL, PostgreSQL, and more. This allows you to switch between different database systems relatively easily without rewriting your data access code.

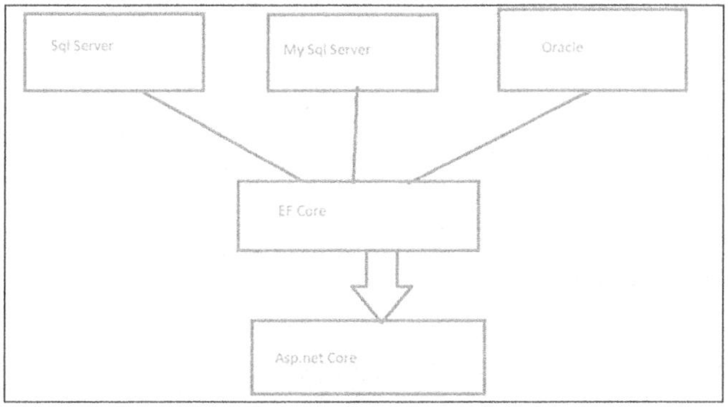

Figure 7.1: EF Core

- **LINQ Integration**

EF Core seamlessly integrates with Language Integrated Query (LINQ), which is a powerful querying language that allows you to write complex queries using C# or VB.NET syntax. This makes querying the database more intuitive and less error-prone.

- **Automatic Change Tracking**

EF Core automatically tracks changes made to objects and generates the necessary SQL statements to persist those changes to the database. This helps to reduce the complexity of managing data changes.

- **Migration Support**

EF Core includes a migration system that helps you manage changes to your database schema over time. It can generate SQL scripts to update the database schema as your application's data model evolves.

- **Testability**

EF Core supports in-memory database providers, which allow you to write unit tests without needing a real database. This can make your testing process more efficient and isolated.

- **Security and Parameterization**

EF Core uses parameterized queries by default, which helps prevent SQL injection attacks. This contributes to the security of your application.

- **Open Source and Active Development**

EF Core is open source and is actively maintained by Microsoft. This means it's continually improving, and the community can contribute to its development and bug fixes.

When Not to Use EF Core

Despite its benefits, it's important to note that EF Core might not be the best choice for every scenario.

For extremely high-performance scenarios or when fine-tuned control over SQL queries is necessary, a more direct approach might be preferred like Ado.net or Dapper approach.

However, for many applications, EF Core offers a great balance between developer productivity and efficient data access.

EF Core Supported Application Types

We can use Entity Framework Core on all DOT NET applications as follows:

- Console Applications
- Windows Applications
- ASP.NET Web Forms
- ASP.NET MVC
- ASP.NET Core MVC
- ASP.NET Core Razor Pages
- Blazor Apps
- WPF
- Xamarin Framework
- Web API
- .NET MAUI

Entity Framework Core Approaches

There are two Entity Framework Core development approaches as follows:

- Database First
- Code First

Database First Approach

In the Database First approach, the domain and context classes are created based on the existing Database. This approach is mainly suitable if our database is ready and we are going to create a domain and context on top of it.

Figure 7.2: *Database First Approach*

Code First Approach

In the Code First approach, the domain and context classes are created by you, and then EF Core creates the database using these classes.

Migration is used whenever EF Core creates or updates the database based on the domain and context classes.

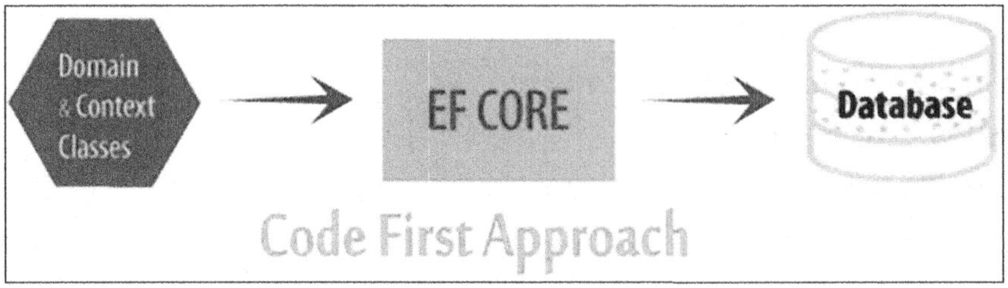

Figure 7.3: *Code First Approach*

Supported Databases

Entity Framework Core works on many databases as follows:

- SQL Server
- MySQL
- PostgreSQL
- SQLite
- SQL Compact
- Firebird
- Oracle
- Db2

CRUD Operation with EF Core in Blazor WebAssembly

In this demo, we will see how to do CRUD operation with the Employee table using EF Core 7.0 in Blazor WebAssembly 7.0.

Note: *If you will use Blazor WebAssembly 8.0, you will not get Asp.net core hosted project template. You need to create two standalone projects, that is, Blazor WebAssembly and Asp.net core. However, our code will be exactly the same.*

Here are the steps:

Step 1: Create the Employee table in the database as follows:

```
CREATE TABLE [dbo].[tblEmp](
      [Id] [int] IDENTITY(1,1) NOT NULL,
      [FirstName] [nvarchar](50) NULL,
      [LastName] [nvarchar](50) NULL,
      [Email] [nvarchar](50) NULL,
      [Salary] [money] NULL,
```

```
 CONSTRAINT [PK_tblEmp] PRIMARY KEY CLUSTERED
(
      [Id] ASC
)WITH (PAD_INDEX = OFF, STATISTICS_NORECOMPUTE = OFF, IGNORE_DUP_KEY
= OFF, ALLOW_ROW_LOCKS = ON, ALLOW_PAGE_LOCKS = ON, OPTIMIZE_FOR_SE-
QUENTIAL_KEY = OFF) ON [PRIMARY]
) ON [PRIMARY]
```

Step 2: Create the Blazor WebAssembly Application as follows:

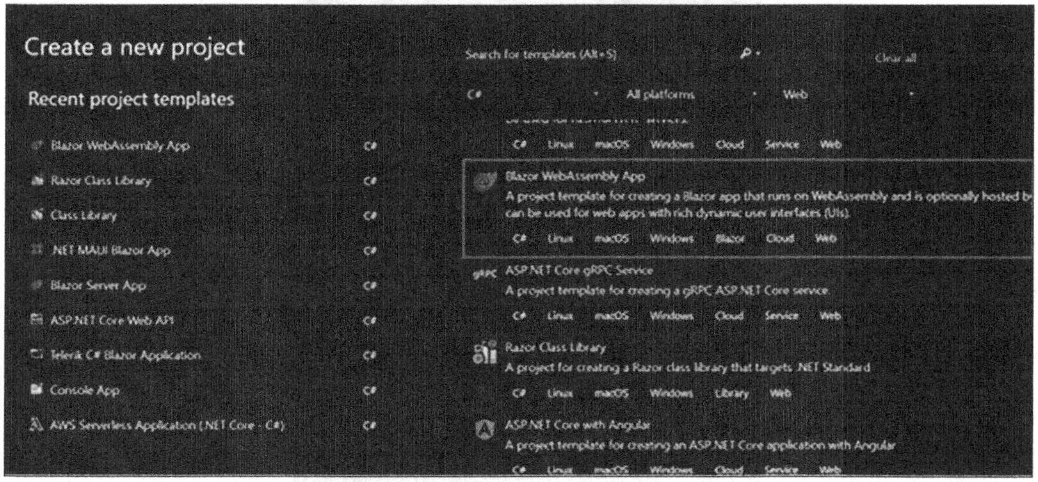

Figure 7.4: *Blazor WebAssembly*

Step 3: Select the `Asp.net Core Hosted` option and create an API project as follows:

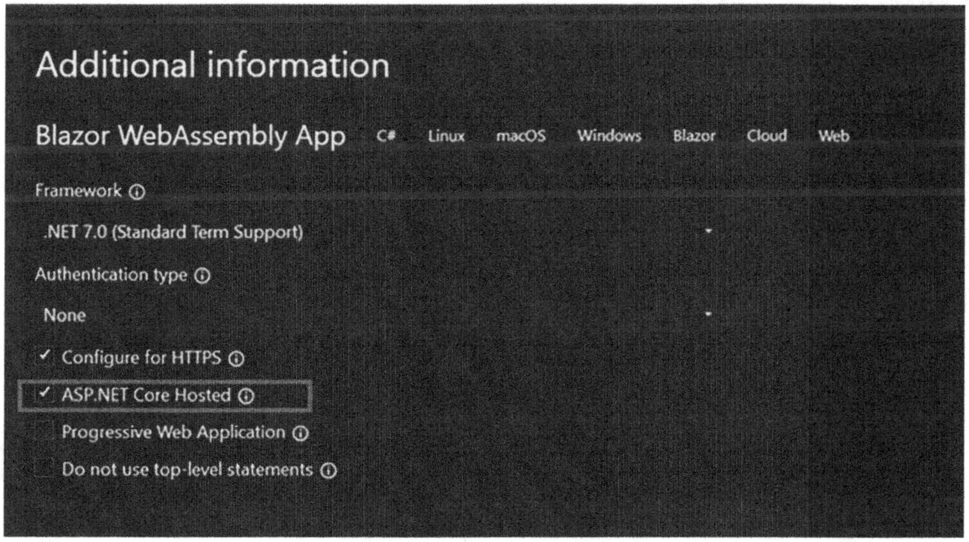

Figure 7.5: *Asp.net Core Hosted*

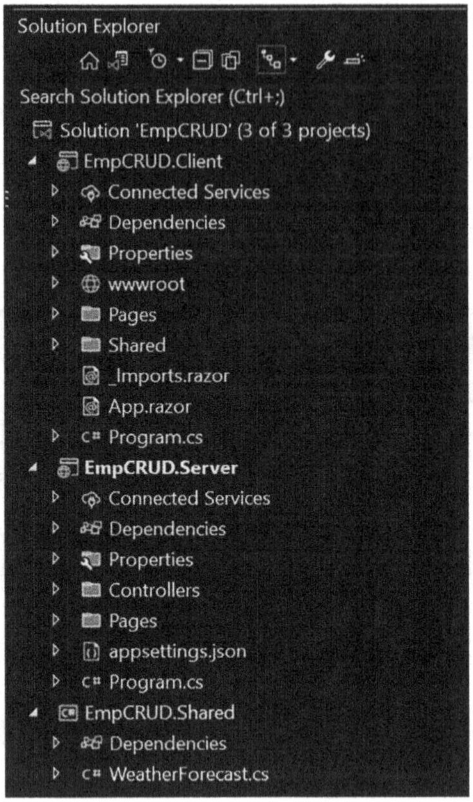

***Figure 7.6**: Project Structure*

Step 4: Go to the Share project folder and create the **Emp** class in the Model folder as follows:

```
using System.ComponentModel.DataAnnotations;

namespace EmpCRUD.Shared.Model
{
    public class Emp
    {
        public int Id { get; set; }
        [Required]
        public string? FirstName { get; set; }
        [Required]
        public string? LastName { get; set; }
        [Required]
        public string? Email { get; set; }
        [Required]
        public decimal? Salary { get; set; }
    }
}
```

Step 5: Now, we will create Data access layers for fetching data from the database. For this task, we have installed **`EF Core Power Tool`** in Visual Studio 2022:

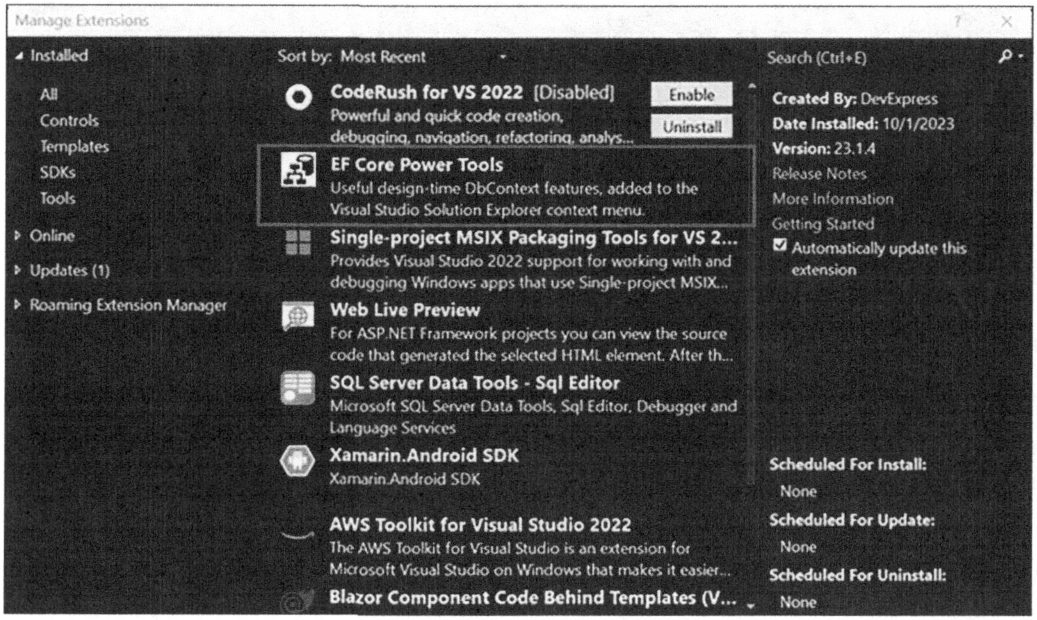

***Figure 7.7:** EF Power Tools*

We will go to the **`EmpCRUD.Server`** and do Reverse Engineering as shown:

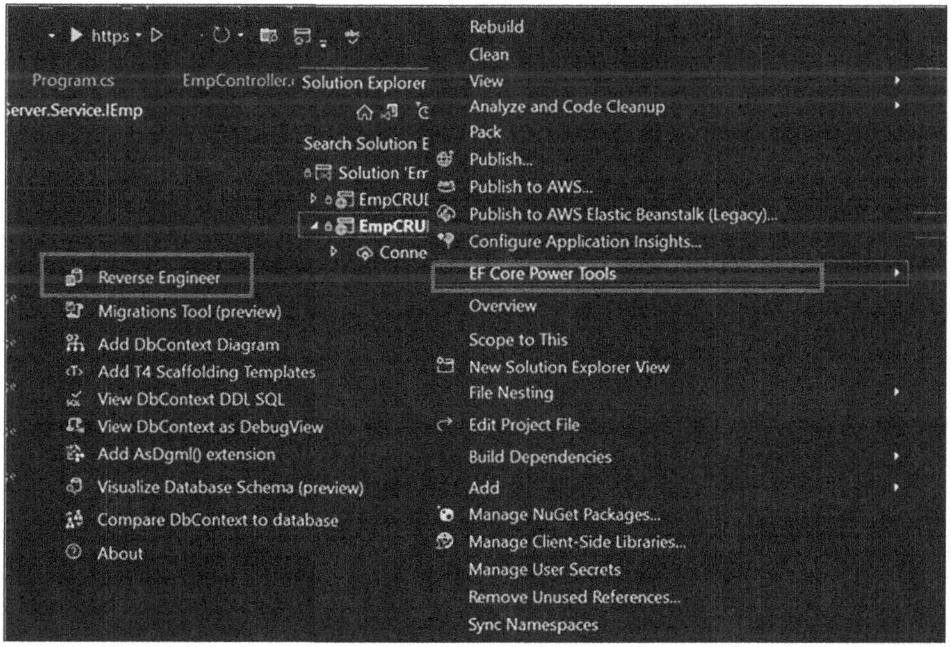

***Figure 7.8:** Reverse Engineer*

Now, it will create the required table mapping class with the Context file for us as follows:

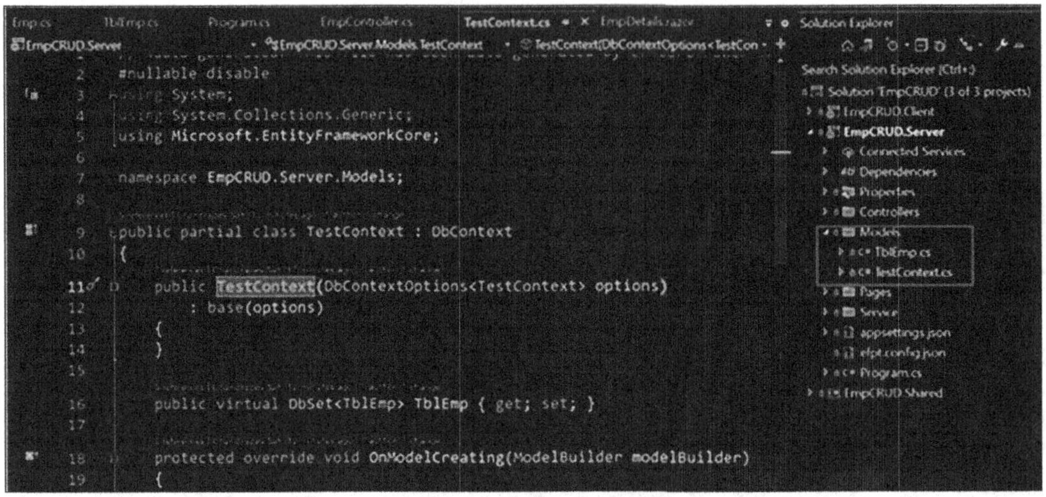

Figure 7.9: *Context File*

Step 6: Create a Service Folder in **`EmpCRUD.Server`** project, and create an **`IEmp.cs`** interface as follows:

```
using EmpCRUD.Server.Models;

namespace EmpCRUD.Server.Service
{
    public interface IEmp
    {
        Task<string> AddEmp(TblEmp emp);
        Task<string> UpdateEmp(TblEmp emp);
        Task<string> DeleteEmp(int Id);
        Task<TblEmp> GetEmpDetails(int Id);
        Task<List<TblEmp>> GetAllEmps();

    }}
```

Step 7: Create the **`EmpService`** for **`IEmp`** Interface as follows:

```
using EmpCRUD.Server.Models;
using Microsoft.EntityFrameworkCore;

namespace EmpCRUD.Server.Service
{

    public class EmpService : IEmp
    {
        private TestContext _dbContext;
```

```
    public EmpService(TestContext context)
    {
        this._dbContext = context;
    }

    public async Task<string> AddEmp(TblEmp emp)
    {
        await _dbContext.TblEmp.AddAsync(emp);
        await _dbContext.SaveChangesAsync();
        return "Data has been added successfully";
    }
    public async Task<List<TblEmp>> GetAllEmps()
    {
        return await _dbContext.TblEmp.ToListAsync();
    }

    public async Task<TblEmp> GetEmpDetails(int Id)
    {
        TblEmp? emp = await _dbContext.TblEmp.FindAsync(Id);

        if (emp == null)
        {
            throw new Exception("Employee not found");
        }
        return emp;
    }

    public async Task<string> UpdateEmp(TblEmp emp)
    {
        _dbContext.Entry(emp).State = EntityState.Modified;
        await _dbContext.SaveChangesAsync();
        return "Data has been updated successfully";
    }

    async Task<string> IEmp.DeleteEmp(int Id)
    {
        var emp = await _dbContext.TblEmp.FindAsync(Id);
        if (emp != null)
        {
            var result = _dbContext.TblEmp.Remove(emp);
            await _dbContext.SaveChangesAsync();
        }
        return "Data Deleted successfully";
    }
}}
```

Step 8: Go to the **API Controller** folder and create an **EmpController** with the given code snippets:

```
using EmpCRUD.Server.Models;
using EmpCRUD.Server.Service;
using Microsoft.AspNetCore.Mvc;

namespace EmpCRUD.Server.Controllers
{
    [Route("api/[controller]")]
    [ApiController]
    public class EmpController : ControllerBase
    {
        private readonly IEmp _IEmp;
        public EmpController(IEmp emp)
        {
            _IEmp = emp;
        }
        // GET: api/<EmpController>
        [HttpGet]
        public async Task<List<TblEmp>> Get()
        {
            return await Task.FromResult(await _IEmp.GetAllEmps());
        }

        // GET api/<EmpController>/5
        [HttpGet("{id}")]
        public async Task<IActionResult> Get(int id)
        {
            return Ok(await _IEmp.GetEmpDetails(id));
        }

        // POST api/<EmpController>
        [HttpPost]
        public async Task<string> post(TblEmp tblEmp)
        {
            return await _IEmp.AddEmp(tblEmp);

        }

        // PUT api/<EmpController>/5
        [HttpPut]
        public async Task<string> Put(TblEmp tblEmp)
        {
            return await _IEmp.UpdateEmp(tblEmp);
        }

        // DELETE api/<EmpController>/5
        [HttpDelete("{id}")]
```

```
        public async Task<string> Delete(int id)
        {
            return await _IEmp.DeleteEmp(id);
        }
    }}
```

Step 9: Now, in the **Program.cs** file, configure the required middleware as follows:

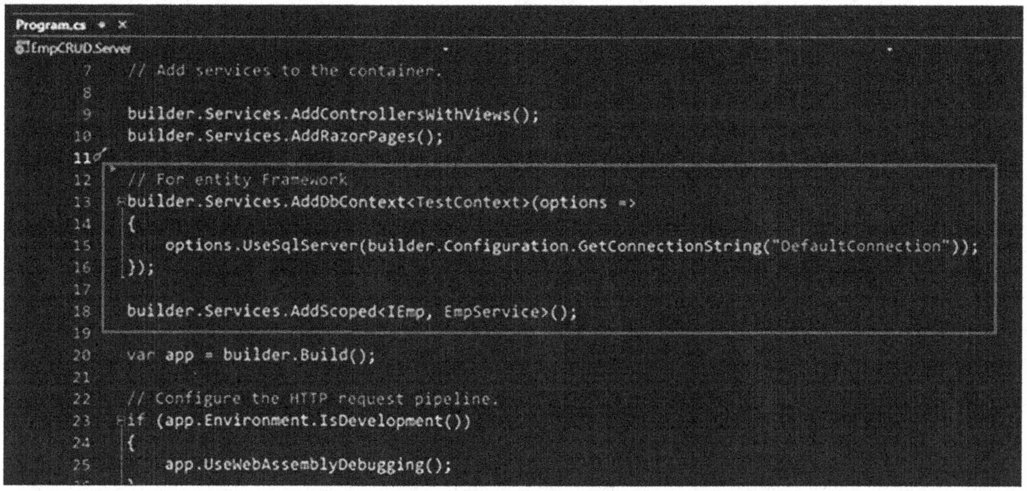

Figure 7.10: *Program.cs*

Step 10: Go to the **appsettings.json** file of **`EmpCRUD.Server`** project and add the connection string as shown:

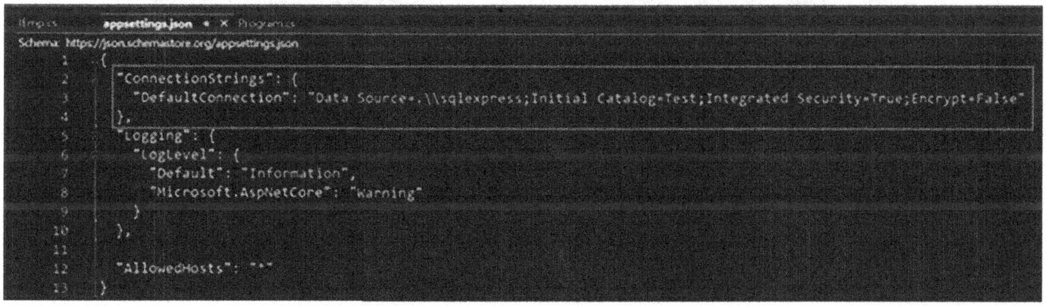

Figure 7.11: *Connection String*

Note: *Do Not store the connection in a JSON file for real-time projects; this is only for demo purposes. For real-time projects, we will store them in a cloud environment.*

Step 11: Now, we will create the UI layer for the Add, Fetch, Edit, and Delete screen in the Blazor Client Project.

AddEmp.Razor

```
@page "/emp/add"
@page "/emp/edit/{empId:int}"
@using EmpCRUD.Shared.Model

@inject HttpClient Http
@inject NavigationManager NavigationManager
<h3>@Title</h3>

<hr />
<EditForm Model="@emp" OnValidSubmit="SaveEmp">
    <DataAnnotationsValidator />
    <div class="mb-3">
        <label for="Name" class="form-label">FirstName</label>
        <div class="col-md-4">
           <InputText class="form-control" @bind-Value="emp.FirstName" />
        </div>
        <ValidationMessage For="@(() => emp.FirstName)" />
    </div>
    <div class="mb-3">
        <label for="Address" class="form-label">LastName</label>
        <div class="col-md-4">
           <InputText class="form-control" @bind-Value="emp.LastName" />
        </div>
        <ValidationMessage For="@(() => emp.LastName)" />
    </div>
    <div class="mb-3">
        <label for="Cellnumber" class="form-label">Email</label>
        <div class="col-md-4">
            <InputText class="form-control" @bind-Value="emp.Email" />
        </div>
        <ValidationMessage For="@(() => emp.Email)" />
    </div>
    <div class="mb-3">
        <label for="Emailid" class="form-label">Salary</label>
        <div class="col-md-4">
           <InputNumber class="form-control" @bind-Value="emp.Salary" />
        </div>
        <ValidationMessage For="@(() => emp.Salary)" />
    </div>
    <div class="form-group">
        <button type="submit" class="btn btn-primary">Save</button>
        <button class="btn btn-light" @onclick="Cancel">Cancel</button>
    </div>
</EditForm>
@code {
    [Parameter]
    public int empId { get; set; }
```

```
    protected string Title = "Add Emp";
    protected Emp emp = new();
    protected override async Task OnParametersSetAsync()
    {
        if (empId != 0)
        {
            Title = "Edit Emp";
            emp = await Http.GetFromJsonAsync<Emp>("api/Emp/" + empId);
        }
    }
    protected async Task SaveEmp()
    {
        if (emp.Id != 0)
        {
            await Http.PutAsJsonAsync("api/Emp", emp);
        }
        else
        {
            await Http.PostAsJsonAsync("api/Emp", emp);
        }
        Cancel();
    }
    public void Cancel()
    {
        NavigationManager.NavigateTo("/fetchempdetails");
    }}
```

Explanation:

In the preceding code snippets, we have created HTML code for the Emp add and edit screen.

We are also calling **`Http.PostAsJsonAsync`** to save data and **`Http.PutAsJsonAsync`** to edit emp data.

Additionally, we are using the **`DataAnnotationsValidator`** for the validation of required input data.

Step 12: Now, we will create the **`EmpDetails.Razor`** screen as follows:

```
@page "/fetchempdetails"
@using EmpCRUD.Shared.Model
@inject HttpClient Http


<h3>EmpDetails</h3>
<div class="row">
    <div class="col-md-6">
        <a href='/emp/add' class="btn btn-primary" role="button">
            <i class="fas fa-user-plus"></i>
            Add User
```

```
        </a>
    </div>
    <div class="input-group col">
        <input type="text" class="form-control" placeholder="Search
user by name"
       @bind="SearchString" @bind:event="oninput" @onkeyup="FilterEmp" />
        @if (SearchString.Length > 0)
        {
            <div class="input-group-append">
                <button class="btn btn-danger" @onclick="ResetSearch">
                    <i class="fas fa-times"></i>
                    ResetSearch
                </button>
            </div>
        }
    </div>
</div>
<br />
@if (empList == null)
{
    <p><em>Loading...</em></p>
}
else
{
    <table class="table table-striped align-middle table-bordered">
        <thead class="table-success">
            <tr>
                <th>ID</th>
                <th>FirstName</th>
                <th>LastName</th>
                <th>Email</th>
                <th>Email</th>
                <th>Action</th>
            </tr>
        </thead>
        <tbody>
            @foreach (var emp in empList)
            {
                <tr>
                    <td>@emp.Id</td>
                    <td>@emp.FirstName</td>
                    <td>@emp.LastName</td>
                    <td>@emp.Email</td>
                    <td>@emp.Salary</td>
                    <td>
                       <a href='/emp/edit/@emp.Id' class="btn btn-
outline-dark" role="button">
                            Edit
                       </a>
```

```
                    <a href='/emp/delete/@emp.Id' class="btn
btn-outline-danger" role="button">
                        Delete
                    </a>
                </td>
            </tr>
        }
    </tbody>

</table>
}
@code {
    protected List<Emp> empList = new();
    protected List<Emp> searchUserData = new();
    protected Emp emp = new();
    protected string SearchString { get; set; } = string.Empty;
    protected override async Task OnInitializedAsync()
    {
        await GetEmp();
    }
    protected async Task GetEmp()
    {
        empList = await Http.GetFromJsonAsync<List<Emp>>("api/Emp");
        searchUserData = empList;
    }
    protected void FilterEmp()
    {
        if (!string.IsNullOrEmpty(SearchString))
        {
            empList = searchUserData
                .Where(x => x.FirstName.IndexOf(SearchString,
StringComparison.OrdinalIgnoreCase) != -1)
                .ToList();
        }
        else
        {
            empList = searchUserData;
        }
    }
    protected void DeleteConfirm(int empId)
    {
        emp = empList.FirstOrDefault(x => x.Id == empId);
    }
    public void ResetSearch()
    {
        SearchString = string.Empty;
        empList = searchUserData;
    }
}
```

Explanation

In the preceding code snippet, we are calling fetch emp details API on page load using the following command:

```
empList = await Http.GetFromJsonAsync<List<Emp>>("api/Emp");
```

After this, we bind the data in a tabular format with Edit and Delete buttons.

We also filter employees from the tabular data. Whenever the user clicks the Edit and Delete screen, we route them to the respective Edit and Delete razor page.

Step 13: Create the **`DeleteEmp.razor`** screen as follows:

```
@page "/emp/delete/{empId:int}"
@using EmpCRUD.Shared.Model
@inject HttpClient Http
@inject NavigationManager NavigationManager

<h2>Delete Emp</h2>
<br />
<div class="form-group">
    <h4>Do you want to delete this user?</h4>
    <table class="table">
        <tbody>
            <tr>
                <td>FirstName</td>
                <td>@emp.FirstName</td>
            </tr>
            <tr>
                <td>LastName</td>
                <td>@emp.LastName</td>
            </tr>
            <tr>
                <td>Email</td>
                <td>@emp.Email</td>
            </tr>
            <tr>
                <td>Salary</td>
                <td>@emp.Salary</td>
            </tr>
        </tbody>
    </table>
</div>
<div class="form-group">
    <input type="submit" value="Delete" @onclick="(async () => await
RemoveEmp(emp.Id))" class="btn btn-danger" />
    <input type="submit" value="Cancel" @onclick="(() => Cancel())"
class="btn btn-warning" />
</div>
```

```
@code {
    [Parameter]
    public int empId { get; set; }
    Emp emp = new Emp();
    protected override async Task OnInitializedAsync()
    {
        emp = await Http.GetFromJsonAsync<Emp>("/api/Emp/" + Convert.
ToInt32(empId));
    }
    protected async Task RemoveEmp(int empId)
    {
        await Http.DeleteAsync("api/Emp/" + empId);
        NavigationManager.NavigateTo("/fetchempdetails");
    }
    void Cancel()
    {
        NavigationManager.NavigateTo("/fetchempdetails");
    }
}
```

Explanation:

In the preceding code snippets, we fetch Emp Details based on **`EmpId`**. We also delete Emp data based on **`EmpId`** using the **`Http.DeleteAsync`** method.

Now, run the application. You will see the output as follows:

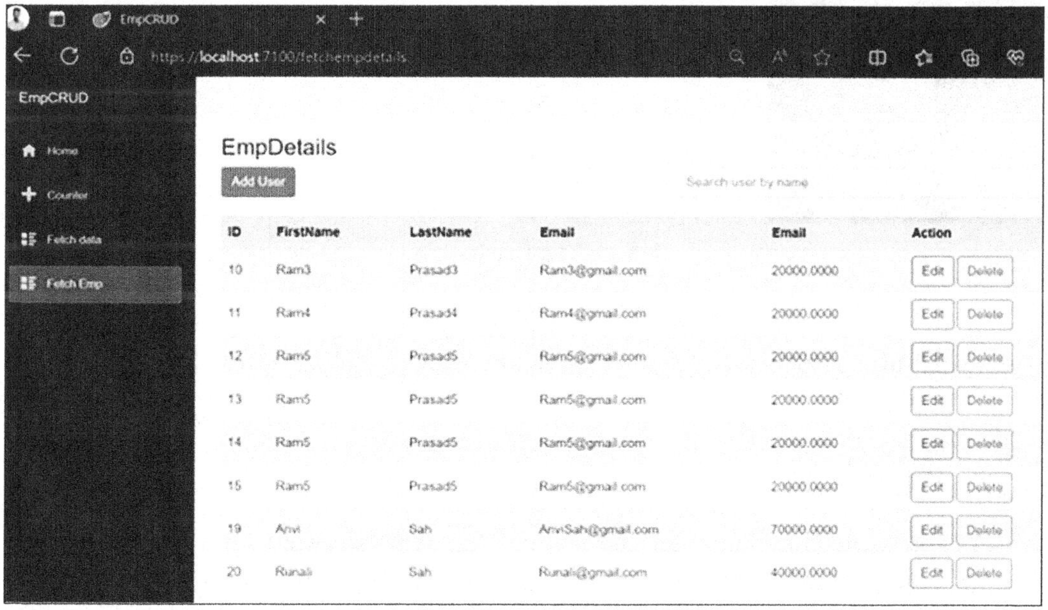

***Figure 7.12:** Output*

Figure 7.13 shows the details of an employee:

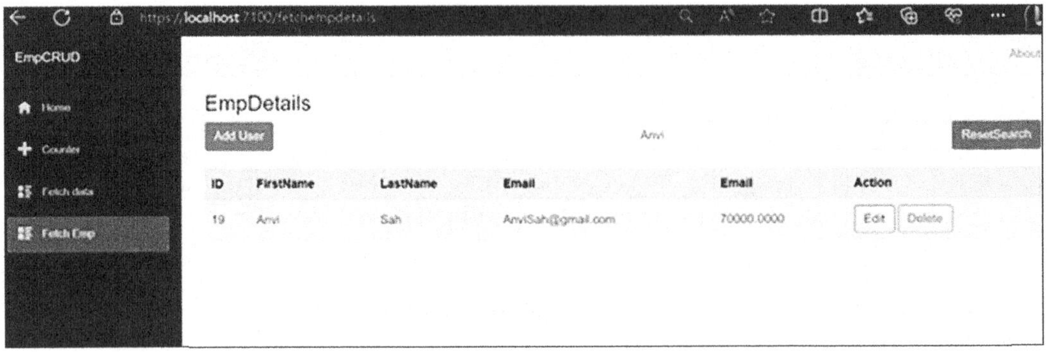

Figure 7.13: *EmpDetails*

Figure 7.14 shows how to delete the details of a user:

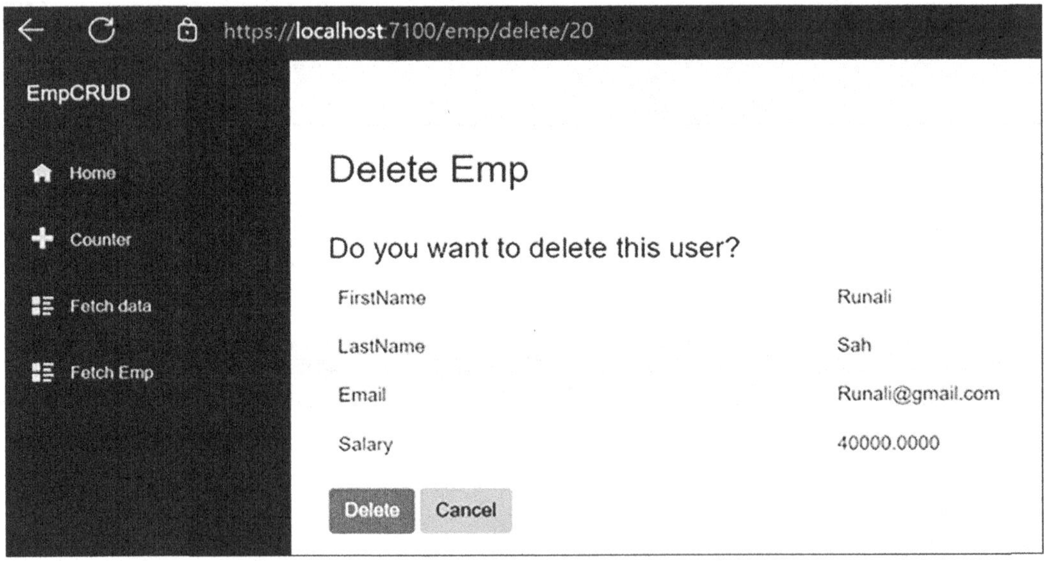

Figure 7.14: *Delete Emp*

Source Code: For the preceding demo project, it can be found at:

https://github.com/ava-orange-education/Practical-Web-Development-with-Blazor-and-.Net-8

Conclusion

In this chapter, we gained familiarity with EF Core. We also explored the benefits of EF Core and learned how to use it in a Blazor WebAssembly application. If we are using **EF Core Power Tool** in Visual Studio 2022, then it will create a scaffolding code first approach for us. In the next chapter, we will learn the validation in Blazor.

Reference

ASP.NET Core Blazor with Entity Framework Core (EF Core) | Microsoft Learn

Multiple Choice Questions

1. What is EF Core in the context of Blazor WebAssembly development?
    a. A front-end JavaScript library
    b. An Object-Relational Mapping (ORM) framework
    c. A server-side rendering framework
    d. A CSS preprocessor
2. Which of the following is true about EF Core in Blazor WebAssembly?
    a. It is used for client-side data manipulation
    b. It provides a bridge between the client and server for database operations
    c. It is primarily used for styling and UI design
    d. It is not compatible with Blazor WebAssembly
3. In a Blazor WebAssembly application, where is EF Core typically used?
    a. On the client side for authentication
    b. On the client side for database operations
    c. On the server side for database operations
    d. None of the above
4. What is the purpose of an Object-Relational Mapping (ORM) framework like EF Core?
    a. It is used to create interactive user interfaces
    b. It provides a way to interact with databases using object-oriented code
    c. It is a version control system for web development
    d. It is used for server-side routing

5. Which programming language is commonly used with EF Core in Blazor WebAssembly development?

    a. JavaScript

    b. C#

    c. Python

    d. Ruby

Answers

1. b
2. b
3. c
4. b
5. b

CHAPTER 8
Validation in Blazor WebAssembly

Introduction

While working with any Blazor Application, you will get requirements to validate the input. Without validation, we can't develop any application.

In the previous web development framework, we used tedious JavaScript code for validation, but in Blazor WebAssembly, we can use a straightforward approach using C# code.

Structure

In this chapter, we will cover the following topics:

- Blazor Form
- Form Validation in Blazor
- Data Annotation in Blazor
- Custom Validation Rules
- Complex or Nested Model Validation in Blazor
- Best Pattern and Practices for Validation in Blazor

Blazor Form

A Blazor Form is a fundamental component in Blazor applications used to handle user input and manage form submissions. It is part of the Blazor framework, which allows developers to build interactive web applications using C# and .NET instead of relying solely on JavaScript.

In Blazor, you can create forms using the **`<EditForm>`** component. The **`<EditForm>`** component wraps the form's content and provides features like form validation, form submission handling, and model binding.

Here's a basic example of a Blazor form:

```
@page "/"
@using BlazorValidation.Model

<PageTitle>Index</PageTitle>
<h3>Form Validation</h3>

<EditForm Model="@myModel" OnValidSubmit="@HandleValidSubmit">
    <DataAnnotationsValidator />
    <ValidationSummary />
    <div>
        <label for="name" class="form-label">Name:</label>
        <InputText id="name" @bind-Value="myModel.Name" class="
form-control" />
        <ValidationMessage For="@(() => myModel.Name)" />
    </div>
    <div>
        <label for="email" class="form-label">Email:</label>
        <InputText id="email" @bind-Value="myModel.Email" class="-
form-control" />
        <ValidationMessage For="@(() => myModel.Email)" />
    </div>
    <div class="form-group">
        <button class="btn btn-outline-primary mt-2">Submit</button>
    </div>
</EditForm>

@code {
    private MyModel myModel = new MyModel();

    private void HandleValidSubmit()
    {
        // Logic to handle form submission when the form is valid
    }
}
```

Model Class

```
public class MyModel
{
    [Required(ErrorMessage = "Name is required")]
    public string Name { get; set; }

    [Required(ErrorMessage = "Email is required")]
    [EmailAddress(ErrorMessage = "Invalid email address")]
    public string Email { get; set; }
}
```

In this example, **`myModel`** is a C# object representing the form data. The form fields are bound to the properties of this object using the **`@bind-Value`** directive. The **`OnValidSubmit`** event is triggered when the form is submitted and is valid, allowing you to handle the submission logic.

Blazor Forms also supports validation through data annotations and provides components like **`<DataAnnotationsValidator>`** and **`<ValidationSummary>`** to display validation messages.

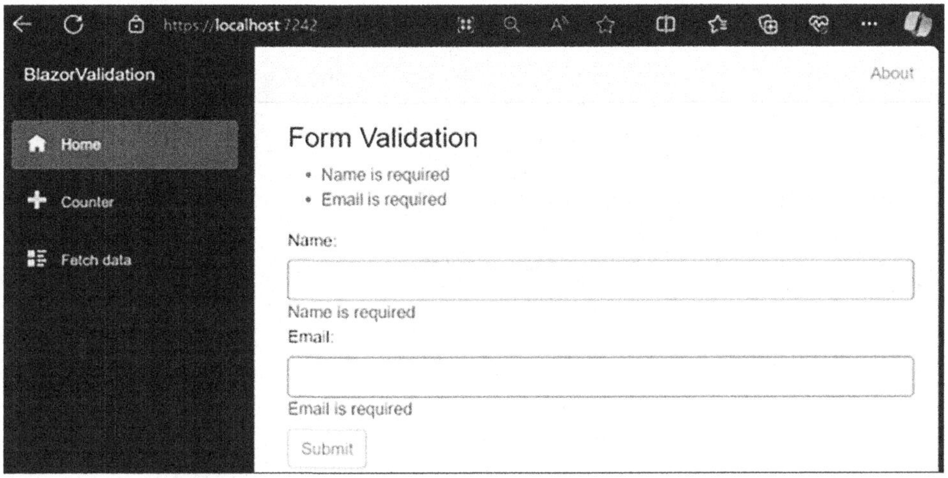

***Figure 8.1**: Form Validation*

Form Validation in Blazor

Form validation in Blazor ensures that user input meets specified criteria before submitting the form. Blazor provides built-in support for both client-side and server-side validation using data annotations.

Here's a brief overview of form validation in Blazor:

- **Data Annotations:** You can use data annotations in your model class to define validation rules. These annotations are attributes applied to the properties of your model class. For example:

```
public class MyModel
{
    [Required(ErrorMessage = "Name is required")]
    public string Name { get; set; }

    [Required(ErrorMessage = "Email is required")]
    [EmailAddress(ErrorMessage = "Invalid email address")]
    public string Email { get; set; }
}
```

In this example, the **[Required]** attribute indicates that the Name and Email properties are required, and **[EmailAddress]** ensures that the Email property is a valid email address.

- **Validation Components:**

<EditForm>: Wraps the form and manages its state.

<DataAnnotationsValidator>: Performs client-side validation based on data annotations.

<ValidationSummary>: Displays a summary of validation errors.

```
<EditForm Model="@myModel" OnValidSubmit="@HandleValidSubmit">
    <DataAnnotationsValidator />
    <ValidationSummary />

    <!-- Form fields and input elements go here -->

    <button type="submit">Submit</button>
</EditForm>
```

- **Validation Messages:**

  You can use the **<ValidationMessage>** component to display error messages associated with specific form fields.

```
<label for="name">Name:</label>
<InputText id="name" @bind-Value="myModel.Name" />
<ValidationMessage For="@(() => myModel.Name)" />
```

This will display the error message if the Name field fails validation.

- **Client-Side Validation:**

Blazor performs client-side validation using the data annotations. The **<DataAnnotationsValidator>** component checks for validation errors on the client side before allowing the form to be submitted.

- **Server-Side Validation:**

Even with client-side validation, it's crucial to perform server-side validation to ensure the integrity and security of your application. The server-side validation can be done in the **OnValidSubmit** event handler or a method called during form submission.

Combining these elements allows you to create a robust form validation system in your Blazor applications, ensuring that user input is accurate and meets the specified criteria.

Data Annotation in Blazor

In Blazor, data annotations are attributes that you can apply to the properties of a model class to define validation rules.

These annotations are part of the **`System.ComponentModel.DataAnnotations`** namespace and provide a declarative way to express validation requirements for your model properties.

Here are some commonly used data annotations in Blazor:

- **`Required` Attribute:**

Indicates that a property is required.

Example:

```
[Required(ErrorMessage = "Name is required")]
public string Name { get; set; }
```

- **`StringLength` Attribute:**

Specifies the maximum and minimum length constraints for a string property.

```
[StringLength(50, MinimumLength = 2, ErrorMessage = "Name must be be-
tween 2 and 50 characters")]
public string Name { get; set; }
```

- **`Range` Attribute:**

Specifies the numeric range constraints for a numeric property.

```
[Range(18, 99, ErrorMessage = "Age must be between 18 and 99")]
public int Age { get; set; }
```

- **`EmailAddress` Attribute:**

Ensures that a string property contains a valid email address.

```
[EmailAddress(ErrorMessage = "Invalid email address")]
public string Email { get; set; }
```

- **`RegularExpression` Attribute:**

Specifies that a string property must match a specified regular expression pattern.

```
[RegularExpression(@"^\d{5}(-\d{4})?$", ErrorMessage = "Invalid ZIP
code")]
public string ZipCode { get; set; }
```

- **`Compare` Attribute:**

Compare the values of two properties for equality.

```
[Compare("Password", ErrorMessage = "Passwords do not match")]
public string ConfirmPassword { get; set; }
```

These annotations help to define validation rules for your model properties. When you use these annotated models in a Blazor application with the **<EditForm>**, **<DataAnnotationsValidator>**, and **<ValidationMessage>** components, Blazor automatically performs client-side validation and displays error messages when validation fails.

It's important to note that while client-side validation is convenient for providing immediate feedback to users, server-side validation should also be implemented to ensure the security and integrity of your application. Blazor makes combining client-side and server-side validation in your forms easy.

Custom Validation in Blazor

Many times, using the Data Annotation rule, we cannot validate all input. In such scenario, we need to create our own validation rule using **ValidationAttribute.**

Let's create a simple demo for **UserName** custom validation rules. If the user selects **UserName** as Admin, we need to display an error message.

For this, we need to create a **UserNameValidation** class as follows:

```
using System.ComponentModel.DataAnnotations;

namespace BlazorValidation.Model
{
    public class UserNameValidation: ValidationAttribute
    {
        protected override ValidationResult IsValid(object value,
ValidationContext validationContext)
        {
            if (value != null)
            {
                string inputValue = value.ToString();
                if (inputValue.Equals("Admin", StringComparison.
OrdinalIgnoreCase))
                {
                    return new ValidationResult("The input value
cannot be 'Admin'.");
                }
            }

            return ValidationResult.Success;
        }
    }
}
```

Now apply this validation attribute to a **Model** class as follows:

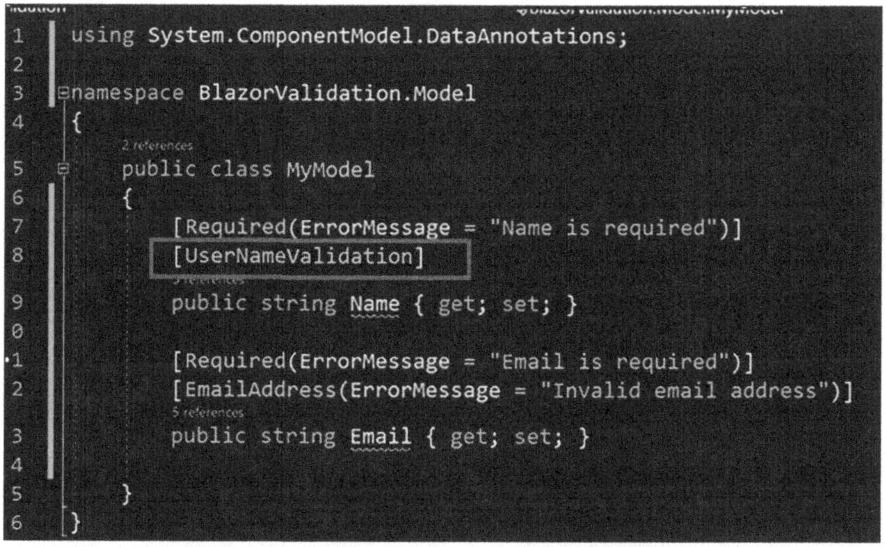

***Figure 8.2**: Applying validation attribute*

Now run the application, and you will see the output as follows:

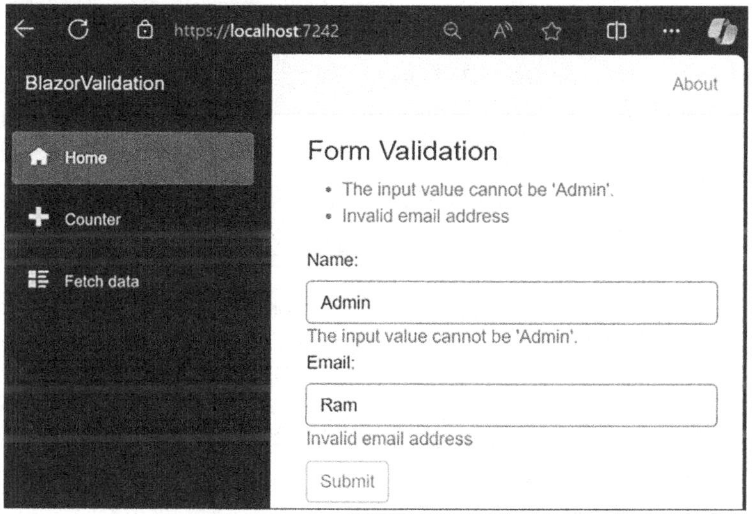

***Figure 8.3**: Form validation output*

Complex or Nested Model Validation in Blazor

Blazor has a built-in **`DataAnnotationsValidator`**. However, the **`DataAnnotations Validator`** only validates top-level properties of the model bound to the form that isn't collection- or complex-type properties.

For validating complex models, we can use: **`Microsoft.AspNetCore.Components.DataAnnotations.Validation`** package

We also need to use **`<ObjectGraphDataAnnotationsValidator />`** inside the **`EditForm`**

```
<EditForm ...>
    <ObjectGraphDataAnnotationsValidator />
    ...
</EditForm>
```

We also need to decorate the model properties with **`[ValidateComplexType]`**

Let's create demo sample code snippets for this.

Step 1: Create the **`Address`** model as follows:

```
using System.ComponentModel.DataAnnotations;

namespace BlazorValidation.Model
{
    public class Address
    {
        [Required]
        public  string Address1 { get; set; }
        public string Address2 { get; set; }
    }
}
```

Step 2: Create the **`Emp`** model class with the **`Address`** nested class.

```
using System.ComponentModel.DataAnnotations;

namespace BlazorValidation.Model
{
    public class Emp
    {
        [Required(ErrorMessage = "Name is required")]
        [UserNameValidation]
        public string Name { get; set; }

        [Required(ErrorMessage = "Email is required")]
        [EmailAddress(ErrorMessage = "Invalid email address")]
        public string Email { get; set; }
        [Required(ErrorMessage = "Address is required")]
        [ValidateComplexType]
        public Address Address { get; set; } = new();

    }
```

Step 3: Create the **Emp** Entry UI screen as follows:

```
@page "/emp"
@using BlazorValidation.Model

<PageTitle>Emp</PageTitle>
<h3>Emp Details</h3>
<EditForm Model="@myModel" OnValidSubmit="@HandleValidSubmit">
    <ObjectGraphDataAnnotationsValidator />
    <ValidationSummary />
    <div>
        <label for="name" class="form-label">Name:</label>
        <InputText id="name" @bind-Value="myModel.Name" class="form-
control" />
        <ValidationMessage For="@(() => myModel.Name)" />
    </div>
    <div>
        <label for="email" class="form-label">Email:</label>
        <InputText id="email" @bind-Value="myModel.Email" class="-
form-control" />
        <ValidationMessage For="@(() => myModel.Email)" />
    </div>
    <div>
        <label for="Address" class="form-label">Address1:</label>
        <InputText id="Address" @bind-Value="myModel.Address.Address1"
class="form-control" />
        <ValidationMessage For="@(() => myModel.Address.Address1)" />
    </div>
    <div>
        <label for="Address" class="form-label">Address2:</label>
        <InputText id="Address" @bind-Value="myModel.Address.Address2"
class="form-control" />
        <ValidationMessage For="@(() => myModel.Address.Address2)" />
    </div>
    <div class="form-group">
        <button class="btn btn-outline-primary mt-2">Submit</button>
    </div>
</EditForm>

@code {
    private Emp myModel = new Emp();

    private void HandleValidSubmit()
    {
        // Logic to handle form submission when the form is valid
    }}
```

Step 4: Run the application and click on the **`Submit`** button.

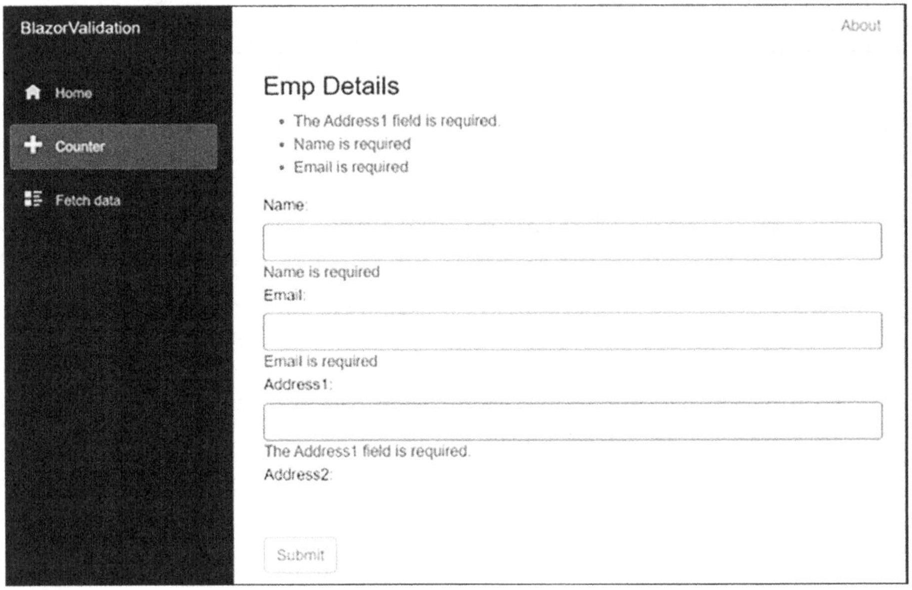

Figure 8.4: *Emp Details Screen*

Best Pattern and Practices for Validation in Blazor

Validating user input is a critical aspect of building reliable and user-friendly applications. In Blazor, you can implement validation using various patterns and practices. Here's a recommended approach and some best practices for validation in Blazor:

1. **Use Data Annotations:**

Leverage the built-in .NET Data Annotations for basic validation rules. This helps to keep your code clean and easy to understand.

```
[Required(ErrorMessage = "Name is required")]
[StringLength(50, ErrorMessage = "Name is too long")]
public string Name { get; set; }
```

2. **Client-Side and Server-Side Validation:**

Implement both client-side and server-side validation to provide a responsive user experience and ensure data integrity.

Client-side validation can be performed using Blazor's built-in validation components, and server-side validation is crucial for security and data consistency.

3. **`EditForm` Component:**

Use the **`<EditForm>`** component to encapsulate your form and handle validation.

Include the **`<DataAnnotationsValidator>`** and **`<ValidationSummary>`** components within the form.

```
<EditForm Model="@myModel" OnValidSubmit="HandleValidSubmit">
    <DataAnnotationsValidator />
    <ValidationSummary />

    <!-- Your form controls and validation messages go here -->
</EditForm>
```

4. **`ValidationMessage` Component:**

Utilize the **`<ValidationMessage>`** component for displaying validation error messages.

Ensure that each input field has a corresponding **`<ValidationMessage>`** with the correct For attribute.

```
<label>Name:</label>
<InputText @bind-Value="myModel.Name" />
<ValidationMessage For="@(() => myModel.Name)" />
```

5. **Custom Validation:**

Implement custom validation logic for scenarios that cannot be handled by standard Data Annotations.

6. **Validation in Event Handlers:**

In your event handlers, such as **`OnValidSubmit`**, check the form's validity before performing any actions.

```
private void HandleValidSubmit()
{
    if (editContext.Validate())
    {
        // Perform actions for a valid form
    }}
```

Conclusion

Validation is one of the critical aspects of building reliable and user-friendly applications. We have also seen that with help of C# Data Annotation attribute, we can create client-side validation. This is one of the simple approaches to implement validation in any web framework.

In the next chapter, we will learn about JavaScript Interop in Blazor.

References

For more details, please refer to the following document:

ASP.NET Core Blazor forms validation | Microsoft Learn

Source Code

https://github.com/ava-orange-education/Practical-Web-Development-with-Blazor-and-.Net-8

Multiple Choice Questions

1. What is the purpose of the **`<DataAnnotationsValidator>`** component in Blazor?
   a. It displays validation error messages for all form fields
   b. It enables client-side validation for Data Annotations attributes
   c. It performs server-side validation for complex objects
   d. It automatically validates all properties of a model
2. Which interface is commonly implemented for performing custom validation on an entire object in Blazor?
   a. `IValidationService`
   b. `IDataAnnotationsValidator`
   c. `IValidatableObject`
   d. `IValidationContext`
3. Which Blazor component is responsible for displaying a summary of validation errors?
   a. `<ValidationSummary>`
   b. `<DataAnnotationsValidator>`
   c. `<ValidationMessage>`
   d. `<EditForm>`

4. In Blazor, what does the **`editContext.Validate()`** method do in a form submission handler?
   a. It triggers client-side validation for all form fields
   b. It performs asynchronous validation for the entire form
   c. It returns a boolean indicating whether the form is valid
   d. It validates only the required fields in the form
5. Which attribute is commonly used for marking a property as required in Blazor validation?
   a. `[Mandatory]`
   b. `[Required]`
   c. `[Validate]`
   d. `[NotNull]`

Answers

1. b
2. c
3. a
4. c
5. b

CHAPTER 9
JavaScript Interop in Blazor

Introduction

JavaScript Interop in Blazor refers to the ability of Blazor to communicate and interact with JavaScript code.

Since Blazor applications run on the browser, there are scenarios where we may need to call JavaScript functions or use JavaScript libraries within our Blazor components. This is where JavaScript Interop comes into play.

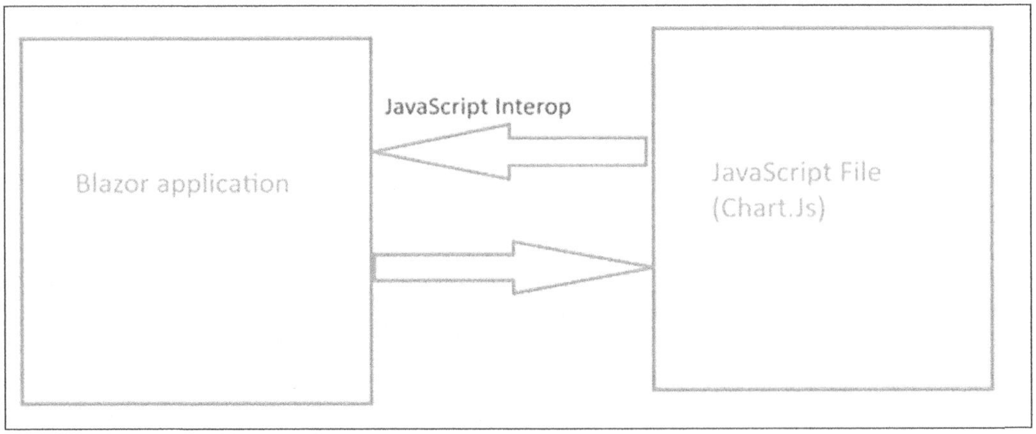

***Figure 9.1**: JavaScript Interop*

In the preceding figure, if we have a Blazor application, we may need to use the Google **Chart.Js** library in Blazor. In this scenario, with the help of JavaScript Interop, we can easily use the **Chart.js** library in the Blazor application.

Structure

In this chapter, we will learn the following topics:

- Calling JavaScript from C#
- Handling Function Return Value
- Passing C# Objects to JavaScript
- Calling C# from JavaScript
- Advanced JavaScript Interop Demo
- Error Handling and Debugging
- Security Considerations
- Performance Optimization

Calling JavaScript from C#

In the Blazor application, we can call the JavaScript function with the help of the **`JSRuntime`** service.

In the following example, we will see how to do it in Blazor application:

Step 1: Create the Blazor WebAssembly application.

Step 2: Go to **`wwwroot`** folder and create the JavaScript file, that is, Demo.js:

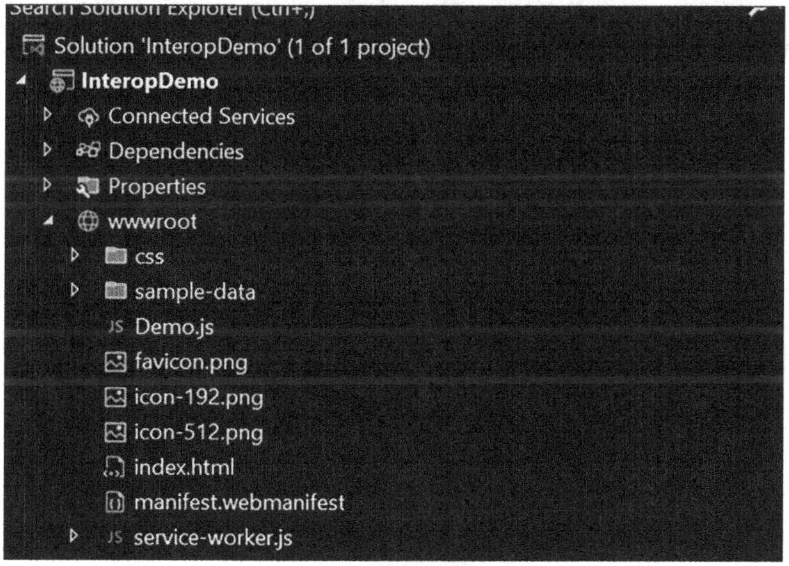

***Figure 9.2**: JavaScript file*

Step 3: Write the JavaScript global function as follows:

```
function helloFunction() {
    alert("Hello Blazor Web Assembly");
}
```

JavaScript global function is attached to window, so we can also write it as follows:

```
window.helloFunction = () => {
    alert("Hello Blazor Web Assembly");
}
```

Step 4: Go to **`index.html`** and register the JavaScript file as follows:

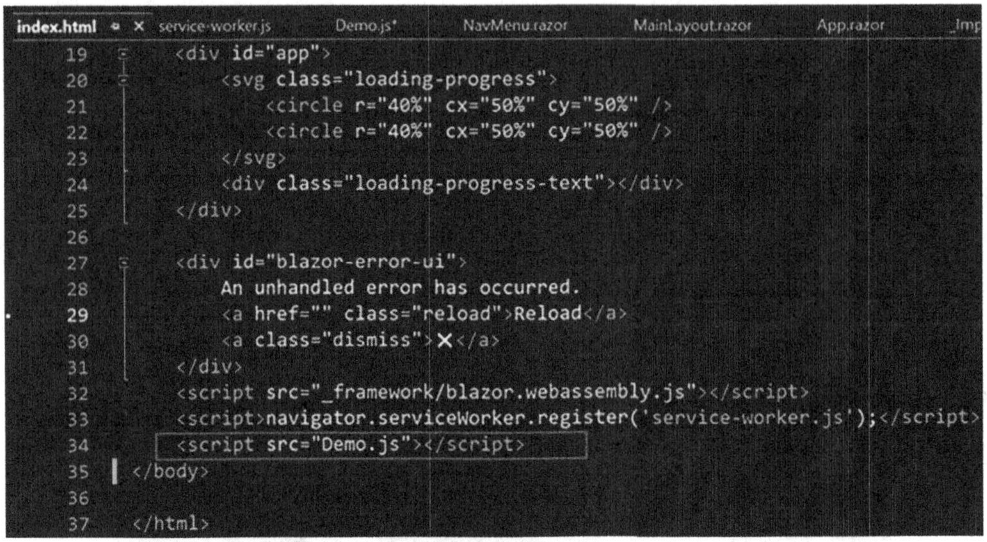

***Figure 9.3**: JavaScript path*

Step 5: Call the JavaScript function from C# with help of **`IJSRuntime`**, as given in the following code:

```
@page "/"
@inject IJSRuntime JS

<h3>JavaScript Interop in Blazor</h3>
<br />
<button @onclick="CallJavaScript">Click Me</button>

@code
{

    private async Task CallJavaScript()
    {
        await JS.InvokeVoidAsync("helloFunction");
    }

}
```

Now run the application, and you will see the output as shown in *Figure* 9.4:

***Figure 9.4**: Output*

Handling Function Return Value

We can handle return value from JavaScript functions like this in C# code.

Write a function to multiply two numbers and return the value to C#:

```
function multiplyNumbers(a, b) {
    return a * b;
}
```

Now call this function in Razor page as follows:

```
@page "/counter"
@inject IJSRuntime JSRuntime
<PageTitle>Counter</PageTitle>

<h3>Handle JavaScript Function Return Value Example</h3>

<button @onclick="CallJavaScript">Call JavaScript Function</button>

<p>Result: @result</p>

@code {
    private int result;

    private async Task CallJavaScript()
    {
        // Call the JavaScript function and capture the return value
        result = await JSRuntime.InvokeAsync<int>("multiplyNumbers",
5, 3);
    }
}
```

Now run the application:

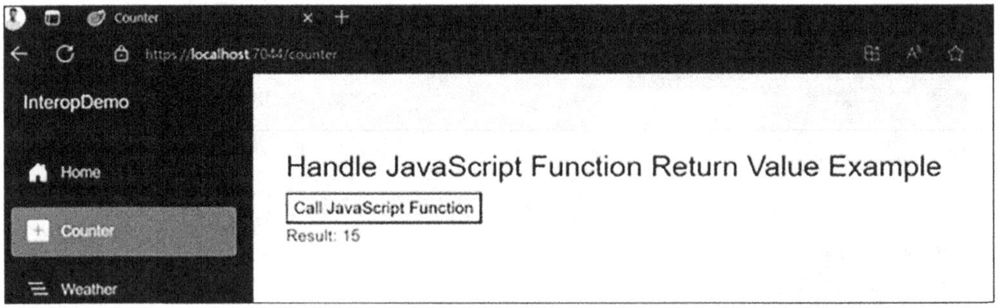

Figure 9.5: *JavaScript function return*

In the preceding example:

- The **`multiplyNumbers`** JavaScript function takes two arguments (a and b) and returns their product.
- In the Blazor component, the **`CallJavaScript`** method is triggered when the button is clicked.
- Inside **`CallJavaScript`**, **`JSRuntime.InvokeAsync<int>`** is used to call the JavaScript function and capture the return value. The function name is specified as **`"myModule.multiplyNumbers`**", and the arguments 5 and 3 are passed.
- The result is then displayed in the HTML using **`@result`**.

Passing C# Objects to JavaScript

Passing C# objects to JavaScript involves serializing the C# object into JSON and then passing the JSON string to a JavaScript function. An example demonstrating how to achieve this in a Blazor component is as follows:

JavaScript Function:

```
function displayPerson(person) {
    console.log("JavaScript function called from C# with person:",
person);
}
```

Razor and C# code

```
@page "/weather"
@using System.Text.Json
@inject IJSRuntime JSRuntime

<h3>Passing C# Object to JavaScript Example</h3>

<button @onclick="PassCSharpObject">Pass C# Object to JavaScript</button>
```

```
@code {
    public class Person
    {
        public string Name { get; set; }
        public int Age { get; set; }
    }

    private async Task PassCSharpObject()
    {
        // Create an instance of the Person class
        var person = new Person
            {
                Name = "Anvi Sah",
                Age = 8
            };

        // Serialize the C# object to a JSON string
        var jsonString = JsonSerializer.Serialize(person);

        // Call the JavaScript function with the serialized JSON string
        await JSRuntime.InvokeAsync<object>("displayPerson", jsonString);
    }
}
```

Now run the application:

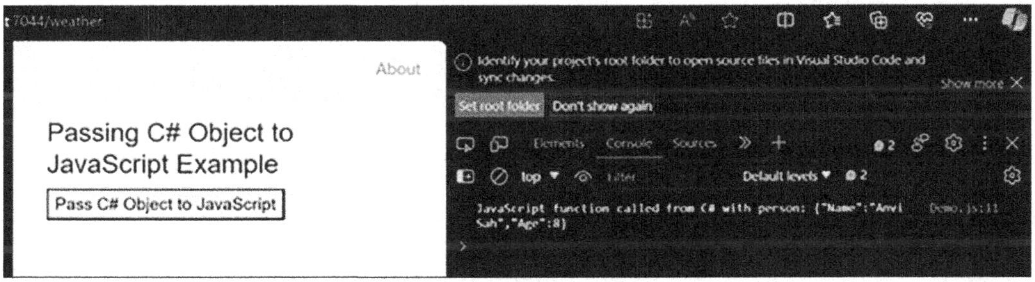

***Figure 9.6**: C# object demo*

In this example:

- The **Person** class is a simple C# class with properties representing a person's name and age.
- The **displayPerson** JavaScript function takes a person parameter, which is expected to be a JSON string representing a person.
- In the Blazor component, the **PassCSharpObject** method is triggered when the button is clicked.
- Inside **PassCSharpObject**, an instance of the **Person** class is created, and it is then serialized into a JSON string using **JsonSerializer.Serialize**.

- The JavaScript function **displayPerson** is then called with the serialized JSON string as an argument using **JSRuntime.InvokeAsync<object>**.

Calling C# from JavaScript

Using **DotNet.invokeMethodAsync** function, we can call the C# method in JavaScript function.

Here is the simple code snippets for this task:

Step 1: Create C# method to reverse the string in Razor Component as follows:

```
@page "/example"
@inject IJSRuntime JSRuntime

<h3>Calling C# from JavaScript Example</h3>

<button @onclick=CallReverse>Click</button>

@code {
    async Task CallReverse()
    {
        await JSRuntime.InvokeVoidAsync("reverseString", "Chandradev");
    }

    [JSInvokable]
    public static Task InteropReverse(string input)
    {
        var result = new String(input.Reverse().ToArray());
        return Task.FromResult(result);
    }}
```

Step 2: Write the JavaScript function to Call C# method as:

```
window.reverseString = function (input) {
    // Call the C# method using DotNet.invokeMethodAsync
    DotNet.invokeMethodAsync("InteropDemo", "InteropReverse", input)
        .then(function (result) {
            alert(result);
        });
```

Now run the application:

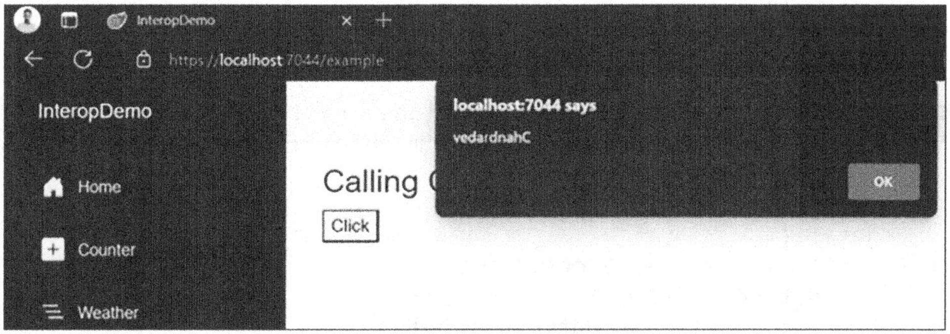

Figure 9.7: *C# from JavaScript*

In the preceding code snippets, we saw that with the help of **`DotNet.invokeMethodAsync`**, we are calling C# method from the JavaScript function.

In C# method, we also need to decorate with **`[JSInvokable]`** attribute. Otherwise, we cannot call the C# method in the JavaScript function.

Advanced JavaScript Interop Demo

In this demo, we will see how to integrate Chartjs library in Blazor application (https://www.chartjs.org/).

Step 1: Register the Chart.js library in Index.html page as:

```
<script src="https://cdnjs.cloudflare.com/ajax/libs/Chart.js/2.9.3/Chart.min.js"></script>
```

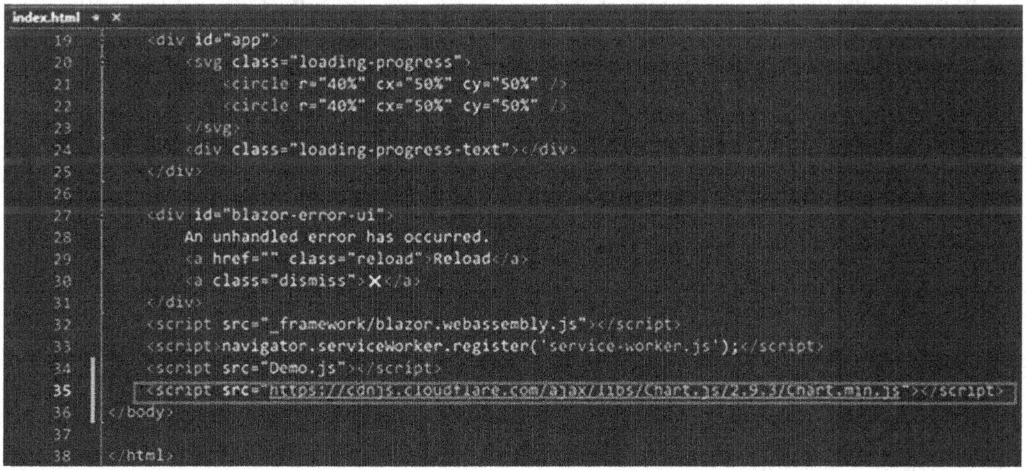

Figure 9.8: *Chart URL*

Step 2: Write JavaScript code for render chart controls as follows:

```
//Chart demo
window.showChart = (chartType, dataOptions) => {
    var ctx = document.getElementById('myChart').getContext('2d');
    var options = {
        type: chartType,
        data: {
            labels: dataOptions.labels,
            datasets: [{
                label: dataOptions.label,
                data: dataOptions.data,
                backgroundColor: dataOptions.color,
                borderColor: dataOptions.color,
                fill: dataOptions.fill
            }]
        }
    };
    new Chart(ctx, options);
```

Step 3: Write the C# code in Razor Component to pass all the required field for chart controls, as shown in the following code:

```
@page "/chart"
@inject IJSRuntime JSRuntime
<h3>Chart Demo</h3>
<canvas id="myChart"></canvas>
@code {
    protected override async Task OnAfterRenderAsync(bool firstRender)
    {
        var dataOptions = new
        {
            labels = new[] { "Jan", "Feb", "Mar", "Apr", "May", "Jun"
},
            data = new[] { 26, 44, 54, 66, 55, 58 },
            label = "Total Sales",
            color = "#57a64a",
            fill = false
        };
        await JSRuntime.InvokeVoidAsync("showChart", "line", dataOp-
tions);
    }}
```

Now run the application:

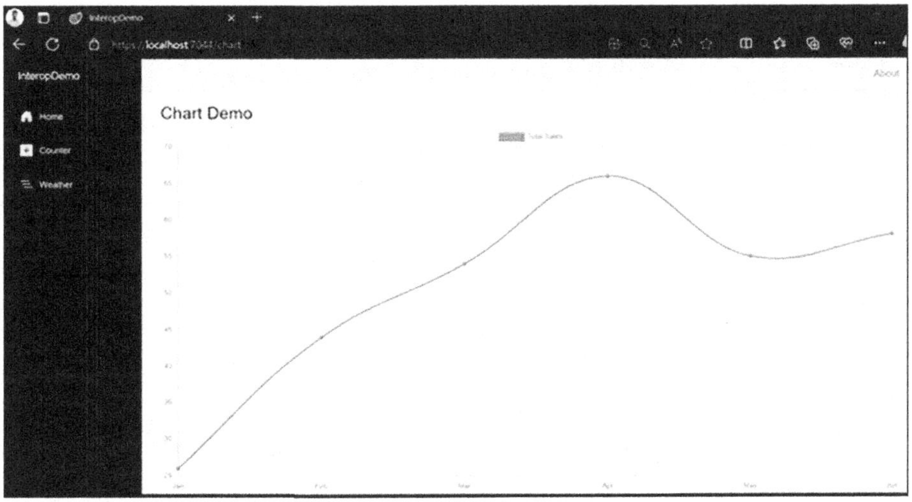

Figure 9.9: *Chart demo*

In the preceding Razor code snippets, the **`InvokeAsync`** method is called in the **`OnAfterRenderAsync`** method instead of a DOM event handler.

`OnAfterRender(Async)` is the place to call JavaScript methods that you want to take place on page or component load, because at this point, the component has completely rendered and DOM elements are available.

Error Handling and Debugging

Handling errors and debugging in JavaScript Interop in Blazor is crucial for ensuring the robustness and reliability of your application. Here are some best practices for error handling and debugging:

- **Error Handling in JavaScript**

Wrap your JavaScript code in **`try-catch`** blocks to handle exceptions gracefully. This is especially important when calling C# methods asynchronously.

```
try {
    // Your JavaScript code here
} catch (error) {
    console.error("An error occurred:", error);}
```

- **Error Handling in C# Methods**

In your C# methods called from JavaScript, implement proper error handling using try-catch blocks. Log or handle exceptions appropriately.

```
[JSInvokable("MyCSharpMethod")]
public async Task<string> MyCSharpMethod(string input)
{
```

```
    try {
        // Your C# code here
        return "Success";
    } catch (Exception ex) {
        Console.Error.WriteLine($"An error occurred: {ex.Message}");
        return "Error";
    }
```

- **Debugging JavaScript Interop**

Use browser developer tools to debug JavaScript code. Set breakpoints, inspect variables, and step through your JavaScript code.

- **Logging from JavaScript to Console**

Utilize **`console.log`**, **`console.error`**, and other console methods in JavaScript to output information that can help in debugging.

```
console.log("This is a log message");
console.error("This is an error message");
```

- **Logging from C# to Browser Console**

Use **`Console.WriteLine`** or **`Console.Error.WriteLine`** in your C# code. These messages will be visible in the browser's console.

```
Console.WriteLine("This is a log message from C#");
Console.Error.WriteLine("This is an error message from C#");
```

- **Inspecting JavaScript Objects**

When passing C# objects to JavaScript, use **`JSON.stringify`** to serialize objects. You can log the serialized JSON string for inspection.

```
var jsonString = JSON.stringify(myCSharpObject);
console.log("C# Object as JSON:", jsonString);
```

- **Verify Method Names and Parameters**

Double-check that the method names and parameters in your JavaScript and C# code match. Typos can lead to invocation errors.

- **Handle Promise Rejections**

Handle promise rejections by attaching a .catch block to your **`DotNet.invokeMethodAsync`** calls. This can help catch errors that occur during the asynchronous invocation.

```
DotNet.invokeMethodAsync("InteropDemo", "SomeMethod", arg1, arg2)
    .then(result => {
        // Handle the result
    })
```

```
    .catch(error => {
        console.error("Error invoking C# method:", error);
    });
```

- **Use Browser Debugging Tools**

Leverage browser debugging tools like Chrome/Edge DevTools or Firefox Developer Tools. Set breakpoints, inspect network requests, and analyze the call stack.

By incorporating these practices, you can enhance the error handling and debugging capabilities of your Blazor application with JavaScript Interop.

Security Considerations

When working with JavaScript Interop in Blazor, it's crucial to consider security implications to protect your application from potential vulnerabilities. Here are some security considerations and best practices:

- **Input Validation**

Validate all input parameters before passing them between C# and JavaScript. This helps prevent injection attacks and ensures that only valid data is processed.

- **Sanitize User Inputs**

If your JavaScript code receives inputs from user interactions or external sources, sanitize the inputs to prevent cross-site scripting (XSS) attacks. Use libraries like `DOMPurify` to sanitize HTML content.

- **Authorization and Authentication**

Ensure that any sensitive operations performed through JavaScript Interop are authorized and authenticated. Verify the user's identity and permissions before executing certain actions.

- **Avoid Eval**

Avoid using eval in JavaScript as it can introduce security vulnerabilities. Instead, use safer alternatives for dynamic code execution.

Using eval (avoid this):

```
function executeDynamicCode(expression) {
    try {
        return eval(expression);
    } catch (error) {
        console.error("Error executing dynamic code:", error);
    }
}

// Example usage
```

```
var result = executeDynamicCode("1 + 1");
console.log("Result:", result);
```

Corrected Code

```
function executeDynamicCode(expression) {
    try {
        // Instead of eval, use a function
        var dynamicFunction = new Function("return " + expression);
        return dynamicFunction();
    } catch (error) {
        console.error("Error executing dynamic code:", error);
    }
}

// Example usage
var result = executeDynamicCode("1 + 1");
console.log("Result:", result);
```

- **Secure JavaScript Execution**

Only execute JavaScript code from trusted sources. Avoid dynamically generating JavaScript code based on untrusted input, as this can lead to code injection vulnerabilities.

- **Content Security Policy (CSP)**

Implement and enforce a Content Security Policy to control which resources can be loaded by your application. This helps mitigate risks associated with malicious scripts.

- **Cross-Origin Resource Sharing (CORS)**

Configure CORS settings appropriately to control which origins are allowed to make requests to your Blazor application. Limit cross-origin requests to trusted domains.

- **Use HTTPS**

Ensure that your application is served over HTTPS. This helps protect against various attacks, including man-in-the-middle attacks.

- **Limit Exposed C# Methods**

Only expose necessary C# methods to JavaScript. Minimize the surface area for potential attacks by only exposing what is required for functionality.

- **Dispose of Object References**

When passing C# objects to JavaScript, manage the lifecycle of JavaScript object references. Dispose of them when they are no longer needed to prevent memory leaks and potential security risks.

- **Logging Sensitive Information**

Avoid logging sensitive information, such as passwords or access tokens, in JavaScript console logs. Ensure that your application's logging mechanisms do not inadvertently expose sensitive data.

- **Updates and Patching**

Regularly update and patch your application dependencies, including JavaScript libraries and frameworks. This helps address security vulnerabilities that may be present in third-party code.

- **Audit and Code Review**

Conduct security audits and code reviews regularly to identify and address potential security issues in your codebase. This includes both C# and JavaScript code.

- **Monitoring and Logging**

Implement robust monitoring and logging mechanisms to detect and respond to security incidents. Log relevant security events and anomalies.

By following these security considerations, you can significantly reduce the risk of security vulnerabilities in your Blazor application that involve JavaScript Interop.

Performance Optimization Tips

Optimizing performance while working with JavaScript Interop in Blazor is crucial for ensuring a smooth and responsive application. Here are some tips for performance optimization:

- **Minimize Interop Calls**

Minimize the number of interop calls between C# and JavaScript. Group multiple operations into a single interop call when possible, to reduce overhead.

- **Batch Interop Calls**

Batch together related interop calls to reduce the communication overhead between C# and JavaScript. This is particularly beneficial when performing multiple operations in quick succession.

- **Use Efficient Data Serialization**

When passing data between C# and JavaScript, use efficient serialization methods. For example, prefer simple types or JSON serialization over more complex serialization mechanisms.

- **Limit Data Size**

Avoid transferring large amounts of data between C# and JavaScript. Limit the amount of data passed in interop calls to only what is necessary for the current operation.

- **Dispose of Object References**

If you use `DotNetObjectReference` to pass C# objects to JavaScript, ensure that you dispose of the object references when they are no longer needed to prevent memory leaks.

- **Use Async/Await Wisely**

Be mindful of using asynchronous interop calls excessively. While asynchronous calls can be beneficial, too many async calls can lead to increased overhead. Use async only when needed.

- **Optimize JavaScript Code**

Optimize your JavaScript code for better performance. Minimize unnecessary computations and ensure that your JavaScript functions are well-optimized.

- **Client-Side Caching**

Consider client-side caching for data that doesn't change frequently. Cache data in JavaScript to avoid unnecessary round trips to the server.

- **Lazy Loading**

Implement lazy loading for components or data that is not immediately required. Load resources or components on demand rather than all at once.

- **Profile and Measure**

Use browser developer tools to profile and measure the performance of your JavaScript code. Identify and address any bottlenecks or performance issues.

- **Compress JavaScript Code**

Minify and compress your JavaScript code before deploying it to production. This reduces the size of the JavaScript files, leading to faster downloads and improved performance.

- **Reduce DOM Manipulations**

Minimize unnecessary DOM manipulations in your JavaScript code. Frequent manipulations can cause reflows and repaints, impacting performance.

- **Avoid Synchronous Calls**

Prefer asynchronous calls over synchronous ones. Synchronous calls can block the UI, leading to a less responsive user experience.

- **Update Dependencies**

Ensure that you are using the latest versions of your JavaScript libraries and dependencies. Newer versions may include performance improvements and optimizations.

- **Benchmark and Test**

Conduct performance benchmarks and tests regularly. Identify areas for improvement and fine-tune your code based on actual performance metrics.

By following these performance optimization tips, you can ensure that your Blazor application with JavaScript Interop delivers a fast and efficient user experience. Remember that performance optimization is an ongoing process, and continuous monitoring and refinement are essential.

Conclusion

In this chapter, we understood that with the help of JavaScript Interop, we can integrate the cool features of any JavaScript library in the Blazor application. We can also call C# method in JavaScript function.

In the real scenario, we will get very few scenarios with a JavaScript library. However, it is good to know the power of JavaScript interop in Blazor for creating interactive and powerful single page applications.
In the next chapter, we will explore Azure service in Blazor.

References

For more details, please refer to the following document:

ASP.NET Core Blazor JavaScript interoperability (JS interop) | Microsoft Learn

(https://learn.microsoft.com/en-us/aspnet/core/blazor/javascript-interoperability/?view=aspnetcore-8.0)

Source Code

https://github.com/ava-orange-education/Practical-Web-Development-with-Blazor-and-.Net-8

Multiple Choice Questions

1. What is JavaScript Interop in the context of Blazor?
    a. A new programming language
    b. A technique for integrating JavaScript code with Blazor applications
    c. A type of serverless computing
    d. A tool for debugging JavaScript in Blazor

2. Which Blazor attribute is used to mark a C# method for invocation from JavaScript?
    a. `[CSharpInvoke]`
    b. `[InvokeJS]`
    c. `[JSInterop]`
    d. `[JSInvokable]`
3. How can you pass C# objects to JavaScript in Blazor?
    a. Using the `DotNet.createObject` function
    b. Directly passing the object as an argument in an interop call
    c. Using the `[JSObject]` attribute
    d. Objects cannot be passed to JavaScript in Blazor
4. What is the purpose of `DotNetObjectReference` in Blazor JavaScript Interop?
    a. To create a reference to a JavaScript object
    b. To reference a .NET object in JavaScript
    c. To invoke C# methods from JavaScript
    d. To dispose of JavaScript objects
5. How can you optimize performance when working with JavaScript Interop in Blazor?
    a. Maximize the number of interop calls to enhance communication
    b. Minimize the size of data transferred in interop calls
    c. Avoid using asynchronous calls in JavaScript
    d. Use synchronous calls for better responsiveness

Answers

1. b
2. d
3. b
4. b
5. b

CHAPTER 10
Azure Service in Blazor

Introduction

Microsoft Azure is a comprehensive cloud computing platform provided by Microsoft. It offers a wide range of services that enable individuals and organizations to build, deploy, and manage applications and services through Microsoft's global network of data centers. Azure provides both Infrastructure as a Service (IaaS) and Platform as a Service (PaaS) solutions, as well as other services for various purposes. In this chapter, we will focus on Azure services that are frequently used while working with Blazor WebAssembly application.

Structure

In this chapter, we will learn the following topics:

- Key Features and Components of Microsoft Azure
- Azure Account Creation Steps
- Static WebSite Deployment and CICD Pipeline
- Creating API Using Azure Function App
- CRUD Operation Using Azure Function
- Deployment of Azure Function
- How to Consume Azure Function in Blazor
- Introduction of Azure App Service
- Deployment of Blazor Application Using Azure App Service
- CICD Pipeline Using Azure App Service

Key Features and Components of Microsoft Azure

Some key features and components of Microsoft Azure include:

- **Compute Services**

Azure offers virtual machines (VMs) for scalable computing power, Azure Kubernetes Service for container orchestration, and Azure Functions for serverless computing.

- **Storage Services**

Azure provides various storage solutions, including Blob Storage for unstructured data, Table Storage for NoSQL data, and Azure SQL Database for relational data.

- **Networking Services**

Azure offers a range of networking services such as Azure Virtual Network for secure connectivity, Azure Load Balancer for distributing incoming network traffic, and Azure VPN Gateway for secure connections to on-premises networks.

- **Database Services**

Azure provides fully managed database services like Azure Cosmos DB, Azure SQL Database, and Azure Database for PostgreSQL, MySQL, and more.

- **AI and Machine Learning**

Azure includes services like Azure Machine Learning for building, training, and deploying machine learning models, as well as cognitive services for adding AI capabilities to applications.

- **Identity and Access Management (IAM)**

Azure Active Directory (Azure AD) is used for managing identities and providing secure access to resources.

- **DevOps Services**

Azure DevOps provides a set of tools for source control, build automation, release management, and more, facilitating the DevOps lifecycle.

- **Internet of Things (IoT)**

Azure IoT Hub allows you to connect, monitor, and manage IoT assets, while other services provide analytics and insights for IoT data.

- **Security and Compliance**

Azure offers a range of security services, including Azure Security Center and Azure Policy, to help protect your applications and data.

- **Analytics and Big Data**

Azure includes services like Azure Synapse Analytics, Azure Data Lake Storage, and HDInsight for processing and analyzing large datasets.

- **Serverless Computing**

Azure Functions enables you to run event-triggered code without explicitly provisioning or managing infrastructure.

As you observed, Azure is very vast topic. However, in this chapter, we will only focus on Azure services that are frequently used while working with Blazor WebAssembly application.

***Figure* 10.1**: *Azure Logo*

Azure Account Creation

Creating an account on Azure Portal is totally free. When you create an account for the first time, you will receive $200 Azure credit free of cost.

To create an Azure account, follow these steps:

1. Visit the Azure Portal:

   Go to the Azure Portal at https://portal.azure.com/

2. Click **`Create a new Azure account`**:

   If you don't have an existing account, click the "**`Start free`**" button to create a new one.

3. Fill in the required information:

   You'll need to provide details such as your email address, password, and other necessary information. Follow the on-screen instructions to complete the sign-up process.

4. Verify your identity:

   Microsoft may require you to verify your identity by providing a phone number for authentication purposes. Follow the prompts to complete this step.

5. Agree to the terms and conditions:

   Read and agree to the terms and conditions of using Azure.

6. Provide payment information:

   Although Azure offers a free tier with limited resources, you may need to provide payment information for verification purposes. Rest assured that you won't be charged unless you explicitly upgrade to a paid plan.

7. Access your Azure Portal:

   Once your account is created, you can log in to the Azure Portal using the credentials you provided during the sign-up process.

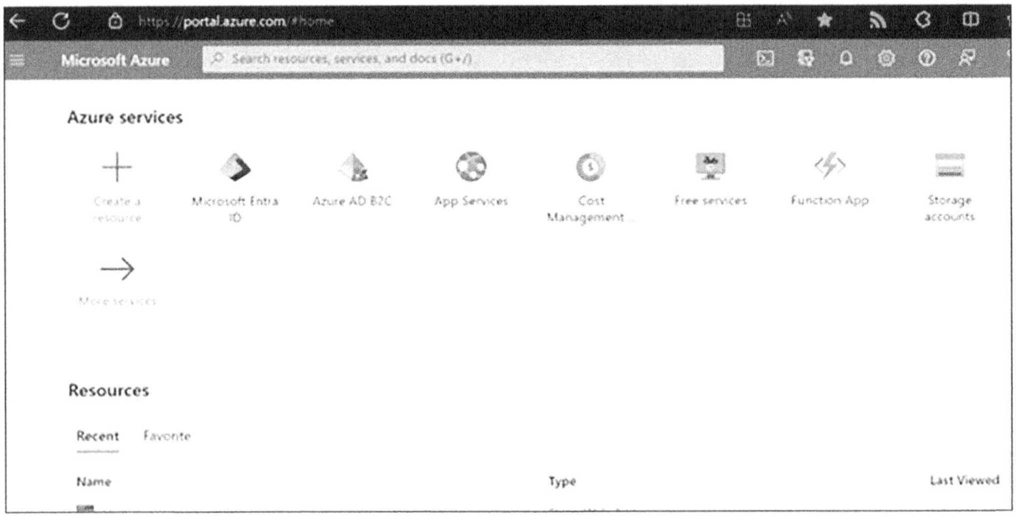

***Figure 10.2**: Azure Portal Dashboard*

Static WebSite Deployment

Blazor WebAssembly is a UI framework similar to Angular, React, and Vue.Js. You can also deploy Blazor WebAssembly as static websites on any cloud provider platform such as Azure, AWS, Google, and so on, which is totally free. You don't have to pay any money for deployment and storage.

If you have created some demo or portfolio project using Blazor WASM and need to share with someone, you can take advantage of this service. It is totally free.

In this demo, we will show one of the easiest approaches using Azure Static Web App.

Step 1: Create the Blazor WebAssembly app using dotnet **`cli`** command as follows:

```
dotnet new blazorwasm -n WasmTest -o app
```

In the preceding command, we create a Blazor WebAssembly application in app folder.

Step 2: Push the code on GitHub Repo.

Step 3: Go to Azure portal and create the `Static Web App` as follows:

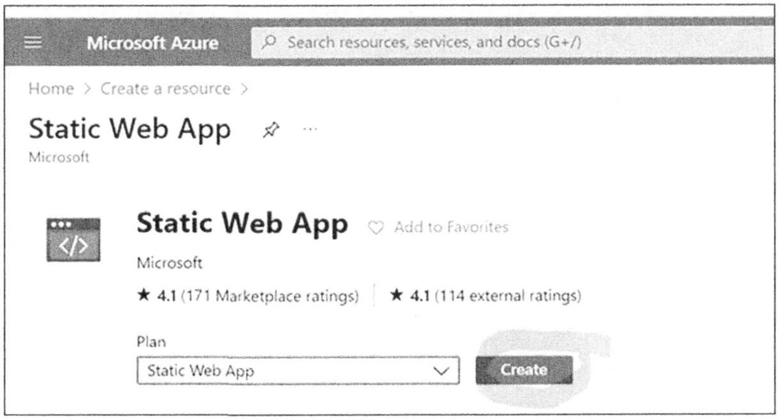

***Figure 10.3**: Static Web App*

Step 4: Fill the mandatory field as shown in *Figure* 10.4:

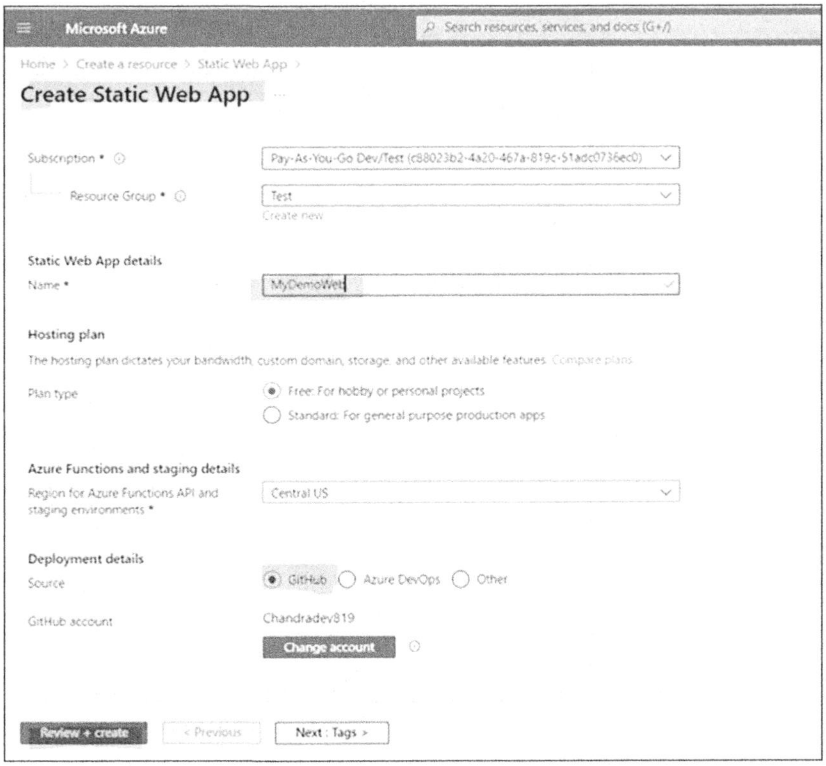

***Figure 10.4**: Create Static Web*

Step 5: Click **`Review + create`** button.

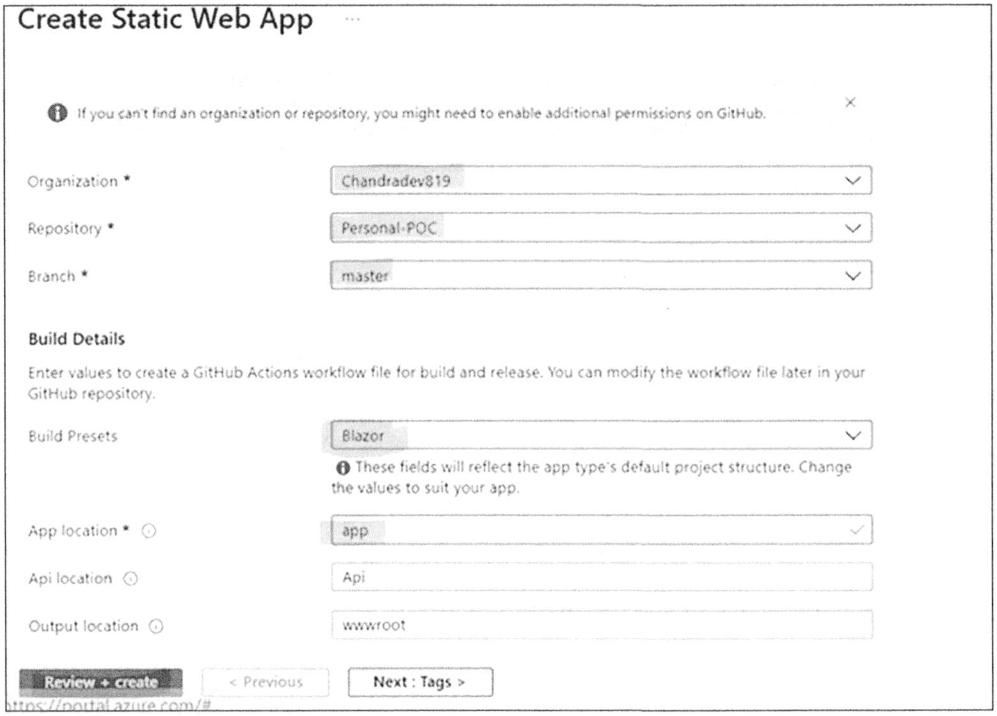

Figure 10.5: *Static Web Review*

Figure 10.6 shows "**`Your deployment is complete`**":

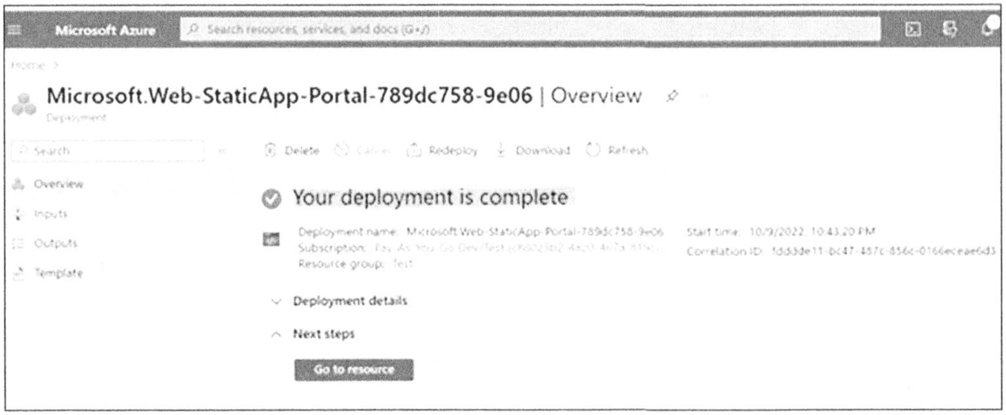

Figure 10.6: *Static Web deployment*

Step 6: Go to your resource and click the generated URL

Figure 10.7: Static Web URL

Now, you will see your website as shown in *Figure 10.8*:

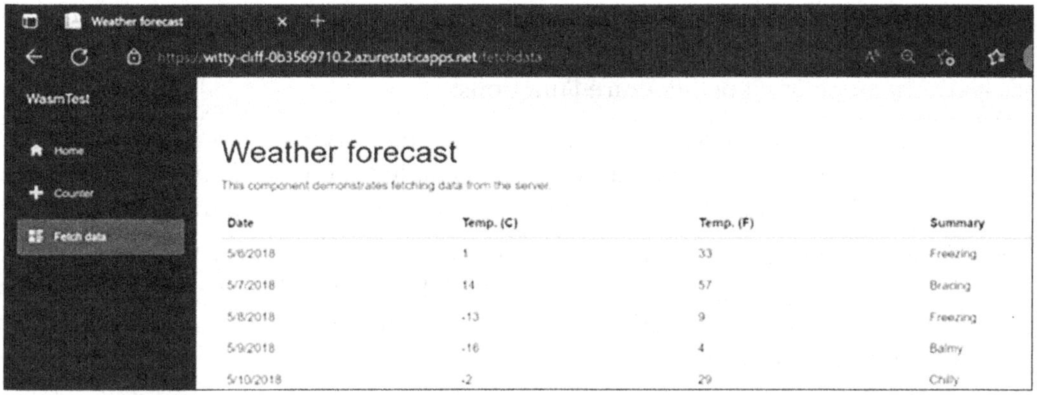

Figure 10.8: Blazor Application

CI/CD Pipeline on GitHub

It will also create a CI/CD pipeline for us on GitHub.

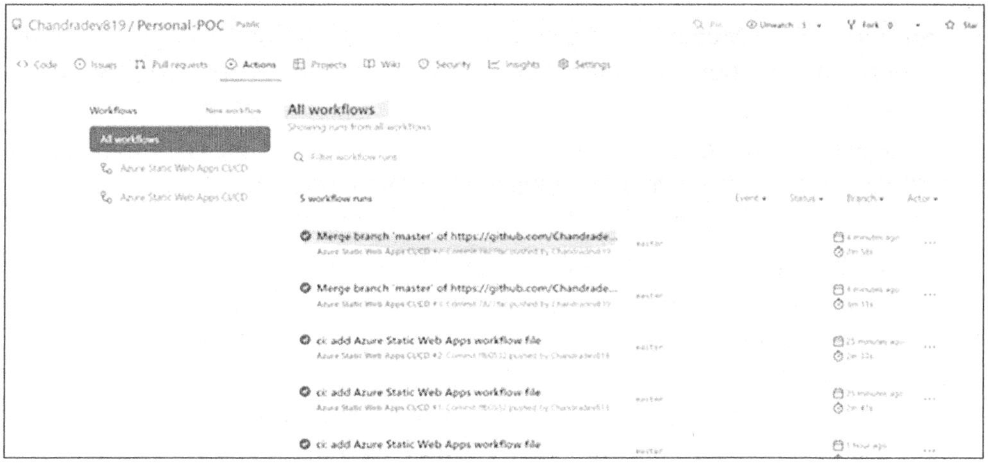

Figure 10.9: CI/CD Pipeline

Azure Function

Azure Function is a serverless computing service offered by Microsoft Azure that allows you to write less code, maintain less infrastructure, and save on costs.

It enables the execution of small units of code, called functions, without the need to manage servers or any other infrastructure.

These functions are triggered by specific events or inputs, allowing developers to respond to events in real time. By utilizing Azure Functions, developers can focus solely on writing code and not worry about infrastructure management.

Benefits of Using Azure Functions

Let's learn the benefits of using Azure Functions:

- **Serverless Computing:** Azure Functions enable serverless computing, allowing you to focus on writing code without managing the underlying infrastructure. This can lead to increased development speed and reduced operational overhead.
- **Cost-Efficiency:** With serverless architecture, you pay only for the compute resources used during the execution of functions. This can result in cost savings compared to traditional server-based approaches where you might pay for idle resources.
- **Scalability:** Azure Functions automatically scale based on demand. Functions can be triggered individually, enabling your application to handle varying workloads efficiently.
- **Event-Driven:** Functions can be triggered by various events such as HTTP requests, timer-based schedules, or events from other Azure services. This makes it suitable for building event-driven architectures and microservices.
- **Support for Multiple Languages:** Azure Functions supports multiple programming languages, including C#, F#, C#, JavaScript, Python, Java, and PowerShell.
- **Integration with Azure Services:** Azure Functions seamlessly integrates with other Azure services, making it easy to connect and interact with services like Azure Storage, Azure SQL Database, or Azure Event Hubs.
- **Rapid Development and Deployment:** The serverless model allows for rapid development and deployment. You can focus on writing the necessary code for your functions without dealing with infrastructure concerns, leading to faster time-to-market.
- **DevOps Integration:** Azure Functions can be easily integrated into your DevOps processes, enabling continuous integration and deployment. This aligns with modern development practices, promoting agility and collaboration.

Different Types of Triggers on Azure Functions

Here is a list of different types of triggers on Azure functions:

- **HTTP Trigger:** This trigger allows your function to be invoked by an HTTP request. It's commonly used for building RESTful APIs or handling HTTP-based events.
- **Timer Trigger:** With a timer trigger, your function can be scheduled to run at specified intervals or according to a cron expression. This is useful for periodic tasks or background processing.
- **Blob Trigger:** This trigger is activated when a new or updated blob is detected in Azure Storage. It's often used for scenarios involving file processing or data ingestion.
- **Queue Trigger:** When a new message arrives in an Azure Storage Queue, a function with a queue trigger can be invoked. This is useful for building decoupled systems and handling asynchronous processing.
- **Event Hub Trigger:** This trigger processes events from Azure Event Hubs, which is a scalable and distributed event streaming platform. It's suitable for handling large-scale event streams.
- **Service Bus Trigger:** With a Service Bus trigger, your function can respond to messages arriving in Azure Service Bus queues or topics. This is useful for building reliable and asynchronous communication between components.
- **Cosmos DB Trigger:** This trigger reacts to changes in Azure Cosmos DB collections, allowing your function to process documents that are inserted or modified in the database.
- **Event Grid Trigger:** Azure Event Grid triggers enable your function to respond to events from various Azure services or custom sources. It provides a flexible and event-driven architecture.
- **GitHub/WebHook Trigger:** This trigger allows your function to respond to events from GitHub repositories, such as code commits or pull requests.
- **Durable Functions Orchestration Trigger:** Durable Functions introduce a special trigger for orchestrations, allowing you to define workflows and manage the state of long-running processes.

These triggers provide a wide range of options for handling different types of events in your applications. As a web developer working with Azure, you can choose the trigger type that best fits the requirements of your projects, whether they involve HTTP requests, scheduled tasks, data changes, or other events.

Creating Azure Function

This is a very vast topic, but in this chapter, a brief introduction about all frequently used Azure services is provided.

We can create the Azure Function using Visual Studio 2022, VS Code, and with Azure Portal website. However, as web developers, we will choose Visual Studio 2022.

Step 1: Create the new project for Azure function as follows:

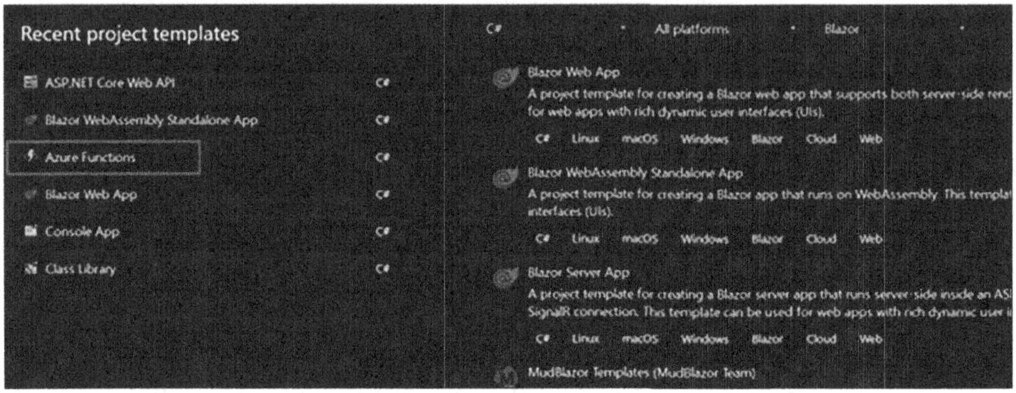

Figure 10.10: *Azure Function*

Here is the template for new project:

Figure 10.11: *Azure Function Project Template*

Figure 10.12 shows the type of Azure Function:

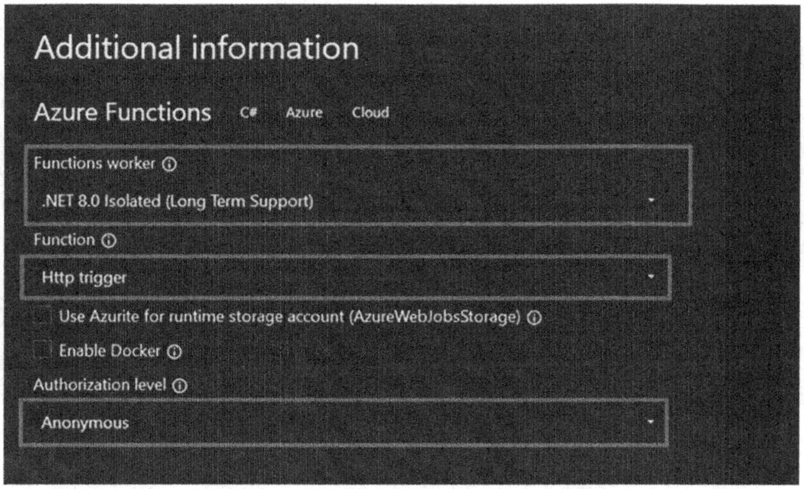

Figure 10.12: *Azure Function Type*

Step 2: Click the **`Create`** Button of the wizard window. Now, it will create basic scaffolding code for Azure function:

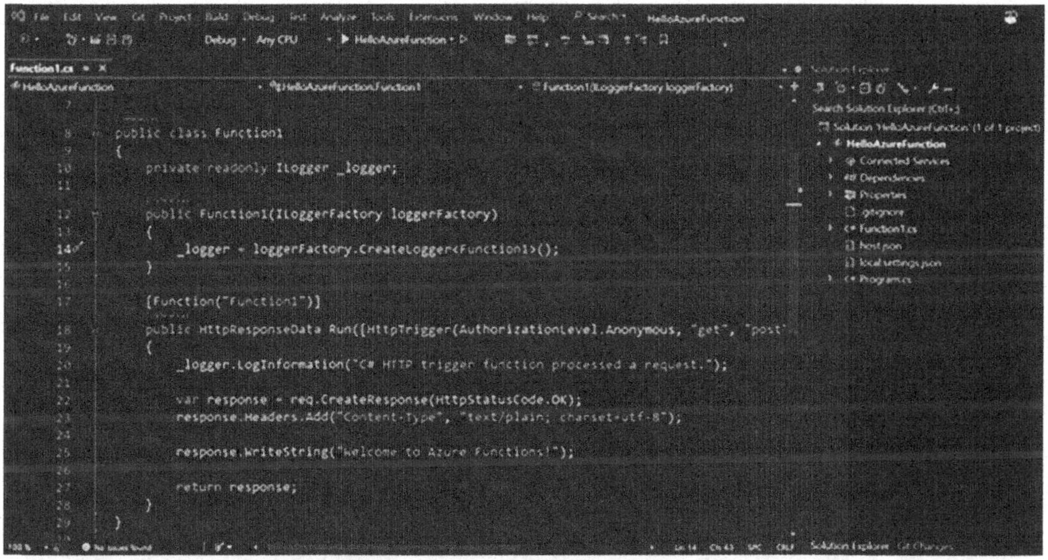

Figure 10.13: *Azure Function Code*

Step 3: Run the application, and you will see command window as follows:

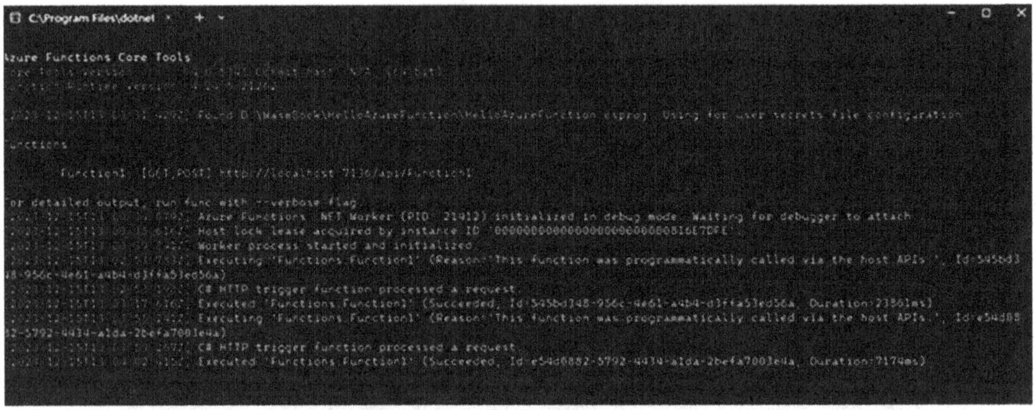

Figure 10.14: *Azure Function Output*

Step 4: Now trigger the given GET and POST method from the postman. It will call the Azure Function code and return "**`Welcome to Azure Functions!`**"

```
[Function("Function1")]
public HttpResponseData Run([HttpTrigger(AuthorizationLevel.Anonymous,
"get", "post")] HttpRequestData req)
{
    _logger.LogInformation("C# HTTP trigger function processed a re-
quest.");

    var response = req.CreateResponse(HttpStatusCode.OK);
    response.Headers.Add("Content-Type", "text/plain; charset=utf-8");

    response.WriteString("Welcome to Azure Functions!");

    return response;}
```

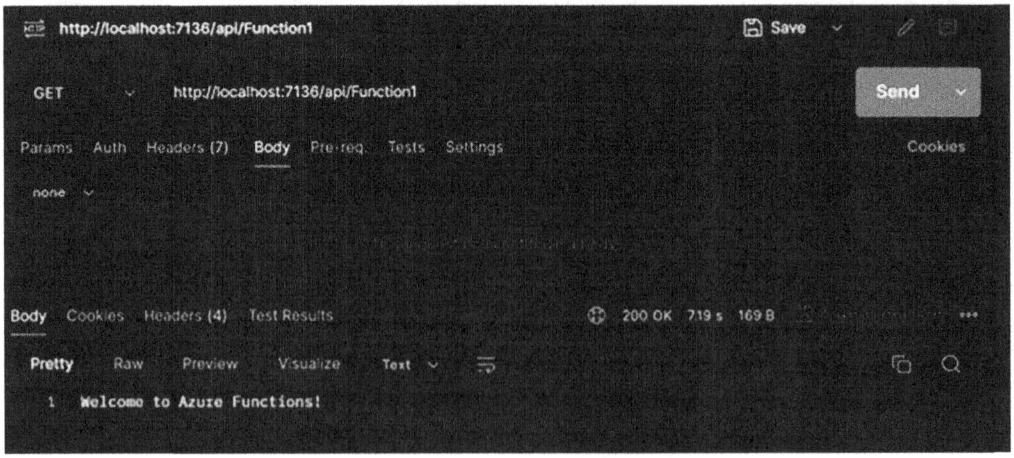

Figure 10.15: *Azure Function Output on Postman*

Http CRUD Operation in Azure Function

Now, we will change the Azure Function name to **`EmpFunction`** and create some in-memory dummy data for demo purposes.

Step 1: Create the **`Employee`** class.

```
public class Employee
{
    public int Id { get; set; }
    public string Name { get; set; }
    public decimal Salary { get; set; }
```

Step 2: Write the Create **`Employee`** Post method as shown here:

```
 public class EmpFunction
    {
        private readonly List<Employee> employeeDataStore = new List
<Employee>();
        private readonly ILogger _logger;

        public EmpFunction(ILoggerFactory loggerFactory)
        {
            _logger = loggerFactory.CreateLogger<EmpFunction>();
            InitializeDummyData();
        }

        // Initialization method to populate dummy data
        private void InitializeDummyData()
        {
            employeeDataStore.Add(new Employee { Id = 1, Name = "John
Doe", Salary = 50000 });
            employeeDataStore.Add(new Employee { Id = 2, Name = "Jane
Smith", Salary = 60000 });
            employeeDataStore.Add(new Employee { Id = 3, Name = "Anvi
Sah", Salary = 70000 });
            // Add more dummy data as needed
        }

        [Function("CreateEmployee")]
        public HttpResponseData CreateEmployee(
            [HttpTrigger(AuthorizationLevel.Anonymous, "post")]
HttpRequestData req)
        {
            _logger.LogInformation("CreateEmployee function processed
a request.");

            var requestBody = req.ReadAsStringAsync().Result;
            var newEmployee = JsonSerializer.Deserialize<Employee>
```

```
(requestBody);

            // Need to Store in actual database
            employeeDataStore.Add(newEmployee);

            var response = req.CreateResponse(HttpStatusCode.OK);
            response.Headers.Add("Content-Type", "application/json;
charset=utf-8");
           response.WriteString(JsonSerializer.Serialize(newEmployee));
            return response;
        }
```

Step 3: Write the code to fetch all employees as shown here:

```
[Function("GetAllEmployees")]
public HttpResponseData GetAllEmployees(
    [HttpTrigger(AuthorizationLevel.Anonymous, "get")] HttpRequestData
req)
{
    _logger.LogInformation("GetAllEmployees function processed a
request.");

    var response = req.CreateResponse(HttpStatusCode.OK);
    response.Headers.Add("Content-Type", "application/json; charset
=utf-8");

    response.WriteString(JsonSerializer.Serialize(employeeDataStore));

    return response;}
```

Step 4: Write the **`UpdateEmployee`** method as shown here:

```
[Function("UpdateEmployee")]
public HttpResponseData UpdateEmployee(
    [HttpTrigger(AuthorizationLevel.Anonymous, "put")] HttpRequestData
req)
{
    _logger.LogInformation("UpdateEmployee function processed a
request.");

    var requestBody = req.ReadAsStringAsync().Result;
    var updatedEmployee = JsonSerializer.Deserialize<Employee>
(requestBody);

    // Find and update the employee based on Id
    var existingEmployee = employeeDataStore.Find(e => e.Id ==
updatedEmployee.Id);
    if (existingEmployee != null)
    {
```

```
        existingEmployee.Name = updatedEmployee.Name;
        existingEmployee.Salary = updatedEmployee.Salary;
    }

    var response = req.CreateResponse(HttpStatusCode.OK);
    response.WriteString("Employee updated.");

    return response;}
```

Step 5: Write the code for **`DeleteEmployee`** as shown here:

```
  [Function("DeleteEmployee")]
        public HttpResponseData DeleteEmployee(
            [HttpTrigger(AuthorizationLevel.Anonymous, "delete")]
HttpRequestData req)
        {
            _logger.LogInformation("DeleteEmployee function processed
a request.");

            var requestBody = req.ReadAsStringAsync().Result;
            var employeeIdToDelete = JsonSerializer.Deserialize
<Employee>(requestBody);

            // Find and remove the employee based on Id
            var employeeToDelete = employeeDataStore.Find(e => e.Id
== employeeIdToDelete.Id);
            if (employeeToDelete != null)
            {
                employeeDataStore.Remove(employeeToDelete);
            }

            var response = req.CreateResponse(HttpStatusCode.OK);
            response.WriteString("Employee deleted.");

            return response;
        }
```

Step 6: Run the application:

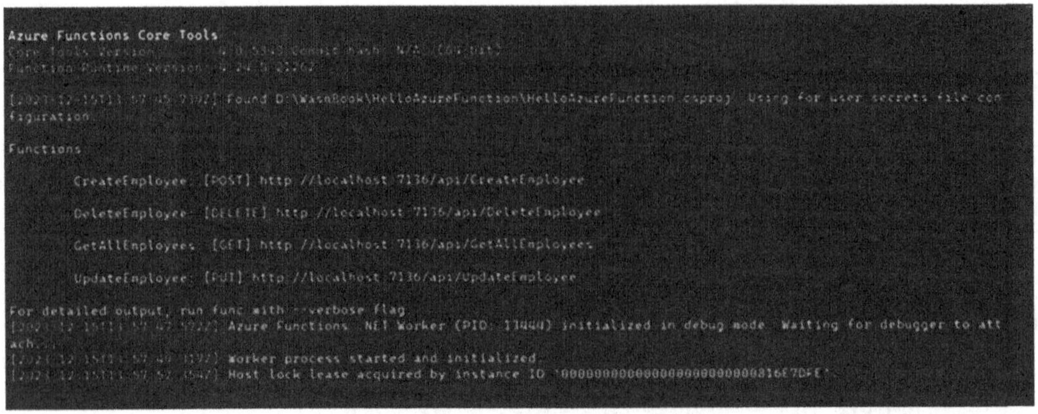

Figure 10.16: *Azure Function Endpoint*

Step 7: Test the given HTTP endpoint using Postman:

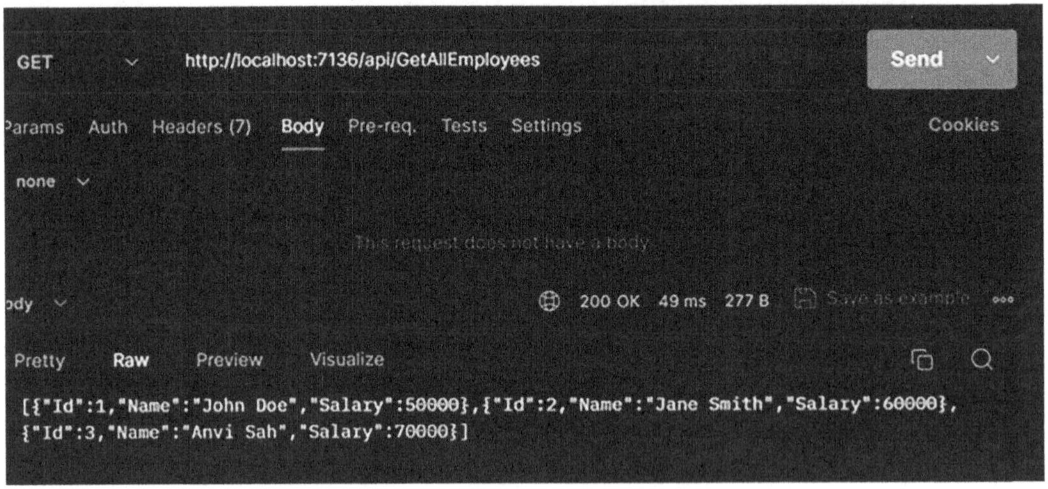

Figure 10.17: *Azure Function GetAllEmployees*

Figure 10.18 shows how to create employee details:

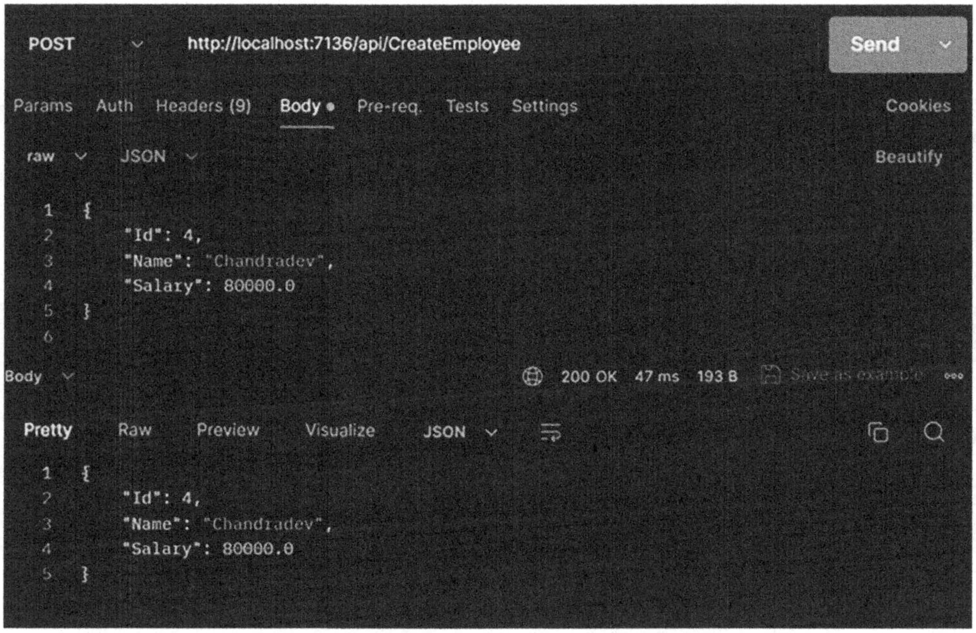

Figure 10.18: *Azure Function CreateEmp*

Figure 10.19 depicts how to delete an employee details:

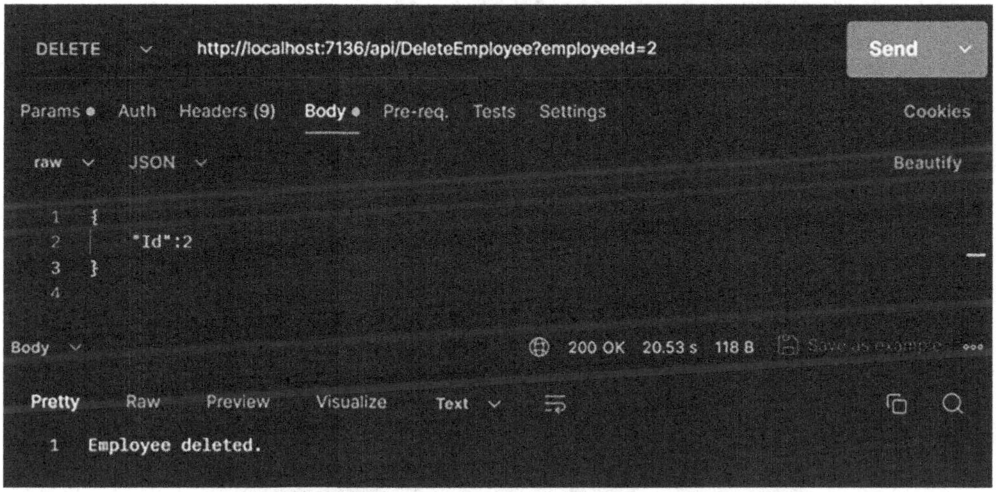

Figure 10.19: *Azure Function DeleteEmp*

Figure 10.20 shows to update employee details:

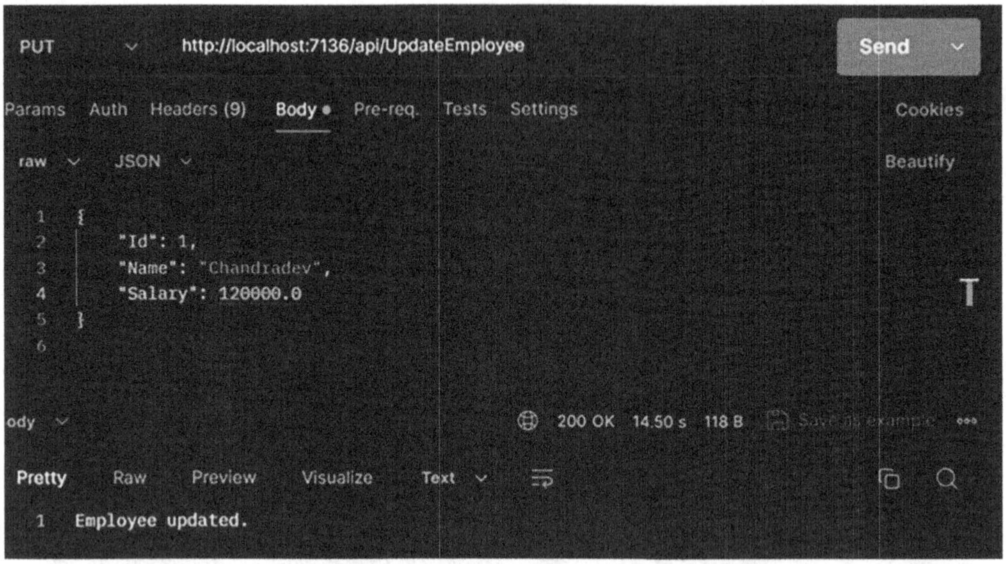

Figure 10.20: *Azure Function UpdateEmp*

In the preceding demo, we saw that with the help of **`HTTPTrigger`**, we can create RESTful APIs.

Azure Function Deployment

We can deploy the Azure Function with the help of Visual Studio 2022 wizard by following these steps:

Step 1: Right click project **`Solution Explorer`** and click **`Publish...`**:

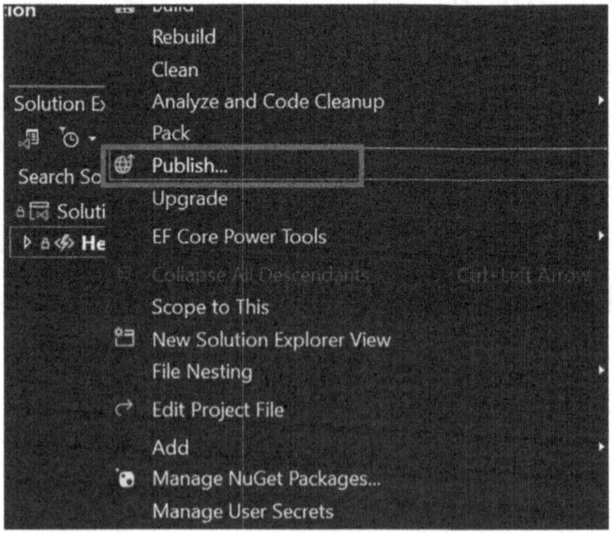

Figure 10.21: *Azure Function Publish – step 1*

Step 2: Select **`Azure`** and click **`Next`**

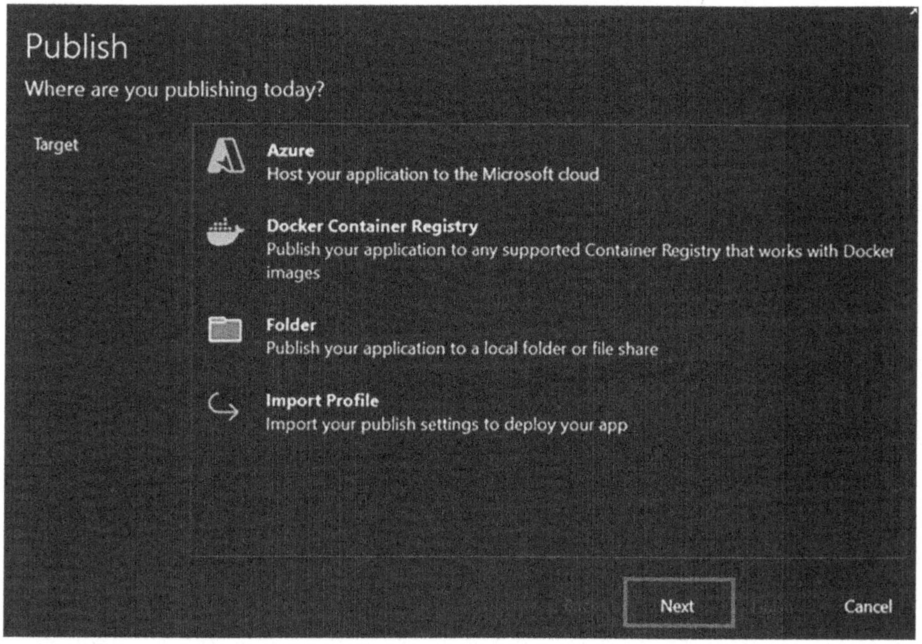

***Figure 10.22**: Azure Function Publish – step 2*

Step 3: *Figure* 10.23 shows the next screen of process:

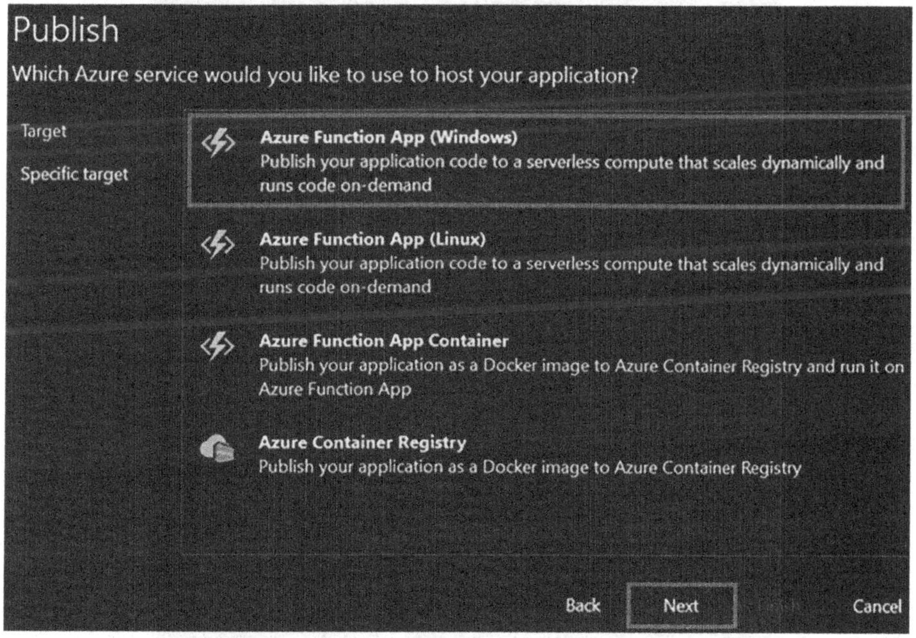

***Figure 10.23**: Azure Function Publish – step 3*

Step 4: As shown in *Figure* 10.24, click **`+ Create new`**:

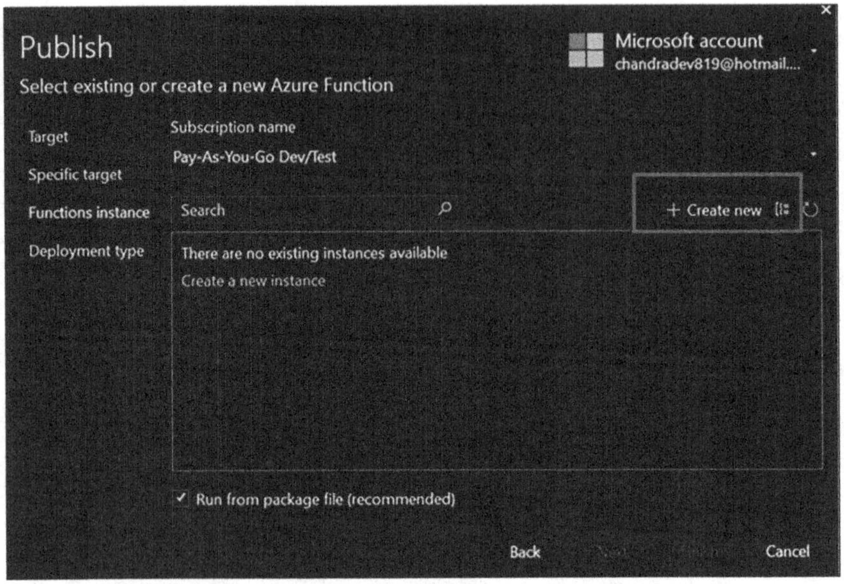

***Figure* 10.24**: *Azure Function Publish – step 4*

Step 5: Then, the following screen will appear:

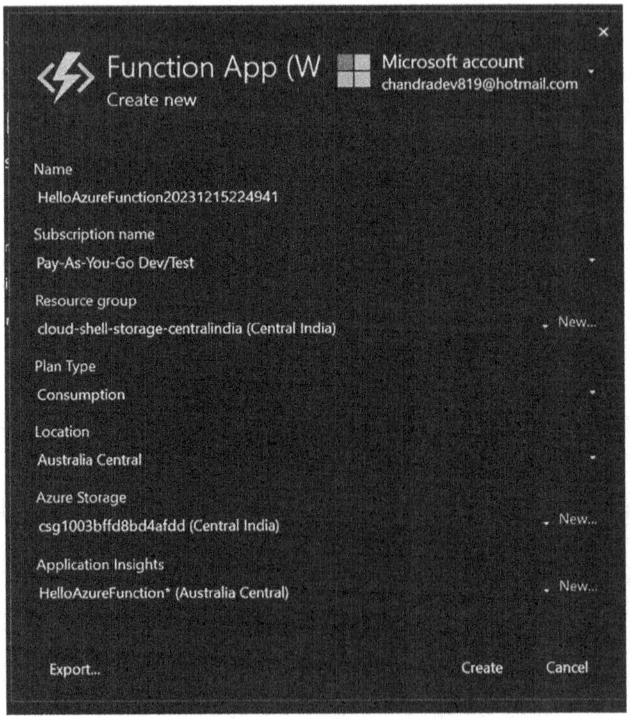

***Figure* 10.25**: *Azure Function Publish – step 5*

Step 6: Click **`Next`**, as shown in *Figure 10.26*:

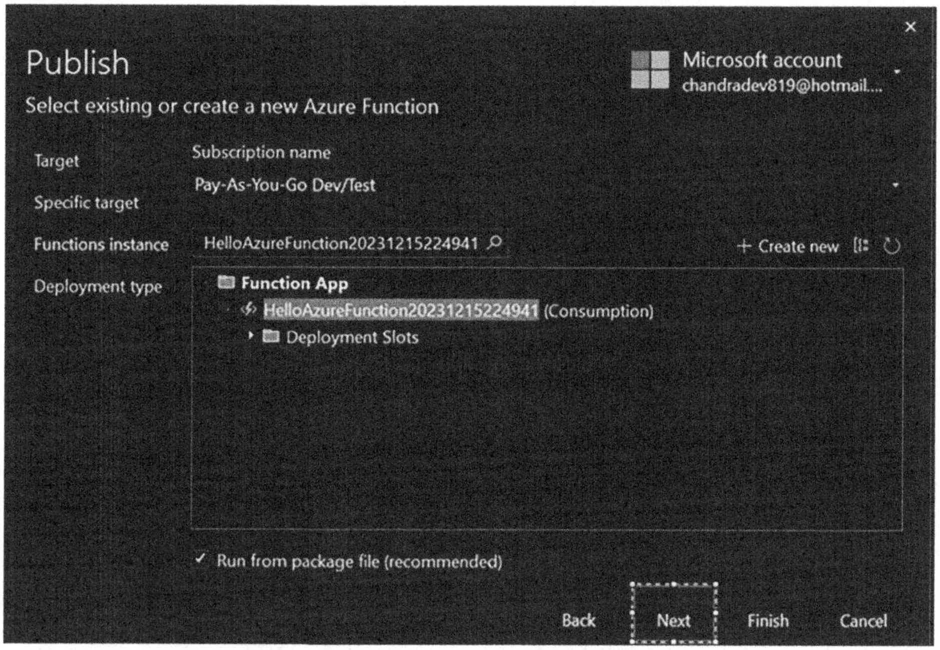

Figure 10.26: *Azure Function Publish – step 6*

Step 7: This is the final step, as shown in *Figure 10.27*, and click **`Finish`**:

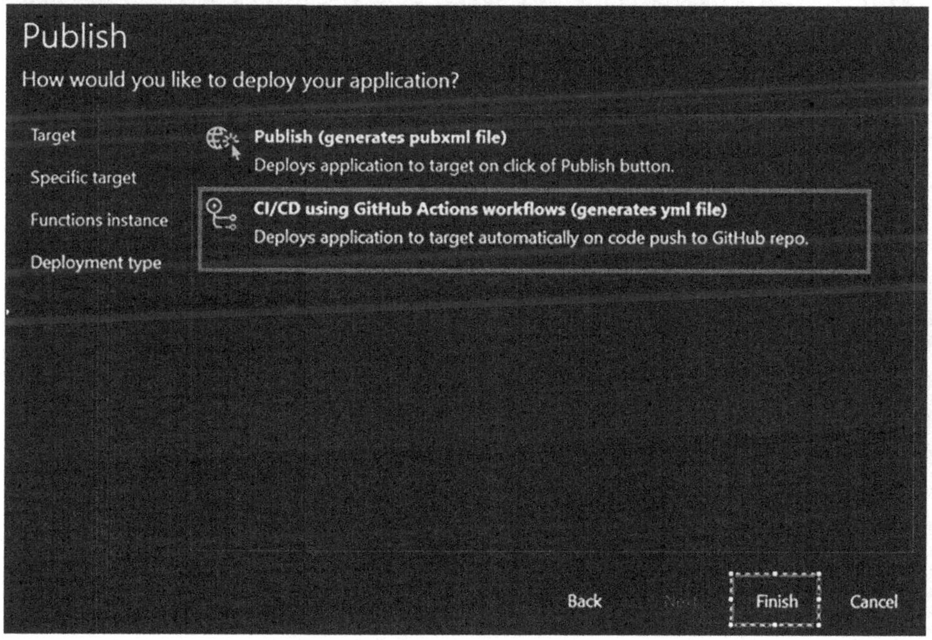

Figure 10.27: *Azure Function Publish – step 7*

Now, this will generate the CICD pipeline on GitHub. Whenever you push any code, it will auto trigger and deploy to Azure.

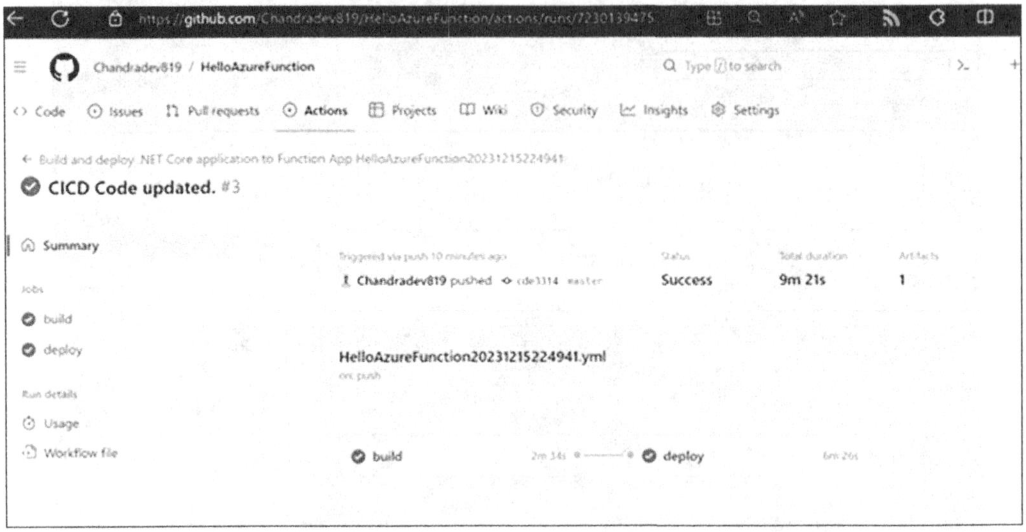

Figure 10.28: Azure Function CICD - 1

Figure 10.29 shows the next step:

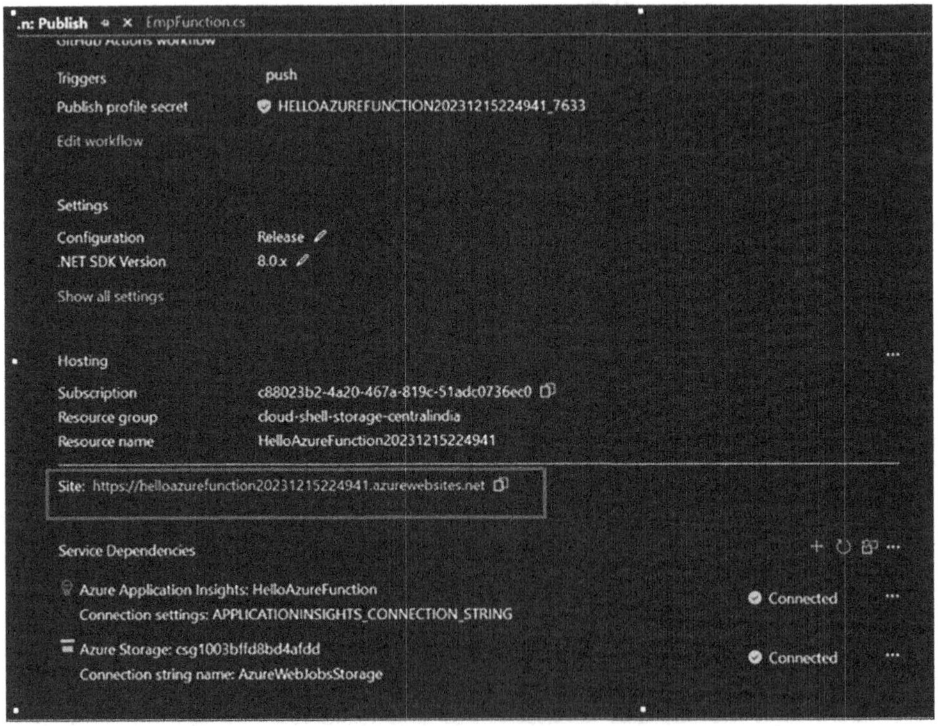

Figure 10.29: Azure Function CICD - 2

Now, our Azure Function code has been deployed to the cloud, and we are ready to use in any web application.

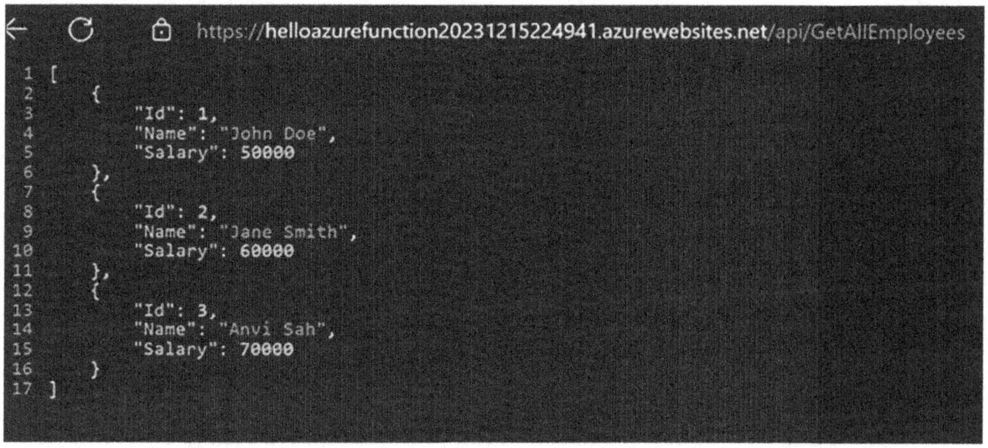

***Figure 10.30**: Azure Function CICD - 3*

In the preceding demo, we saw that with the help of a Visual Studio 2022 wizard, we are able to deploy the Azure Function on the cloud. It also created CICD pipeline and application insight.

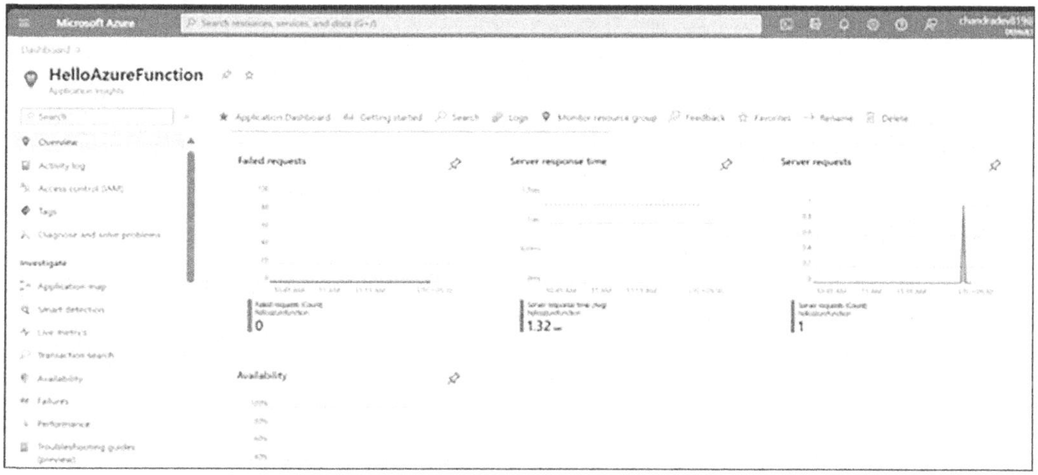

***Figure 10.31**: Azure Function Application Insight*

Consuming Azure Function in Blazor WebAssembly

Azure Function is web API endpoint, and we can consume Azure Function endpoints similar to web API using "**`HttpClient`**". Here is a complete code snippet for API call:

```
@inject HttpClient Http

@code {
    private string result;

    private async Task CallAzureFunction()
    {
        // Replace "YourFunctionUrl" with the actual URL of your Azure
Function
        var functionUrl = "https://your-function-url.azurewebsites.
net/api/YourFunction";

        var response = await Http.GetAsync(functionUrl);

        if (response.IsSuccessStatusCode)
        {
            result = await response.Content.ReadAsStringAsync();
        }
        else
        {
            result = $"Error: {response.StatusCode}";
        }
    }
}

<div>
    <button @onclick="CallAzureFunction">Call Azure Function</button>
    <p>@result</p>
```

Azure App Service

Azure App Service is a fully managed platform for building, deploying, and scaling web apps. It supports various programming languages, including C#, which you mentioned in your profile. As a senior web developer working with Azure, you might find Azure App Service useful for hosting your Blazor applications.

Azure App Service offers features such as automatic scaling, continuous integration and deployment (CI/CD), and easy integration with Azure services.

It supports following app deployment:

- Web App (Asp.net webform, Asp.net MVC, Asp.net core, and Blazor)
- Static Web App (AngularJs, Angular, ReactJs, VueJs, Blazor WASM, and so on)
- Web App +Database
- WordPress Website deployment

Now, in our demo, we will see how to deploy our Blazor Application with the help of Web App Service.

App Deployment with CICD Pipeline

Creating CICD pipeline on Azure portal for Blazor or Asp.net core project is very simple and straightforward.

Step 1: Create the **`App Services`** on Azure portal:

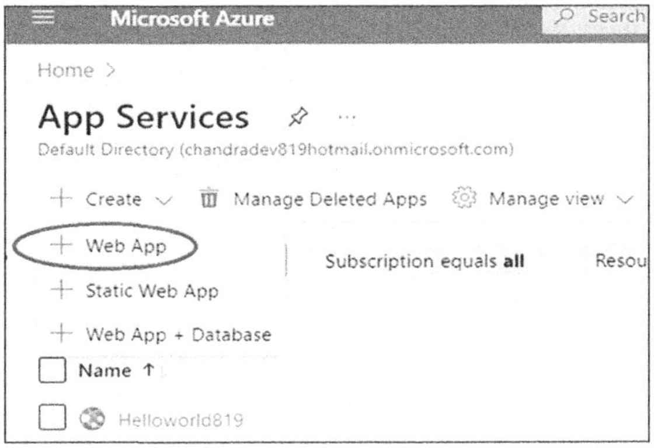

***Figure 10.32**: Web App*

Step 2: Fill all the required mandatory field as shown in the following figure:

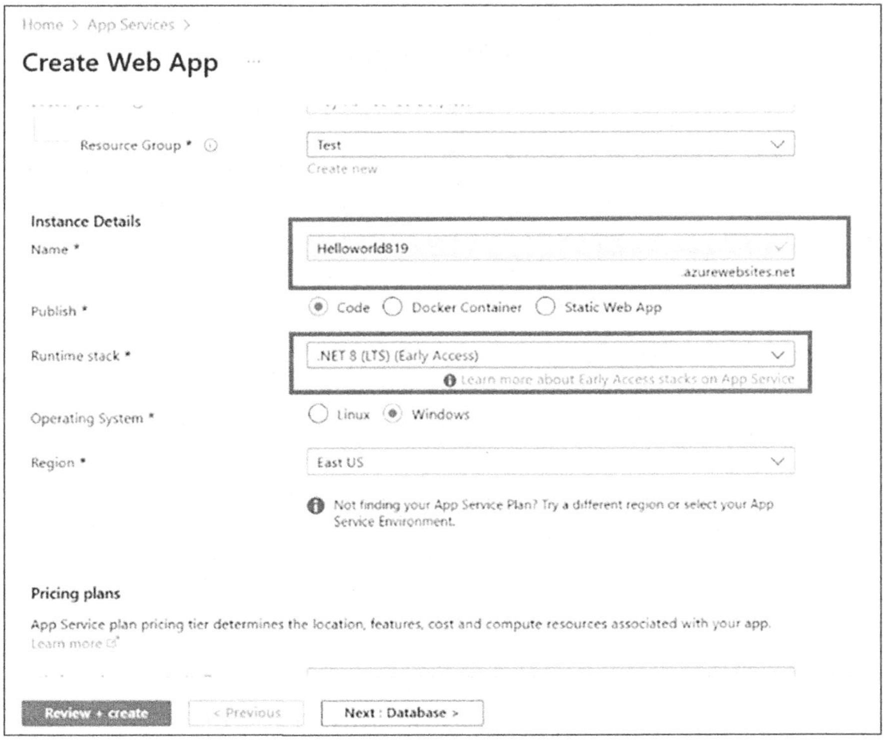

***Figure 10.33**: Web App*

Step 3: Enable GitHub Action settings, as given in the following image. This will help us to create a CICD pipeline.

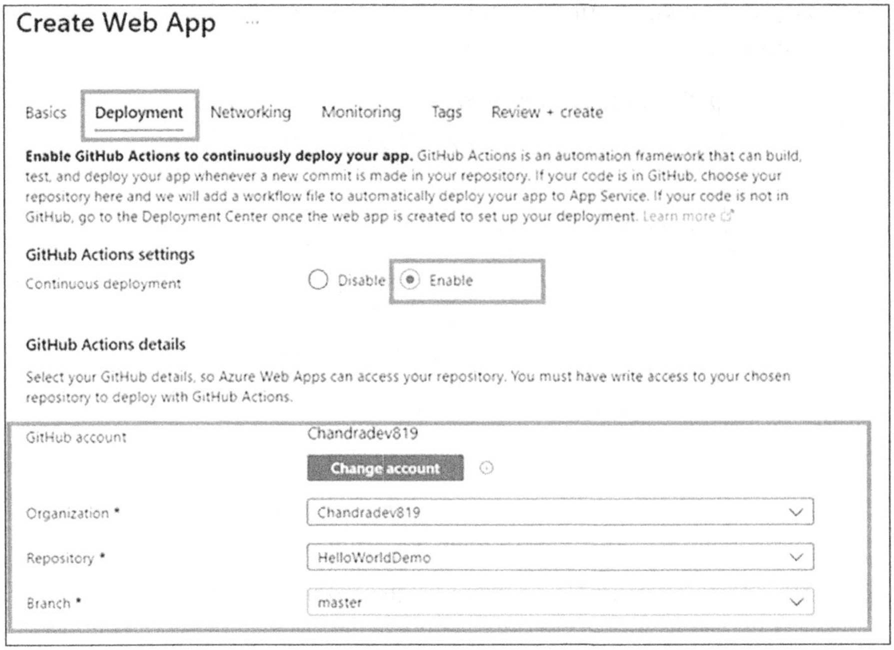

***Figure 10.34**: Web App*

Step 4: Now click Create Web App.

If you come to the GitHub repo, you will see that the Azure Web App deployment wizard has already added a **yaml** file, which will trigger the deployment process for us.

***Figure 10.35**: Web App*

Step 5: Now change the code on source code and push to GitHub repo. The CICD process will trigger.

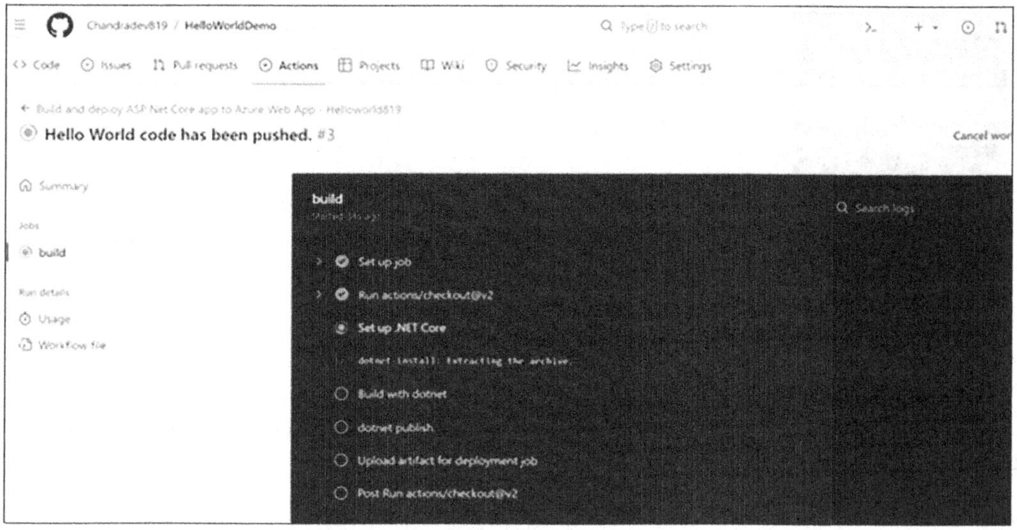

***Figure 10.36**: Web App (1)*

Now, the code has been pushed:

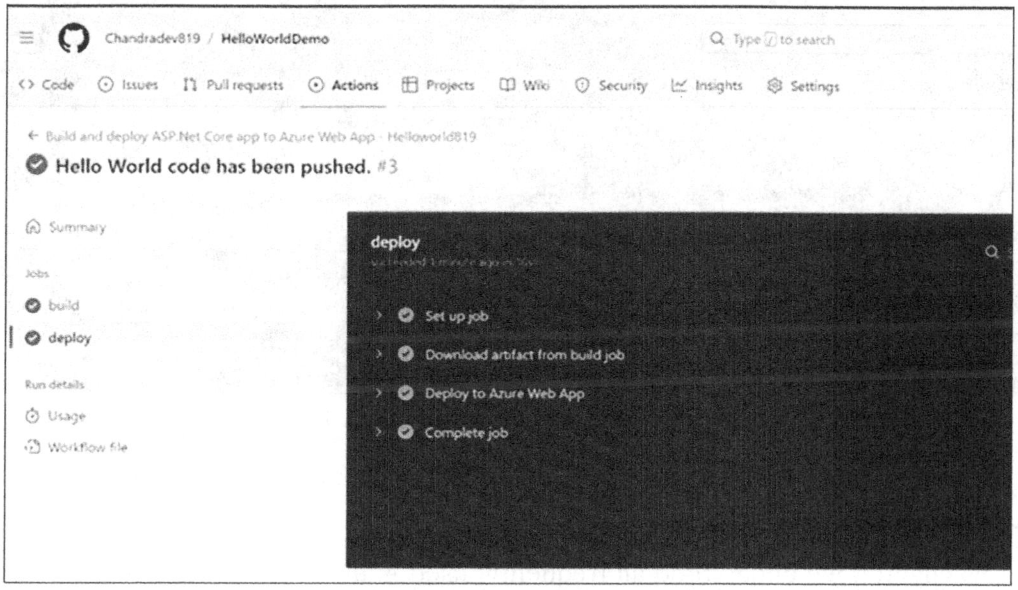

***Figure 10.37**: Web App (2)*

Step 6: Now run the created Web App. We will see output as follows:

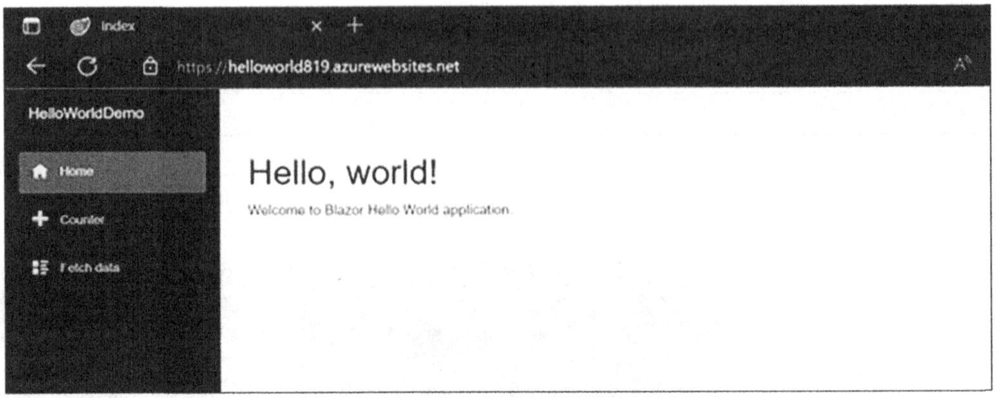

Figure 10.38: *Blazor app*

In the preceding demo, we saw that without writing a single line of code, Azure Portal can create a CICD pipeline for us. It will hardly take 5–10 min to deploy an application with the CICD pipeline.

We can also do the same task with help of Visual Studio 2022 Wizard.

Figure 10.39: *Visual Studio Wizard*

Conclusion

In this chapter, we understood all frequently used Azure Service while doing Blazor web development. It is a very essential skill for any .Net Developer. We also learned various tips and tricks of the Visual Studio 2022 wizard.

We gained insights on how to create a CICD pipeline for any web application without writing any code. These skills are time saving and thus make them more productive for any developer. The upcoming chapter will explain the readers about security challenges in Blazor.

References

For more details, please refer to the following document:

https://learn.microsoft.com/en-us/azure/azure-functions/

Azure Key Vault documentation | Microsoft Learn

Azure documentation | Microsoft Learn

Source Code

https://github.com/ava-orange-education/Practical-Web-Development-with-Blazor-and-.Net-8

Multiple Choice Questions

1. What is the primary purpose of Azure Functions?
   a. Hosting static websites
   b. Managing virtual machines
   c. Running serverless compute functions
   d. Storing relational databases
2. What is the smallest unit of execution in Azure Functions?
   a. Virtual Machine
   b. Container
   c. Function
   d. Application
3. What is the primary purpose of Azure Key Vault?
   a. Hosting web applications
   b. Storing and managing sensitive information such as secrets, keys, and certificates
   c. Running serverless functions
   d. Analyzing big data

4. What is the primary purpose of Azure App Service?
    a. Storing and managing large datasets
    b. Building and deploying containerized applications
    c. Creating and hosting web apps and APIs
    d. Managing virtual networks
5. What type of data is Azure Blob Storage designed to store?
    a. Structured data in tables
    b. Large binary objects like images, videos, and documents
    c. Real-time streaming data
    d. Relational databases

Answers

1. c
2. c
3. b
4. c
5. b

CHAPTER 11
Security in Blazor WebAssembly

Introduction

Developing web applications always comes with security challenges, and Blazor WebAssembly is no exception. However, understanding the security considerations specific to client-side technology is essential to ensure your applications are safe and secure.

As you know, Blazor WASM is client-side technology and runs on a browser sandbox like other JavaScript libraries. So, if we do not implement proper security in Blazor WebAssembly, then hackers can easily hijack your application, and it would be a big loss to you and your organization.

Structure

In this chapter, we will cover the following topics:

- Introduction to Authentication and Authorization
- Authentication and Authorization Using OIDC
- Authentication and Authorization Using Azure AD
- Authentication and Authorization Using Google
- Custom Token-Based Authentication in Blazor WASM
- Tips and Tricks While Implementing Security
- Common Mistakes While Implementing Security

Authentication and Authorization

Authentication and authorization are essential to building secure web applications, including those developed with Blazor WebAssembly. Let's understand these terms in more detail::

Authentication

Authentication is the process of verifying the identity of a user, ensuring that the person or system trying to access a resource is who they claim to be. In the context of Blazor WebAssembly, authentication typically involves validating user credentials, such as a username and password.

Blazor WebAssembly supports various authentication methods, including:

- **ASP.NET Core Identity**
  ASP.NET Core Identity is a membership system that adds login functionality to your application. It provides features like user registration, password recovery, and user profile management.
- **External Providers (OAuth/OpenID Connect)**
  You can integrate external authentication providers like Google, Facebook, or Azure AD to allow users to log in using their existing accounts from these providers.
- **Token-based Authentication**
  Use JSON Web Tokens (JWT) or other token-based authentication mechanisms to secure communication between the client and server. Tokens are typically issued upon successful authentication and sent with each authorization request.

Authorization

Authorization is the process of determining what actions or resources a user can access once their identity is verified through authentication. In other words, it defines permissions and controls access to specific functionalities or data.

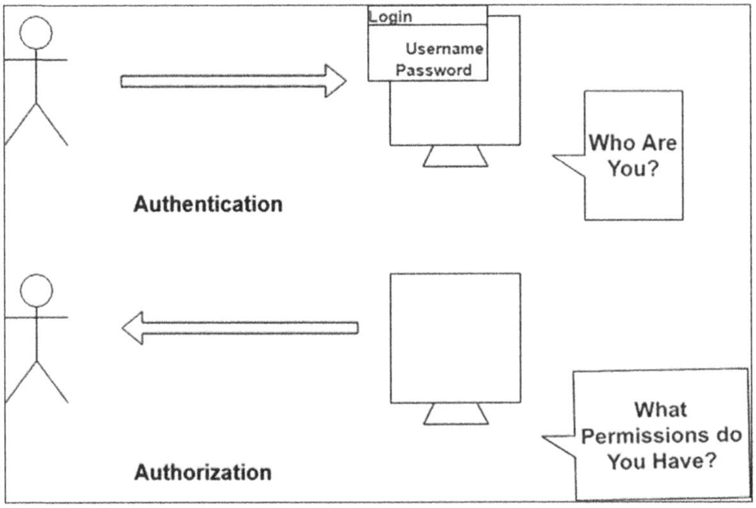

Figure 11.1: *Authentication and Authorization Process*

Authentication and Authorization Using OIDC

OIDC stands for OpenID Connect, which is an identity layer built on top of the **OAuth 2.0** authorization framework. It is a standard protocol for authentication and single sign-on (SSO) on the web.

Blazor WebAssembly supports authenticating and authorizing apps using OpenID Connect **(OIDC)** via the **`Microsoft.AspNetCore.Components.WebAssembly.Authentication`** library.

The library can authenticate against any third-party Identity Provider (IP) that supports OIDC, which are called OpenID Providers (OP).

The authentication support in the Blazor WebAssembly Library (Authentication.js) is built on top of the Microsoft Authentication Library (MSAL, msal.js).

OIDC is an authentication protocol built on top of OAuth 2.0, designed for secure and standardized user authentication. OIDC-compliant identity providers include Azure AD, Google, Facebook, Okta, or Auth0, and so on.

Now, we will see how to implement the implementation of Azure AD Authentication in Blazor WebAssembly.

Step 1: Create the Blazor WebAssembly 8.0 as follows:

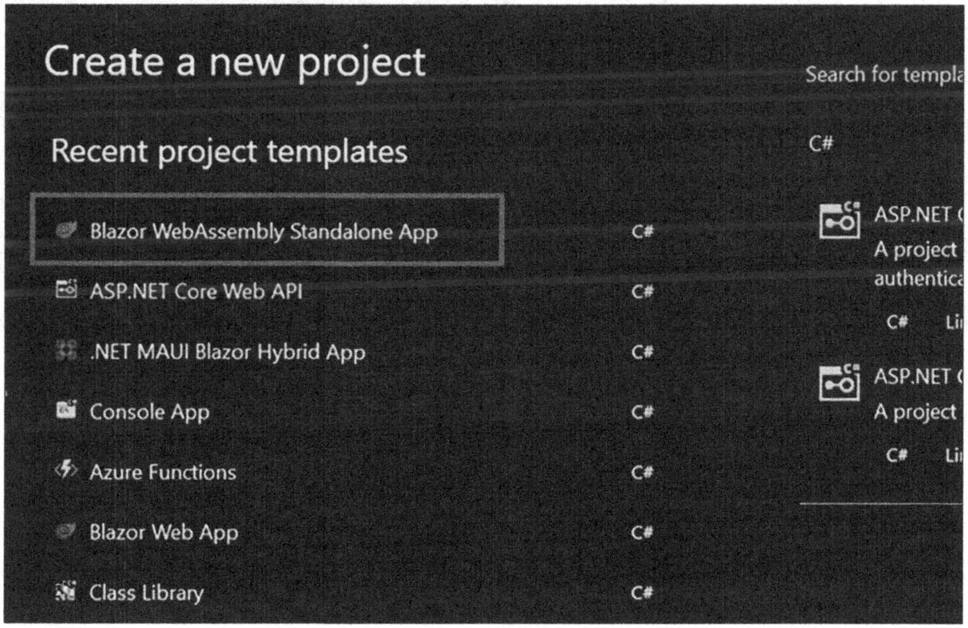

***Figure 11.2:** Blazor Wasm Project Template*

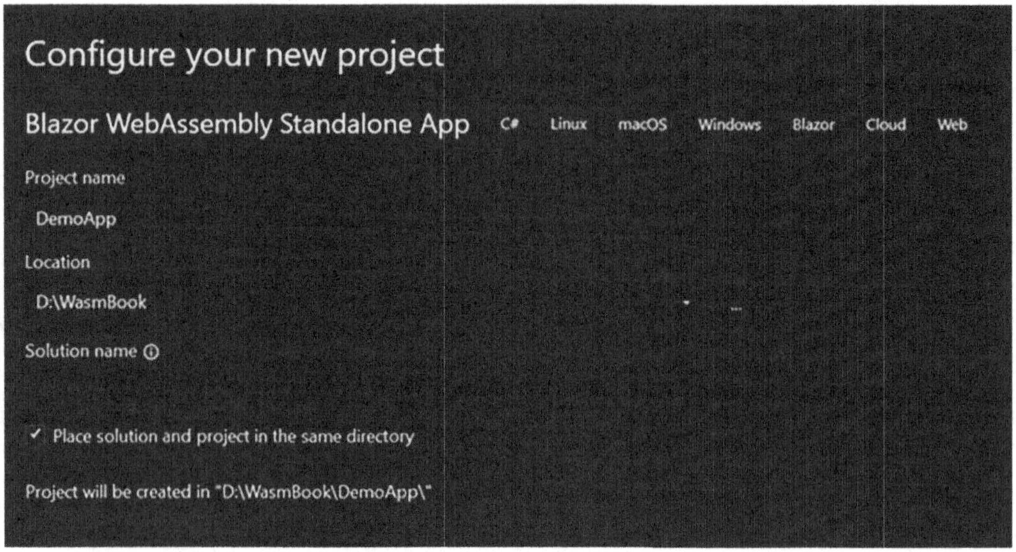

Figure 11.3: *Folder Location*

Step 2: Select the **`Microsoft identity platform`** as shown in the following figure:

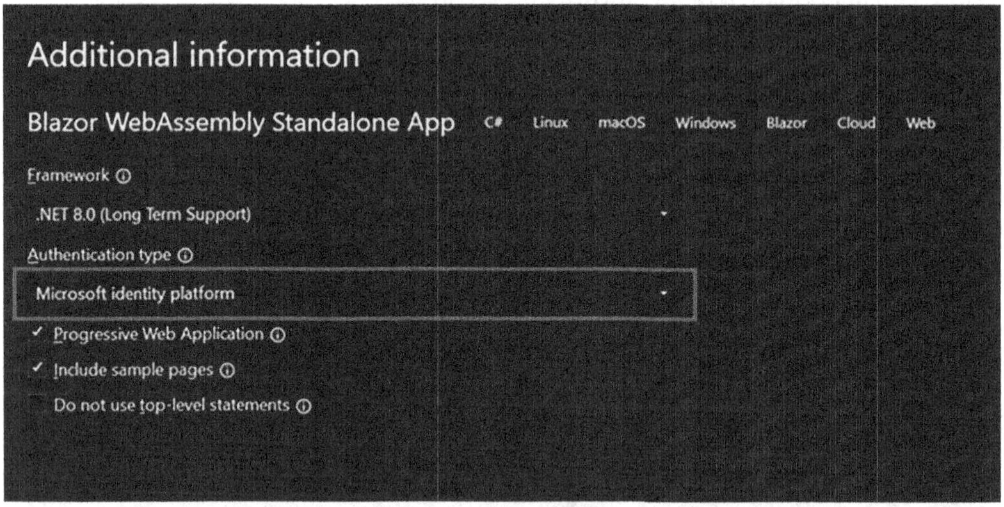

Figure 11.4: *Microsoft Identity*

Step 3: Now configure the application as given in Visual Studio Wizard:

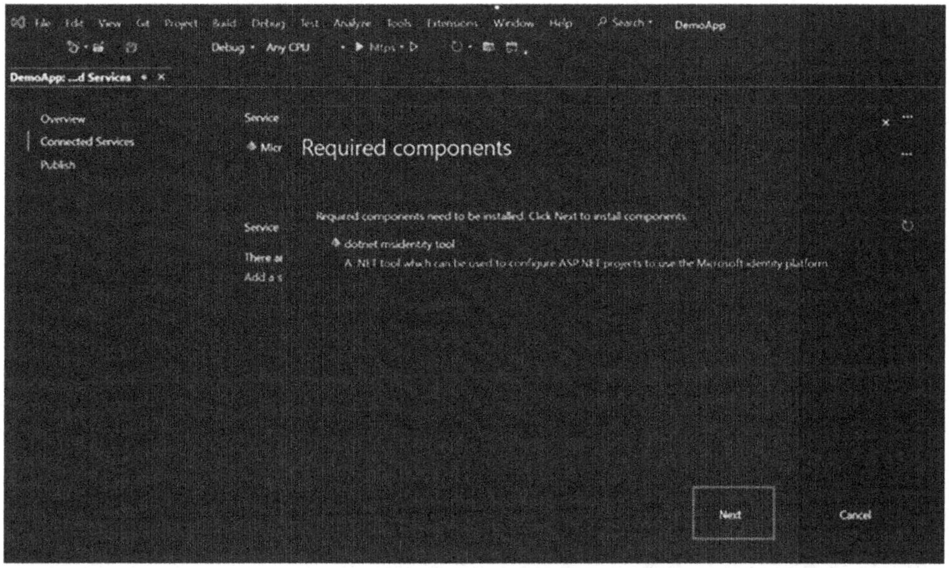

Figure 11.5: *Next Wizard*

Step 4: If this wizard will not create the JSON file, then create an **`appsettings.json`** file and keep the **`TenantId`** and **`ClientId`** here. It will be there in the **`wwwroot`** folder.

```
{
  "AzureAd": {
    "Authority": "",
    "ClientId": "",
    "ValidateAuthority": true

  }}
```

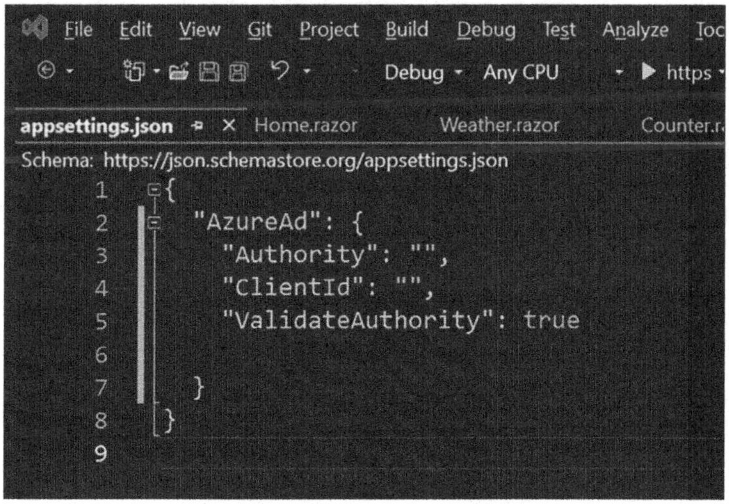

Figure 11.6: *appsetting.json file*

Step 5: Go to the Azure portal and select "**`Microsoft Entra ID`**":

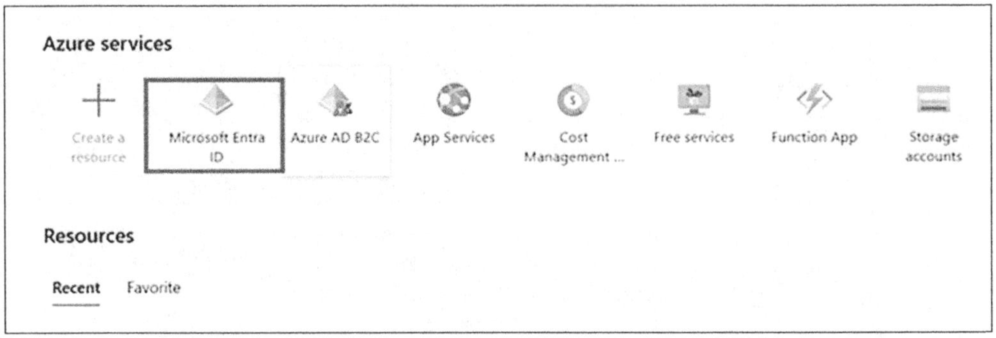

Figure 11.7: *Azure Portal*

In *Figure* 11.8, click **`+ Add`** > **`App registration`**

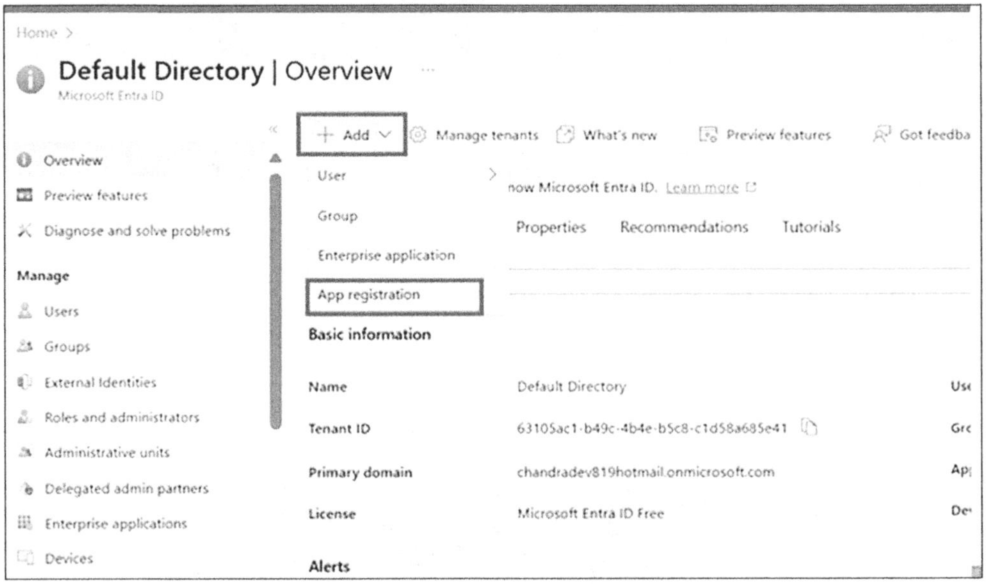

Figure 11.8: *App Registration*

Step 6: Click the **`Register`** button:

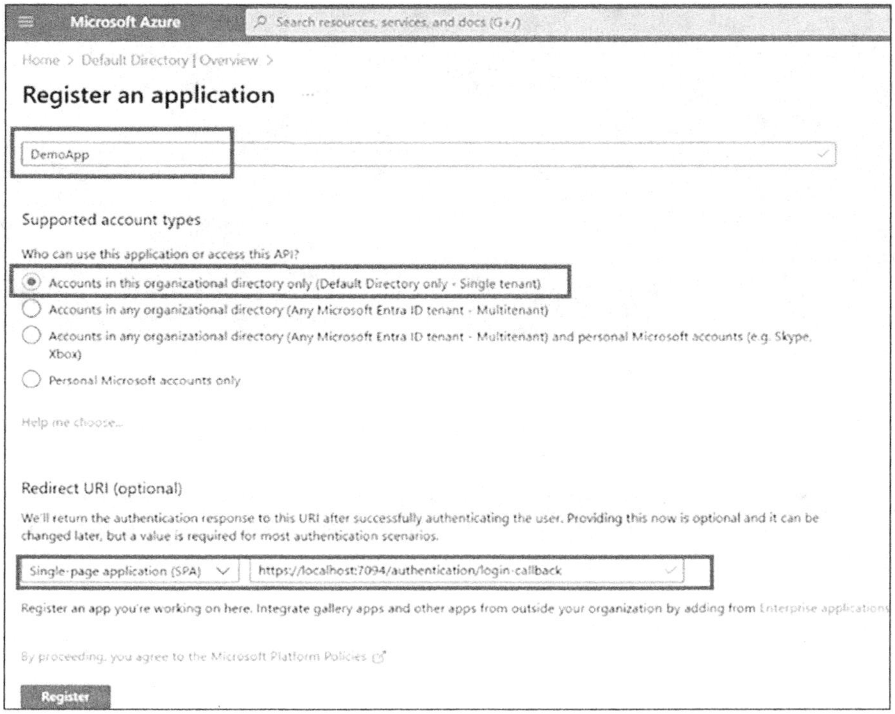

Figure 11.9: *Create Application*

Step 7: After clicking the **`Register`** button, you will see the following screen. We need to copy **`ClientId`** and **`TenentId`** from here.

Figure 11.10: *Client and tenentId*

Step 8: Keep this **`ClientId`** and **`TenentId`** on **`appsettings.json`** as follows:

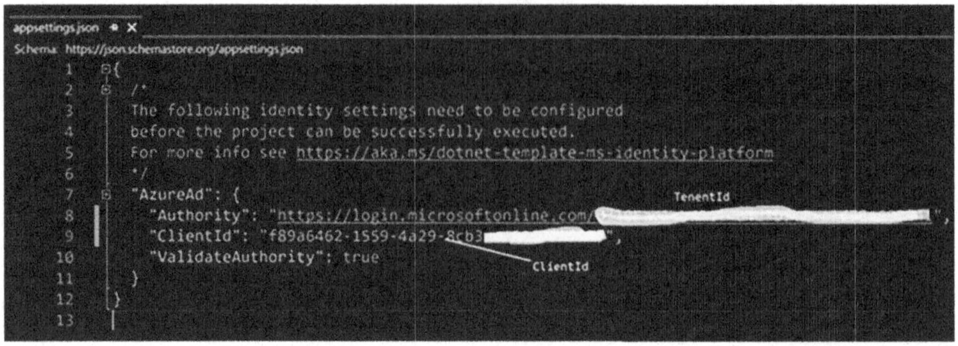

Figure 11.11: *Client and tenentId in appsetting.json file*

Step 9: Go to the Authentication section and check on both **`Access Token`** and **`ID Token`**, as given in the following figure:

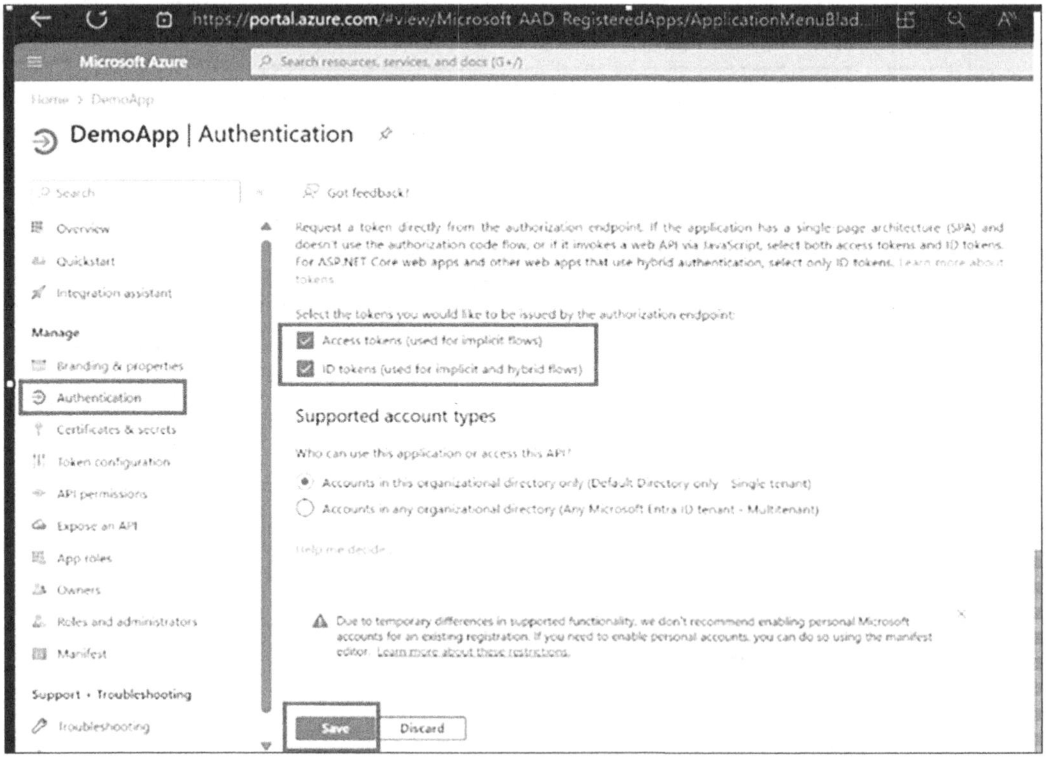

Figure 11.12: *Authentication on Azure Portal*

Step 10: Run the application. You will see authentication and authorization out of box with help of **`Microsoft.Authentication.WebAssembly.Msal`**.

This library is specifically designed to enable authentication and authorization in Blazor WebAssembly applications.

Within this namespace, you will find classes and components that facilitate the integration of authentication features into your Blazor WebAssembly applications. MSAL helps you implement secure authentication workflows using protocols like OAuth 2.0 and OpenID Connect.

Figure 11.13: *Final Output*

If you want to create the Blazor WebAssembly application with the help of the dotnet CLI command with **`ClientId`** and **`TenentId`**, then you can write as follows:

```
dotnet new blazorwasm --auth SingleOrg -o DemoApp --client-id
"981fc724-c146-4ced-b693-ec9f3b13cefb" --tenant-id "63105ac1-b49c-
4b4e-b5c8-c1d58a685e41" -f net8.0
```

The aforementioned CLI command will create the same Blazor WebAssembly with all inbuilt security features.

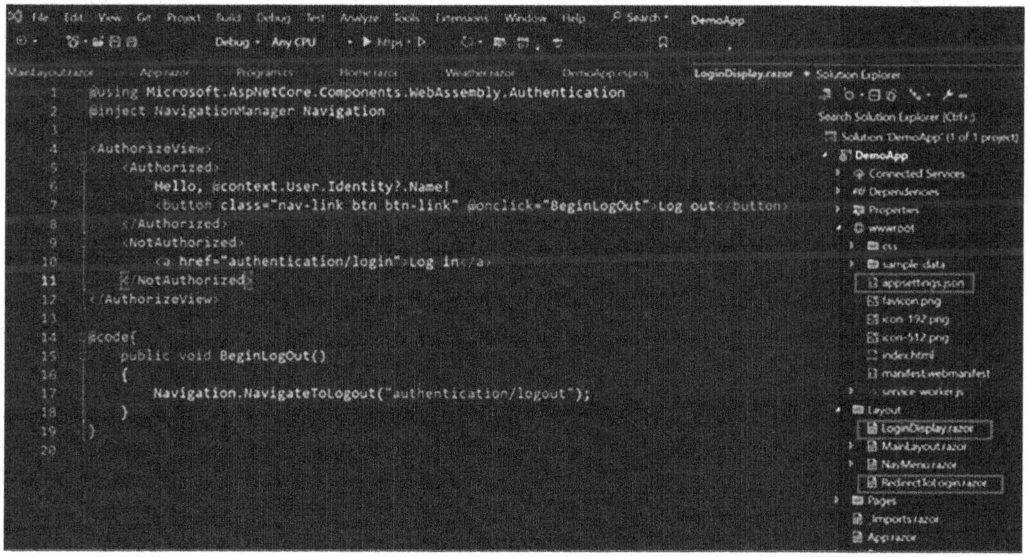

Figure 11.14: *Blazor WASM Project*

Exploring Practical Use Scenario of Microsoft Entra ID

We can use the following scenario:

1. **Single Sign-On (SSO):** It enables single sign-on, allowing users to access multiple applications with a single set of credentials. This is beneficial for both user convenience and security.
2. **Authentication and Authorization for Applications:** When developing applications that require secure authentication and authorization mechanisms, Azure AD can be used to manage user identities and control access to resources.
3. **Enterprise-Level Identity Management**: Azure AD is well-suited for enterprise-level identity management, offering features such as multi-factor authentication, conditional access policies, and comprehensive identity protection.
4. **API Protection:** If your applications involve APIs, Azure AD can secure those APIs by authenticating and authorizing users and applications that attempt to access them.
5. **Microsoft 365 Integration:** If your organization uses Microsoft 365 services, Azure AD provides a unified identity platform that integrates with Microsoft 365, making it easier to manage user identities across various Microsoft services.
6. **Security and Compliance:** Azure AD includes robust security features, such as risk-based conditional access, identity protection, and compliance reporting, making it suitable for applications that require a high level of security and compliance.
7. **B2B and B2C Scenarios:** Azure AD supports both business-to-business (B2B) and business-to-consumer (B2C) scenarios. You can use Azure AD B2B to enable collaboration with external users, and Azure AD B2C for building customer-facing applications with identity and access management.
8. **Integrating with On-Premises Active Directory:** If your organization has an on-premises Active Directory, Azure AD can be integrated to extend identity and access management to the cloud while maintaining a connection with the on-premises infrastructure.

Note: Now Azure AD name has been changed to Microsoft Entra ID.

Google Authentication and Authorization in Blazor WebAssembly

Using OpenID Connect (OIDC), we can also integrate Google authentication and authorization in the Blazor WebAssembly application.

`Microsoft.AspNetCore.Components.WebAssembly.Authentication` library plays a major role for doing all authentication and authorization tasks for us.

For this, all processes will be the same except for the Azure Portal configuration. Here, we need to configure on the Google Developer Portal.

Step 1: Create the Blazor WebAssembly application with **`Microsoft Identity platform`** as follows:

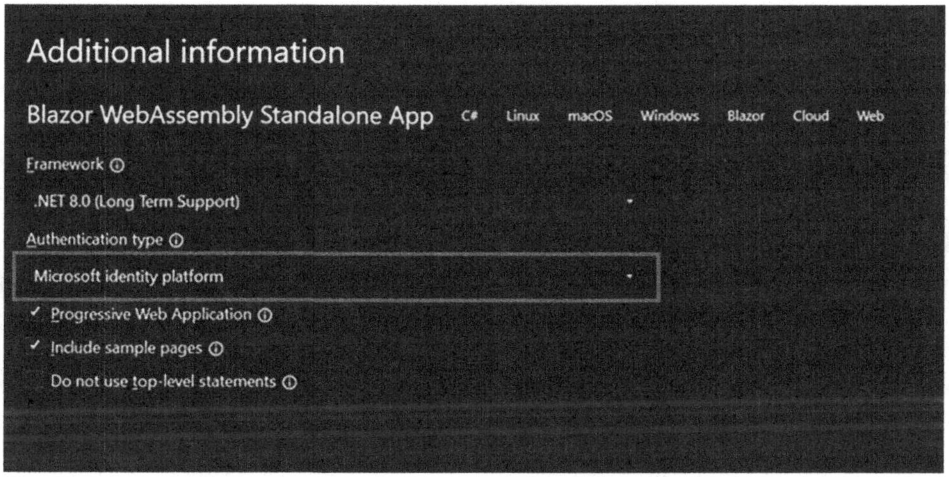

***Figure 11.15**: Blazor WebAssembly Application*

This will create all the required scaffolding code for us for doing authentication and authorization.

Step 2: Create a Google API Console project to obtain a client ID and client secret to configure the Google authentication in our application.

For a detailed explanation, please go through the following post:

Integrating Google Sign-In into your web app | Authentication | Google for Developers

Figure 11.16: *Google API Console Project*

Step 3: Go to the **`appsetting.json`** file, change the Authority and Client Id as shown here:

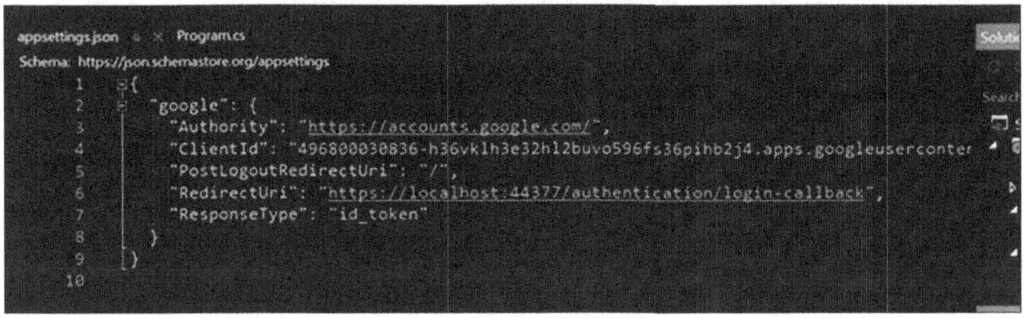

Figure 11.17: *Appsetting File*

Step 4: Change the Google key on program file as shown here:

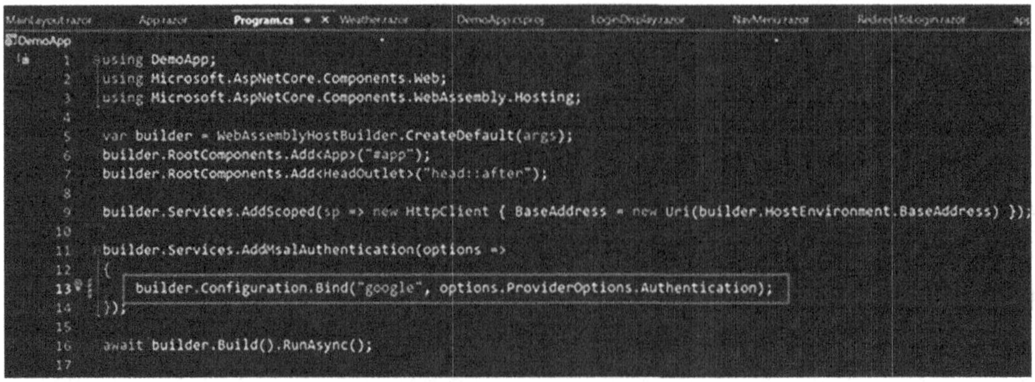

Figure 11.18: *Dependency Injection*

Step 5: Run the application:

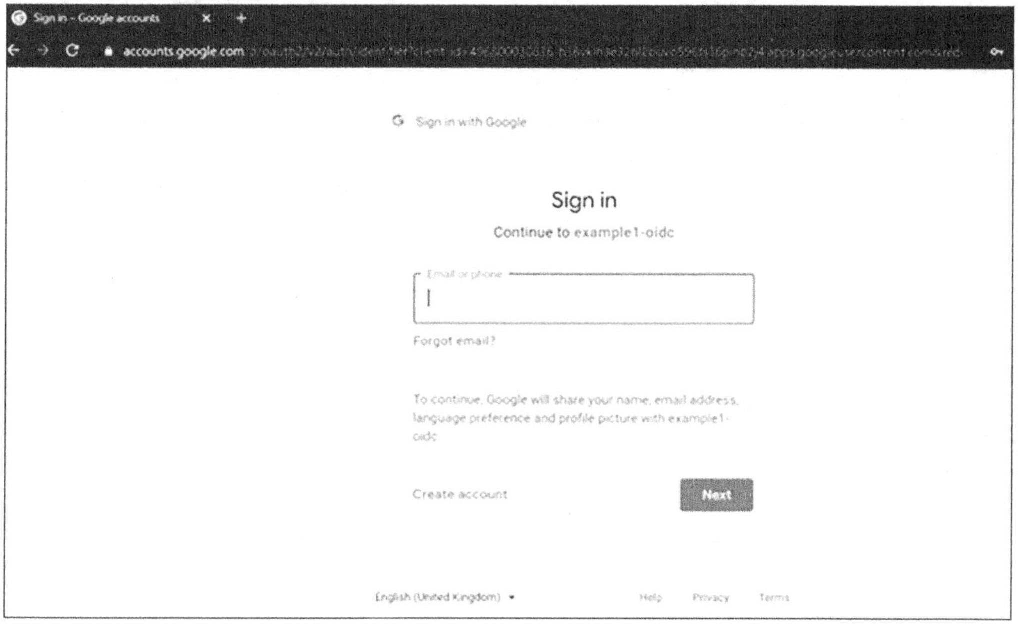

Figure 11.19: *Google Login*

Step 6: After clicking Next, we get the following screen:

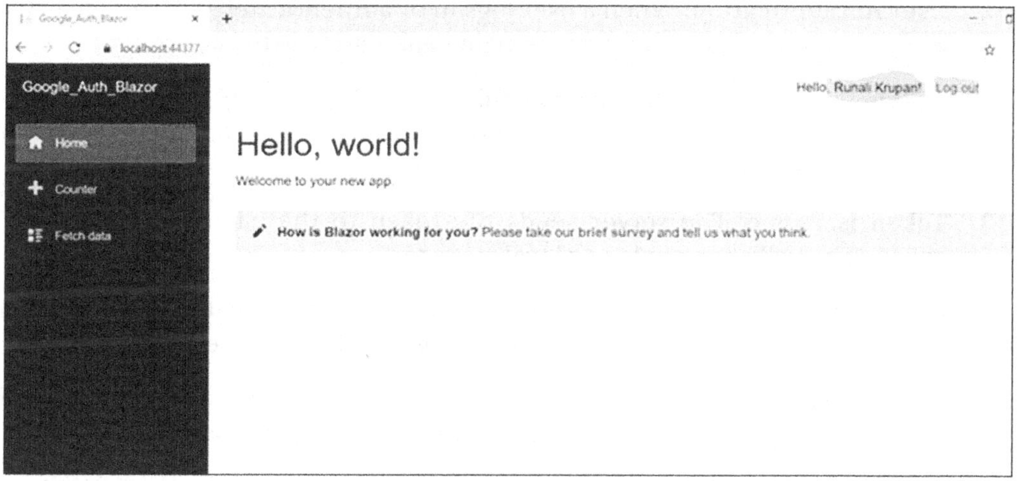

Figure 11.20: *Login Demo*

In the preceding demo, we saw that with the help of **OpenID Connect (OIDC),** we are able to integrate any third-party authentication and authorization in our Blazor WebAssembly application.

Custom Token-Based Authentication in Blazor WebAssembly

Token-based authentication is a security mechanism widely used in web development to authenticate users and authorize their access to resources. It involves the use of tokens, which are typically generated by a server upon successful authentication and then sent to the client. The client includes this token in subsequent requests to prove its identity.

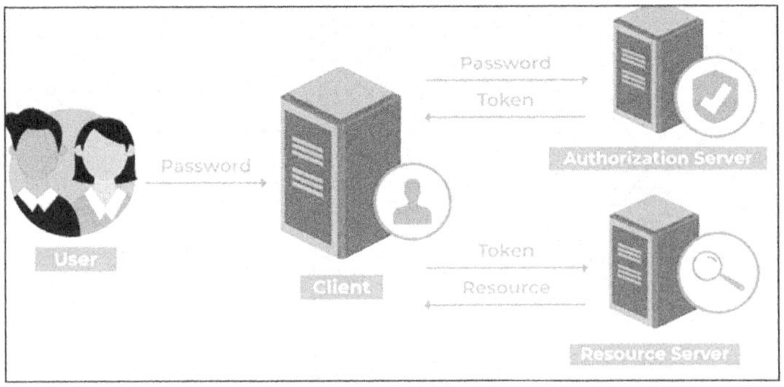

Figure 11.21: *Token-Based Authentication*

Here's a brief overview of how token-based authentication works:

1. **User Authentication:** When a user logs in or authenticates, the server verifies their credentials (for example, username and password).
2. **Token Generation:** Upon successful authentication, the server generates a unique token (often a JSON Web Token or JWT) that contains information about the user and their roles or permissions.
3. **Token Issuance:** The server sends the token to the client, which stores it securely, usually in a cookie or local storage.
4. **Subsequent Requests:** The client includes the token in the headers of its requests to the server. This token serves as proof of the user's identity.
5. **Token Verification:** The server, upon receiving a request, verifies the token's authenticity and checks if the user has the required permissions to access the requested resource.

Token-based authentication offers several advantages, including:

- **Statelessness:** The server doesn't need to store session information, making it scalable and easy to maintain.
- **Cross-Origin Resource Sharing (CORS):** Tokens can be easily included in HTTP headers, allowing for cross-origin requests.

- **Security:** Tokens can be encrypted and signed, adding an extra layer of security.
- **Decoupling:** Since the client holds the token, it can be used to access multiple services without the need to re-enter credentials.

Now, let's create a Token-Based Authentication demo.

Asp.net Core Web API

Here are the steps to create web API project:

Step 1: Create the web API application project

Figure 11.22: *Web API Project*

Here is the next screen:

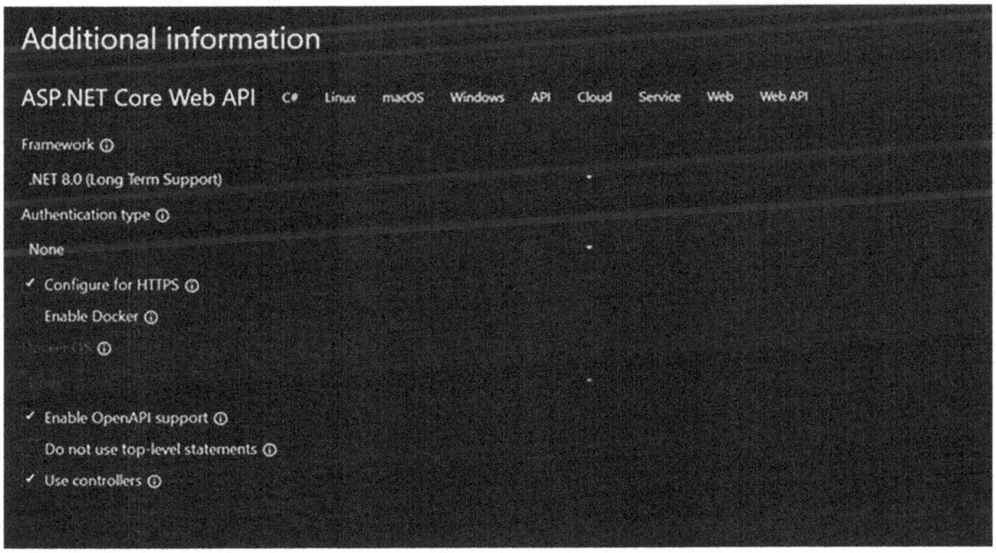

Figure 11.23: *Web API Project Template*

Step 2: Install the **`Microsoft.AspNetCore.Authentication.JwtBearer`** NuGet package.

It is commonly used to secure APIs by validating JWTs received from clients. The **`JwtBearer`** authentication handler reads the JWT from the request's Authorization header, validates it, and sets the user on the **`HttpContext`** based on the information in the token.

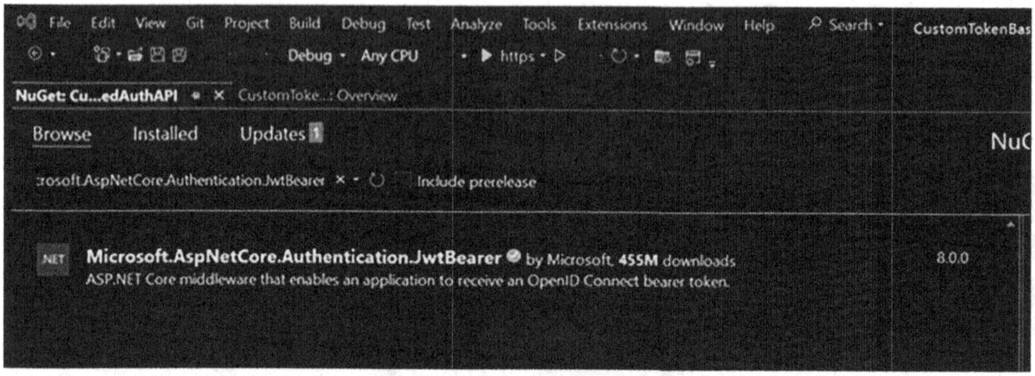

***Figure 11.24:** NuGet Package*

Step 3: Now, we will create a required model class for the login page.

`Login.cs` Class:

```
using System.ComponentModel.DataAnnotations;

namespace CustomTokenBasedAuthAPI.Model
{
    public class Login
    {
        [Required]
        public string? Email { get; set; }
        [Required]
        public string? Password { get; set; }
    }
```

`LoginResult.cs` Class:

```
namespace CustomTokenBasedAuthAPI.Model
{
    public class LoginResult
    {
        public string? Token { get; set; }
        public DateTime Expiry { get; set; }
    }}
```

Step 4: Add an **appSettings.json** file to the API project with the following content:

```
{
  "Logging": {
    "LogLevel": {
      "Default": "Information",
      "Microsoft.AspNetCore": "Warning"
    }
  },
  "Jwt": {
    "Key": "ITNN8mPfS2ivOqr1eRWK0Rac3sRAchQETRTTTEdG8BUy0pK4vQ3\",",
    "Issuer": "CustomTokenBasedAuthAPI",
    "Audience": "CustomTokenBasedAuthAPIAudience"
  },
  "AllowedHosts": "*"
}
```

Step 5: Go to the **program.cs** file and add this configuration for authentication:

```
// Add services to the container.
ConfigurationManager configuration = builder.Configuration;
builder.Services.AddAuthentication(JwtBearerDefaults.Authentication-
Scheme).AddJwtBearer(options =>
{
    options.TokenValidationParameters = new TokenValidationParameters
    {
        ValidateIssuer = true,
        ValidateAudience = true,
        ValidateLifetime = true,
        ValidateIssuerSigningKey = true,
        ValidIssuer = configuration.GetValue<string>("Jwt:Issuer"),
        ValidAudience = configuration.GetValue<string>("Jwt:Audience"),
        IssuerSigningKey = new SymmetricSecurityKey(Encoding.UTF8.
GetBytes(configuration.GetValue<string>("Jwt:Key")))
    };
});

builder.Services.AddCors(policy =>
{
    policy.AddPolicy("CorsPolicy", opt => opt
        .AllowAnyOrigin()
        .AllowAnyHeader()
        .AllowAnyMethod());
});
```

For keeping the Authorization header on the swagger page, configure the middleware pipeline as follows:

```
//for keeping Authorization on Swagger
builder.Services.AddSwaggerGen(option =>
{
    option.SwaggerDoc("v1", new OpenApiInfo { Title = "CustomToken-
Based API", Version = "v1" });
    option.AddSecurityDefinition("Bearer", new OpenApiSecurityScheme
    {
        In = ParameterLocation.Header,
        Description = "Please enter a valid token",
        Name = "Authorization",
        Type = SecuritySchemeType.Http,
        BearerFormat = "JWT",
        Scheme = "Bearer"
    });
    option.AddSecurityRequirement(new OpenApiSecurityRequirement
    {
        {
            new OpenApiSecurityScheme
            {
                Reference = new OpenApiReference
                {
                    Type=ReferenceType.SecurityScheme,
                    Id="Bearer"
                }
            },
            new string[]{}
        }
    });
});
```

Then add authentication and authorization middleware to the request pipeline in the Configure method. Ensure that they are added after Routing and before EndPoint configuration:

```
app.UseCors("CorsPolicy");
app.UseAuthorization();
app.UseAuthorization();
```

Step 6: Add an [Authorize] attribute to the existing **`WeatherForecast`** controller:

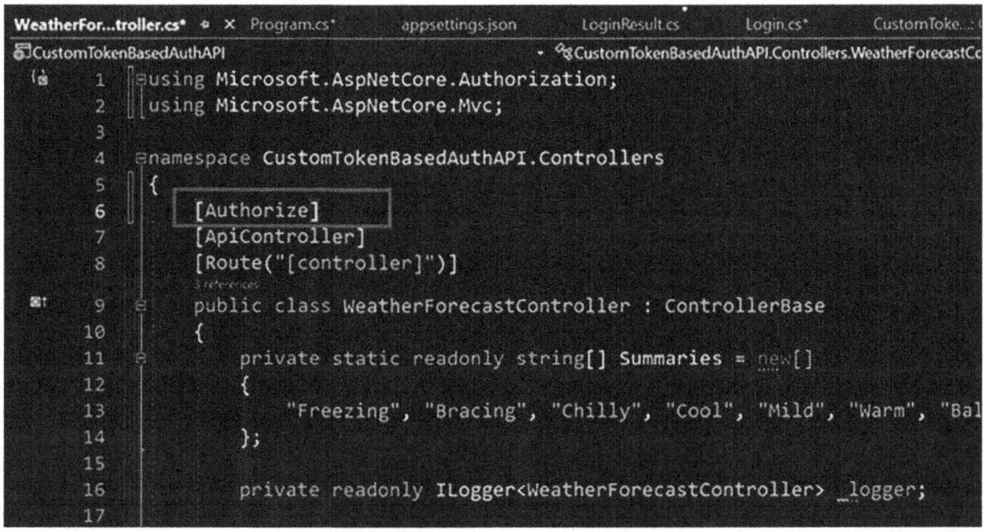

Figure 11.25: *[Authorize] attribute*

As you know, after keeping the Authorize attribute on top of any controller, we can access outside without a valid token. It will be a secured API controller.

Step 7: Now, we will create a login controller for validating users and generating JWT token:

```
using CustomTokenBasedAuthAPI.Model;
using Microsoft.AspNetCore.Mvc;
using Microsoft.IdentityModel.Tokens;
using System.IdentityModel.Tokens.Jwt;
using System.Security.Claims;
using System.Text;

namespace CustomTokenBasedAuthAPI.Controllers
{
    [Route("api/[controller]")]
    [ApiController]
    public class LoginController : ControllerBase
    {
        private readonly IConfiguration _configuration;
        public LoginController(IConfiguration configuration) => _config-
uration = configuration;

        [HttpPost]
        public LoginResult Login(Login objlogin)
        {
            // we are keeping 1 minute token expiry period
            // In real scenario, we can keep longer period
            var expiry = DateTime.Now.AddMinutes(1);
            return ValidateCredentials(objlogin) ? new LoginResult {
```

```
Token = GenerateJWT(objlogin.Email, expiry), Expiry = expiry } : new
LoginResult();
        }

        // Used for Validating User credentials
        bool ValidateCredentials(Login credentials)
        {
            bool success = false;
           // We are hardcoding the EmailId and Password for demo purposes.
            if (credentials.Email == "Admin@gmail.com" && credentials.
Password == "Admin")
            {
                success = true;
            }
            return success;
        }

        // this is used for generating JWT Token
        private string GenerateJWT(string email, DateTime expiry)
        {
            var securityKey = new SymmetricSecurityKey(Encoding.UTF8.
GetBytes(_configuration["Jwt:Key"]));
            var token = new JwtSecurityToken(
                _configuration["Jwt:Issuer"],
                _configuration["Jwt:Audience"],
                new[] { new Claim(ClaimTypes.Name, email) },
                expires: expiry,
                signingCredentials: new SigningCredentials(securi-
tyKey, SecurityAlgorithms.HmacSha256)
            );
            var tokenHandler = new JwtSecurityTokenHandler();
            return tokenHandler.WriteToken(token);
        }
    }
}
```

For the purpose of demonstration, the token expiry is set to 1 minute.

The Web API entry point validates the credentials. In this example, we have given hardcoded value. However, in a real-time project, you can validate in the actual database table.

Step 8: Run the application and pass the valid **`EmailId`** and **`Password`**. It will generate a Bearer token with some expiry period.

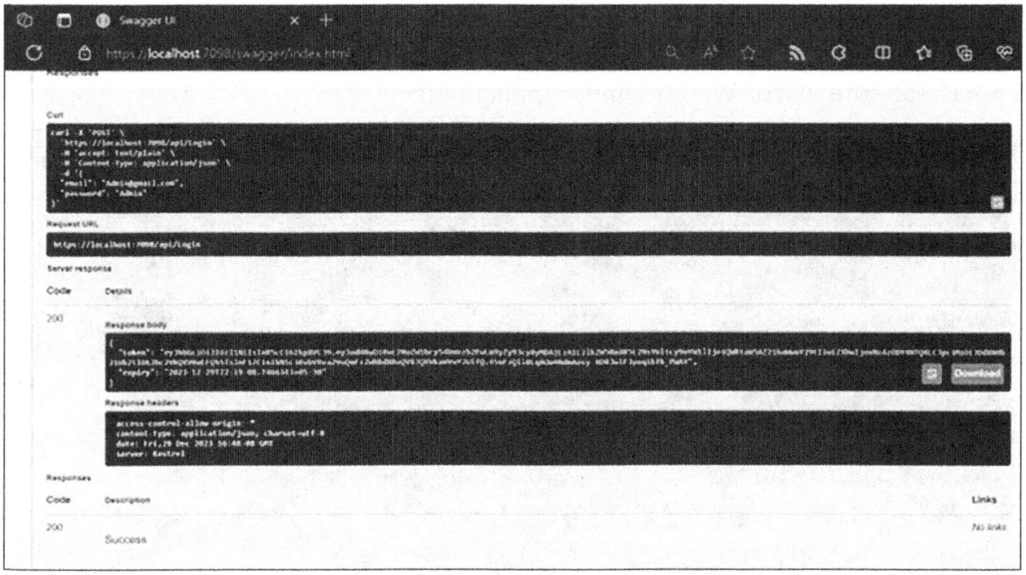

Figure 11.26: *Postman Demo*

Now, we will pass the token on Swagger authorize header and then trigger the weather forecast controller endpoint. We will see the expected data.

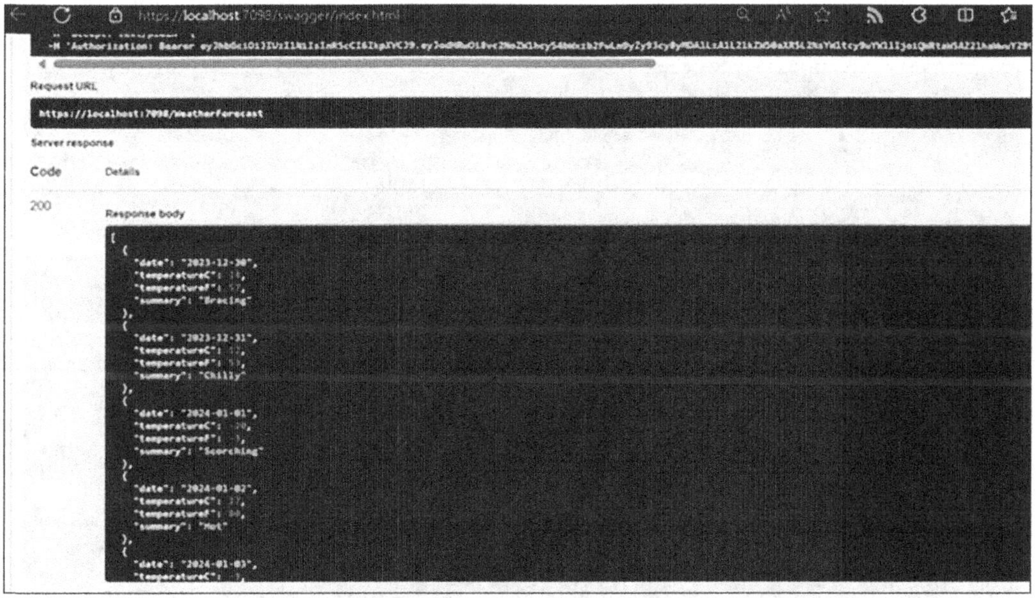

Figure 11.27: *Postman Output*

We have completed the web API part. Now, we will create a Blazor WebAssembly project and consume the token-based API endpoint. For this task, we can perform the following steps.

Blazor WASM Client Side

Step 1: Create the Blazor WebAssembly application:

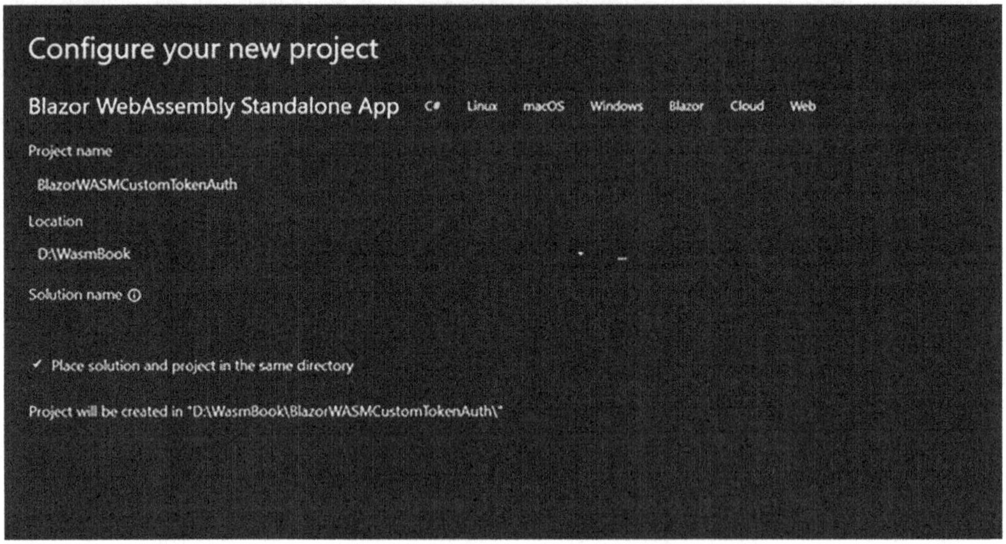

Figure 11.28: *Project Template*

Figure 11.29 shows the additional information:

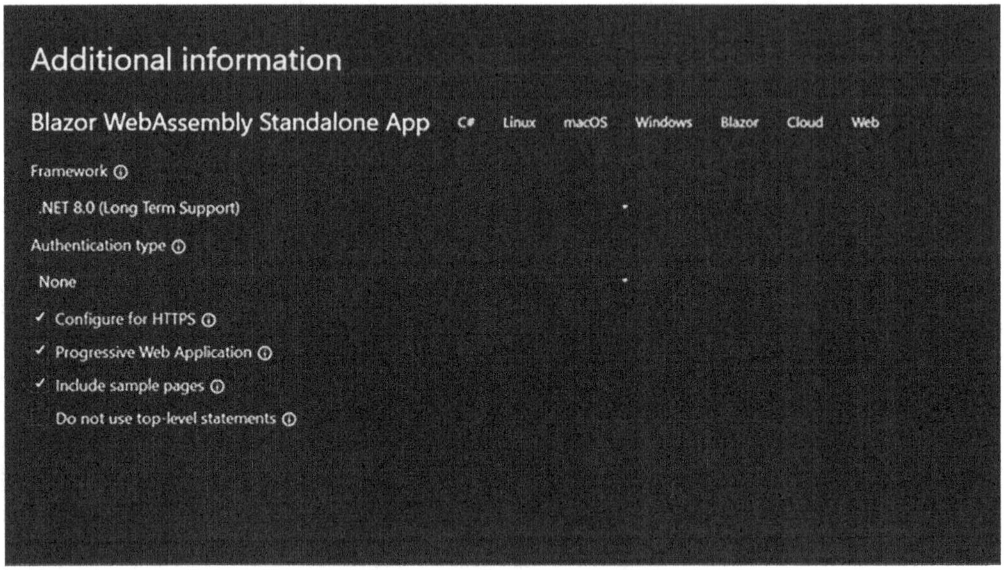

Figure 11.29: *Project Wizard*

Step 2: Install the **`Microsoft.AspNetCore.Components.Authorization`** NuGet package.

Figure 11.30: *NuGet Package*

Step 3: Create the Helper Folder and create **`TokenAuthenticationStateProvider`** class and write code as shown here:

```
using Microsoft.AspNetCore.Components.Authorization;
using Microsoft.JSInterop;
using System.Security.Claims;
using System.Text.Json;

namespace BlazorWASMCustomTokenAuth.Helper
{
    public class TokenAuthenticationStateProvider : Authentication-
StateProvider
    {
        private readonly IJSRuntime _jsRuntime;

        public TokenAuthenticationStateProvider(IJSRuntime jsRuntime)
        {
            _jsRuntime = jsRuntime;
        }

        public async Task SetTokenAsync(string token, DateTime expiry
= default)
        {
            if (token == null)
            {
                await _jsRuntime.InvokeAsync<object>("localStorage.
removeItem", "authToken");
                await _jsRuntime.InvokeAsync<object>("localStorage.
removeItem", "authTokenExpiry");
            }
            else
            {
                await _jsRuntime.InvokeAsync<object>("localStorage.
setItem", "authToken", token);
                await _jsRuntime.InvokeAsync<object>("localStorage.
setItem", "authTokenExpiry", expiry);
```

```
            }

            NotifyAuthenticationStateChanged(GetAuthentication-
StateAsync());
        }

        public async Task<string> GetTokenAsync()
        {
            var expiry = await _jsRuntime.InvokeAsync<object>("lo-
calStorage.getItem", "authTokenExpiry");
            if (expiry != null)
            {
                if (DateTime.Parse(expiry.ToString()) > DateTime.Now)
                {
                    return await _jsRuntime.InvokeAsync<string>("local
Storage.getItem", "authToken");
                }
                else
                {
                    await SetTokenAsync(null);
                }
            }
            return null;
        }


        public override async Task<AuthenticationState> GetAuthenti-
cationStateAsync()
        {
            var token = await GetTokenAsync();
            var identity = string.IsNullOrEmpty(token)
                ? new ClaimsIdentity()
                : new ClaimsIdentity(ParseClaimsFromJwt(token), "jwt");
           return new AuthenticationState(new ClaimsPrincipal(identity));
        }

        private static IEnumerable<Claim> ParseClaimsFromJwt(string jwt)
        {
            var payload = jwt.Split('.')[1];
            var jsonBytes = ParseBase64WithoutPadding(payload);
            var keyValuePairs = JsonSerializer.Deserialize<Dictio-
nary<string, object>>(jsonBytes);
            return keyValuePairs.Select(kvp => new Claim(kvp.Key, kvp.
Value.ToString()));
        }

        private static byte[] ParseBase64WithoutPadding(string base64)
        {
```

```
            switch (base64.Length % 4)
            {
                case 2: base64 += "=="; break;
                case 3: base64 += "="; break;
            }
            return Convert.FromBase64String(base64);
        }
    }
}
```

Here's a high-level explanation of the code:

1. **Constructor:**
   - The class has a constructor that takes an IJSRuntime parameter. This parameter is used to interact with the JavaScript code from C#.
2. **SetTokenAsync method:**
   - This method is used to set the authentication token in the local storage of the browser.
   - If the token is null, it removes both the authentication token and its expiry from the local storage.
   - If the token is not null, it stores the token and its expiry in the local storage.
   - Finally, it notifies that the authentication state has changed.
3. **GetTokenAsync method:**
   - Retrieves the authentication token and its expiry from the local storage.
   - If the token is not expired, it returns the token; otherwise, it removes the token and returns null.
4. **Get+AuthenticationStateAsync method:**
   - Overrides the base method to provide the current authentication state.
   - Call the GetTokenAsync method to get the authentication token.
   - Creates a ClaimsIdentity based on the parsed claims from the JWT token.
   - Returns an AuthenticationState object with a ClaimsPrincipal based on the obtained identity.
5. **`ParseClaimsFromJwt` method:**
   - Parses the claims from the JWT token's payload.
   - It decodes the payload, converts it to a JSON string, and deserializes it into a dictionary of key-value pairs.
   - Creates and returns a list of Claim objects from the dictionary.

6. **`ParseBase64WithoutPadding` method:**
   - Adjusts the base64 string if it has incorrect padding and converts it to a byte array.

Overall, this class is responsible for managing the authentication state in a Blazor WASM application by storing and retrieving JWT tokens from the local storage, and providing the authentication state to the application. The JWT token is used to represent the user's claims and authentication status.

Step 4: Register the **`AuthenticationStateProvider`** with the dependency injection in Program.cs file as shown here.

```
builder.Services.AddScoped<TokenAuthenticationStateProvider>();
builder.Services.AddScoped<AuthenticationStateProvider>(provider => provider.GetRequiredService<TokenAuthenticationStateProvider>
```

Figure 11.31: *Dependency Injection*

```
using BlazorWASMCustomTokenAuth;
using BlazorWASMCustomTokenAuth.Helper;
using Microsoft.AspNetCore.Components.Authorization;
using Microsoft.AspNetCore.Components.Web;
using Microsoft.AspNetCore.Components.WebAssembly.Hosting;



var builder = WebAssemblyHostBuilder.CreateDefault(args);
builder.RootComponents.Add<App>("#app");
builder.RootComponents.Add<HeadOutlet>("head::after");
builder.Services.AddScoped(sp => new HttpClient { BaseAddress = new
Uri(builder.HostEnvironment.BaseAddress) });

builder.Services.AddAuthorizationCore();
builder.Services.AddScoped<TokenAuthenticationStateProvider>();
builder.Services.AddScoped<AuthenticationStateProvider>(provider =>
provider.GetRequiredService<TokenAuthenticationStateProvider>());

await builder.Build().RunAsync();
```

Step 5: Create the login page as follows:

```
@page "/login"
@inject HttpClient Http
@inject TokenAuthenticationStateProvider AuthStateProvider
@inject ILogger<Login> Logger

<h3>Login</h3>

<div class="container col-6">
    @if (loginFailure)
```

```
    {
        <div class="alert alert-danger">Your credentials did not work.
Please try again.</div>
    }
    <div class="card">
        <div class="card-body">
            <h5 class="card-title">Login</h5>
            <EditForm Model="credentials" OnValidSubmit="SubmitCre-
dentials">
                <DataAnnotationsValidator />

                <div class="form-group">
                    <label>Email address</label>
                    <InputText class="form-control" @bind-Value="cre-
dentials.Email" />
                    <ValidationMessage For="@(()=> credentials.Email)"
/>
                </div>
                <div class="form-group">
                    <label>Password</label>
                    <InputText type="password" class="form-control" @
bind-Value="credentials.Password" />
                    <ValidationMessage For="@(()=> credentials.Pass-
word)" />
                </div>
                <button type="submit" class="btn btn-outline-primary
btn-sm">Submit</button>
            </EditForm>
        </div>
    </div>
</div>

@code {
    BlazorWASMCustomTokenAuth.Model.Login credentials = new Blazor-
WASMCustomTokenAuth.Model.Login();
    bool loginFailure;
    EditForm loginform { get; set; }
    async Task SubmitCredentials()
    {
        var response = await Http.PostAsJsonAsync("https://local-
host:7098/api/login", credentials);
        var result = await response.Content.ReadFromJsonAsync<Login-
Result>();
        loginFailure = result?.Token == null;
        if (!loginFailure)
        {
            await AuthStateProvider.SetTokenAsync(result.Token,
result.Expiry);
```

```
        }
    }
}
```

Step 6: Go to the **App.razor** file and write code as follows:

```
<CascadingAuthenticationState>
    <Router AppAssembly="@typeof(Program).Assembly">
        <Found Context="routeData">
            <AuthorizeRouteView RouteData="@routeData" DefaultLay-
out="@typeof(MainLayout)">
                <NotAuthorized>
                  <BlazorWASMCustomTokenAuth.Pages.Login/>
                </NotAuthorized>
            </AuthorizeRouteView>
        </Found>
        <NotFound>
            <LayoutView Layout="@typeof(MainLayout)">
                <p>Sorry, there’s nothing at this address.</p>
            </LayoutView>
        </NotFound>
    </Router>
</CascadingAuthenticationState>
```

In the preceding code, we are using **CascadingAuthenticationState**, this will ensure that the authentication state is available to all components within its scope. The authentication state typically contains information about the current user's identity and authentication status.

If the user is not authenticated, the child content of the **NotAuthorized** component is displayed, that is, the login component that you just created.

Step 7: Go to **MainLayout.razor** page and write the code for logout button as follows:

```
@inherits LayoutComponentBase
@using Microsoft.AspNetCore.Components.Authorization
@inject TokenAuthenticationStateProvider TokenProvider

<div class="page">
    <div class="sidebar">
        <NavMenu />
    </div>

    <main>
        <div class="top-row px-4">
            <AuthorizeView>
                Logged in as @context.User.Identity.Name
                <button class="btn btn-sm btn-outline-dark" @onclick="@
```

```
(() => TokenProvider.SetTokenAsync(null))">Logout</button>
            </AuthorizeView>
        </div>

        <article class="content px-4">
            @Body
        </article>
    </main>
</div>
```

Step 8: Now, go to **`Weather.razor`** page and change the code for fetching data from Weather Forecast API as follows:

```
private WeatherForecast[]? forecasts;

protected override async Task OnInitializedAsync()
{
    var token = await TokenProvider.GetTokenAsync();
    if (token != null)
    {
        Http.DefaultRequestHeaders.Authorization = new Authentication-
HeaderValue("Bearer", token);
        forecasts = await Http.GetFromJsonAsync<WeatherFore-
cast[]>("https://localhost:7098/WeatherForecast");
    }
}
```

Note: *Make sure to keep `@attribute [Authorize]` on the top of the page. Here is the complete code snippet.*

```
@page "/weather"
@inject HttpClient Http
@using System.Net.Http.Headers
@inject TokenAuthenticationStateProvider TokenProvider
@attribute [Authorize]

<PageTitle>Weather</PageTitle>

<h1>Weather</h1>

<p>This component demonstrates fetching data from the server.</p>

@if (forecasts == null)
{
    <p><em>Loading...</em></p>
}
else
{
```

```
    <table class="table">
        <thead>
            <tr>
                <th>Date</th>
                <th>Temp. (C)</th>
                <th>Temp. (F)</th>
                <th>Summary</th>
            </tr>
        </thead>
        <tbody>
            @foreach (var forecast in forecasts)
            {
                <tr>
                    <td>@forecast.Date.ToShortDateString()</td>
                    <td>@forecast.TemperatureC</td>
                    <td>@forecast.TemperatureF</td>
                    <td>@forecast.Summary</td>
                </tr>
            }
        </tbody>
    </table>
}

@code {
    private WeatherForecast[]? forecasts;

    protected override async Task OnInitializedAsync()
    {
        var token = await TokenProvider.GetTokenAsync();
        if (token != null)
        {
            Http.DefaultRequestHeaders.Authorization = new Authenti-
cationHeaderValue("Bearer", token);
            forecasts = await Http.GetFromJsonAsync<WeatherFore-
cast[]>("https://localhost:7098/WeatherForecast");
        }
    }

    public class WeatherForecast
    {
        public DateOnly Date { get; set; }

        public int TemperatureC { get; set; }

        public string? Summary { get; set; }
```

```
        public int TemperatureF => 32 + (int)(TemperatureC / 0.5556);
    }
}
```

Step 9: Run the application and go to **`weatherforecast`** page. It will route to login page:

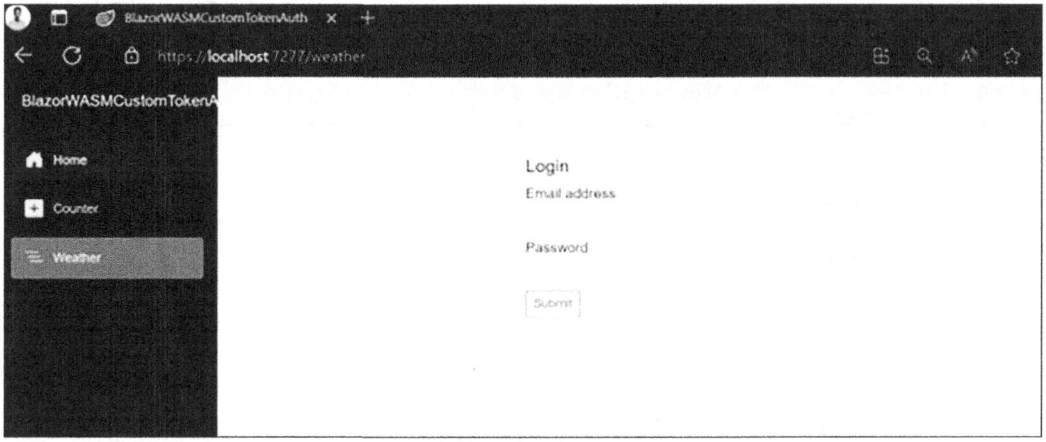

Figure 11.32: *Output*

After login, you can see the following screen:

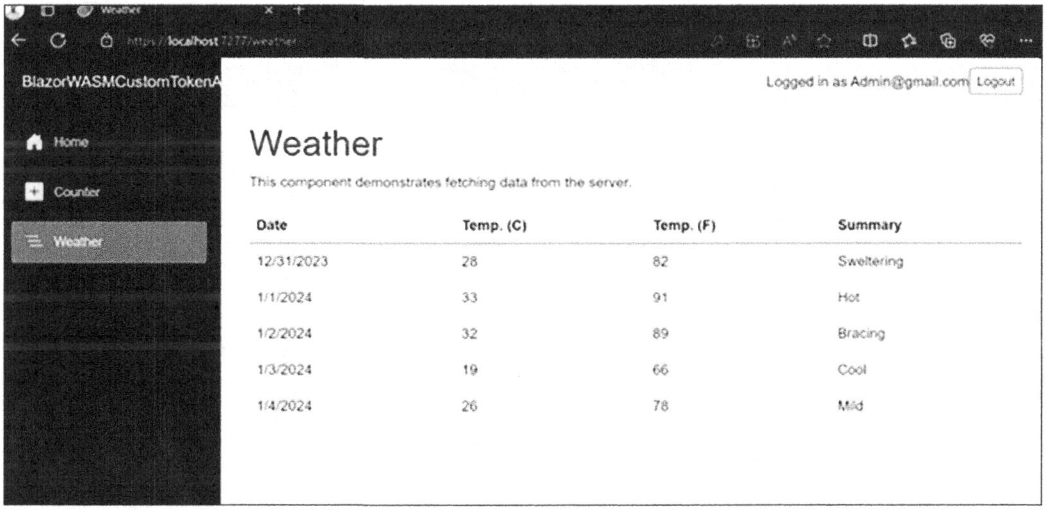

Figure 11.33: *Output*

Note: *Keep in mind that you are running Web API and Blazor WASM Project at the same time. Otherwise, it will not work.*

In the preceding demo, we saw how to consume bearer token-based API endpoints in the Blazor WebAssembly application.

Tips and Tricks While Implementing Security in Blazor WebAssembly

Implementing security in Blazor WebAssembly is crucial to ensure the protection of your application and user data. Here are some tips and tricks to enhance security:

- **Authentication and Authorization:**

Use the built-in authentication and authorization mechanisms provided by Blazor. Leverage the AuthorizeView component to control access to components based on user roles.

- **JWT (JSON Web Tokens):**

Consider using JWT for secure token-based authentication. JWTs can be issued by your authentication server and used to validate the identity of the user in subsequent requests.

- **HTTPS:**

Always use HTTPS to encrypt data transmitted between the client and the server. This helps protect sensitive information from being intercepted during communication.

- **Secure API Endpoints:**

Ensure that your API endpoints are secure by implementing proper authentication and authorization checks. Validate input parameters on the server side to prevent injection attacks.

- **CORS (Cross-Origin Resource Sharing):**

Configure CORS settings appropriately to control which domains can access your Blazor WebAssembly application. This helps prevent unauthorized access from malicious websites.

- **Content Security Policy (CSP):**

Implement a Content Security Policy to mitigate the risk of cross-site scripting (XSS) attacks. This restricts the types of content that your application can load.

- **Data Validation:**

Validate user input on both the client and server sides to prevent security vulnerabilities such as injection attacks and cross-site scripting.

- **Logging and Monitoring:**

Implement comprehensive logging to track security-related events and monitor the application for unusual activities. Regularly review logs to identify potential security threats.

- **Dependency Scanning:**

Regularly scan and update dependencies to patch known security vulnerabilities. Use tools to automate this process and ensure you are using the latest and secure versions of libraries.

- **Session Management:**

Manage user sessions securely. Use token-based authentication with appropriate expiration times and implement session logout functionality.

- **Secure Storage:**

Be cautious with client-side storage. Avoid storing sensitive information in local storage or cookies, and use secure methods like **`HttpOnly`** cookies for storing authentication tokens.

When a cookie is marked as "**`HttpOnly`**," it means it is not accessible through client-side scripts, such as JavaScript. This restriction is designed to enhance the web application's security by preventing certain types of attacks, particularly those related to cross-site scripting (XSS).

In the context of storing authentication tokens, marking cookies as **`HttpOnly`** is a best practice to protect sensitive information, such as user authentication tokens, from being accessed by malicious scripts.

- **Security Headers:**

Set security headers in your application, such as Content Security Policy (CSP), Strict-Transport-Security (HSTS), and X-Content-Type-Options, to enhance overall security.

Common Mistakes While Implementing Security in Blazor WebAssembly

Developing secure Blazor WebAssembly applications is crucial, and developers should be aware of common mistakes to avoid potential security vulnerabilities. Here are some frequently encountered mistakes:

- **Insufficient Authentication and Authorization:**

Mistake: Failing to properly implement authentication and authorization mechanisms, or misconfiguration roles and permissions, can lead to unauthorized access to sensitive functionalities.

Solution: Use the built-in authentication and authorization features of Blazor, and thoroughly test user roles and permissions.

- **Insecure Data Transmission:**

Mistake: Neglecting to use HTTPS can expose sensitive data to interception during transmission.

Solution: Always use HTTPS to encrypt data between the client and server, ensuring a secure communication channel.

- **Client-Side Trust:**

Mistake: Relying too much on client-side validation without validating input on the server side can lead to security issues.

Solution: Implement server-side validation to ensure that user inputs are properly validated and secure against attacks like injection.

- **Lack of Input Validation:**

Mistake: Failing to validate and sanitize user inputs can expose the application to injection attacks.

Solution: Validate and sanitize all user inputs on the server side to prevent injection vulnerabilities.

- **Cross-Site Scripting (XSS):**

Mistake: Not properly validating and sanitizing user inputs can lead to XSS vulnerabilities, allowing attackers to inject malicious scripts.

Solution: Implement proper input validation, sanitize user inputs, and use Content Security Policy (CSP) headers to mitigate XSS risks.

- **Insecure Storage of Secrets:**

Mistake: Storing sensitive information, such as API keys or connection strings, directly in client-side code or in an insecure manner.

Solution: Store sensitive information securely on the server side and use environment variables or secure storage mechanisms for secrets.

- **Client-Side Trust for Business Logic:**

Mistake: Relying on client-side logic for critical business rules without server-side verification can expose the application to manipulation.

Solution: Perform critical business logic and validation on the server side to prevent client-side tampering.

- **Over Reliance on Client-Side Security:**

Mistake: Depending solely on client-side security measures without considering server-side security checks.

Solution: Implement a defense-in-depth strategy with both client-side and server-side security measures.

- **Ignoring Security Headers:**

Mistake: Neglecting to set security headers, such as Content Security Policy (CSP) and Strict-Transport-Security (HSTS), can leave the application vulnerable.

Solution: Set appropriate security headers to enhance the overall security posture of the application.

- **Not Regularly Updating Dependencies**

Mistake: Failing to update dependencies and libraries can result in using versions with known security vulnerabilities.

Solution: Regularly update dependencies to patch known vulnerabilities and enhance the security of the application.

Developers should stay informed about the latest security best practices, conduct regular security audits, and follow secure coding guidelines to minimize the risk of introducing security vulnerabilities in Blazor WebAssembly applications.

Conclusion

In this chapter, we understood how to implement different types of security approach in Blazor WebAssembly application. We also learned tips and tricks while implementing security. All the latest security related concepts are kept in a very simplified way in this book.

If you are reading the chapter and are unable to implement it in your project, then feel free to download the source code from GitHub and play with it.

References

ASP.NET Core Blazor authentication and authorization | Microsoft Learn

Source Code

https://github.com/ava-orange-education/Practical-Web-Development-with-Blazor-and-.Net-8

Multiple Choice Questions

1. What is the purpose of marking cookies as "`HttpOnly`" in Blazor WebAssembly?
    a. Enhancing SEO
    b. Enabling cross-origin resource sharing
    c. Preventing cross-site scripting (XSS) attacks
    d. Improving client-side performance
2. Which of the following is a common security vulnerability that can be mitigated by using Content Security Policy (CSP) in a Blazor WebAssembly application?
    a. Cross-Site Scripting (XSS)
    b. Cross-Site Request Forgery (CSRF)
    c. SQL Injection
    d. Man-in-the-Middle (MitM) attacks
3. What is the purpose of setting the "Secure" attribute on cookies in a Blazor WebAssembly application?
    a. Preventing cookie theft
    b. Enabling cookie access from JavaScript
    c. Allowing cross-origin requests
    d. Enhancing cookie expiration
4. Which of the following is a recommended practice for securing API endpoints in a Blazor WebAssembly application?
    a. Implementing weak authentication
    b. Using plain text for data transmission
    c. Validating and authorizing requests on the server side
    d. Storing sensitive information in client-side cookies
5. What does HTTPS provide in the context of security for Blazor WebAssembly?
    a. Protection against XSS
    b. Encryption of data transmitted between the client and server

   c. Prevention of SQL injection attacks

   d. Enhanced client-side performance

6. In Blazor WebAssembly, what role does the "**`AuthorizeView`**" component play in terms of security?

   a. Enforcing HTTPS connections

   b. Defining security policies

   c. Controlling access to components based on user authentication

   d. Setting CSP headers

Answers

1. c
2. a
3. a
4. c
5. b
6. c

Index

M

N

P

R

S

W

Made in the USA
Coppell, TX
17 October 2026

93086757R00136